P9-ECQ-503

Other McGraw-Hill Books of Interest

ISBN	AUTHOR	TITLE
0-07-006551-9	Bosler	*CLIST Programming*
0-07-044129-4	Murphy	*Assembler for COBOL Programmers: MVS, VM*
0-07-006533-0	Bookman	*COBOL II for Programmers*
0-07-046271-2	McGrew, McDaniel	*In-House Publishing in a Mainframe Environment*
0-07-051265-5	Ranade et al.	*DB2: Concepts, Programming, and Design*
0-07-054594-4	Sanchez, Canton	*IBM Microcomputers: A Programmer's Handbook*
0-07-002467-7	Aronson, Aronson	*SAS System: A Programmer's Guide*
0-07-002673-4	Azevedo	*ISPF: The Strategic Dialog Manager*
0-07-007248-5	Brathwaite	*Analysis, Design, and Implementation of Data Dictionaries*
0-07-009816-6	Carathanassis	*Expert MVS/XA, JCL: A Guide to Advanced Techniques*
0-07-015231-4	D'Alleyrand	*Image Storage and Retrieval Systems*
0-07-016188-7	Dayton	*Integrating Digital Services*
0-07-017606-X	Donofrio	*CICS: Debugging, Dump Reading, and Problem Determination*
0-07-018966-8	Eddolls	*VM Performance Management*
0-07-033571-0	Kavanagh	*VS COBOL II for COBOL Programmers*
0-07-040666-9	Martyn, Hartley	*DB2/SQL: A Professional Programmer's Guide*
0-07-050054-1	Piggott	*CICS: A Practical Guide for System Fine Tuning*
0-07-050686-8	Prasad	*IBM Mainframes: Architecture and Design*
0-07-051144-6	Ranade, Sackett	*Introduction to SNA Networking: Using VTAM/NCP*
0-07-051143-8	Ranade, Sackett	*Advanced SNA: A Professional's Guide to VTAM/NCP*

Database Experts Series

ISBN	AUTHOR	TITLE
0-07-020631-7	Hoechst et al.	*Guide to Oracle*
0-07-033637-7	Kageyama	*CICS Handbook*
0-07-016604-8	DeVita	*The Database Experts' Guide to FOCUS*
0-07-055170-7	IMI Systems, Inc.	*DB2 and SQL/DS: A User's Reference*
0-07-023267-9	Larson	*The Database Experts' Guide to DATABASE 2*
0-07-039002-9	Lusardi	*Database Experts' Guide to SQL*
0-07-048550-X	Parsons	*The Database Experts' Guide to IDEAL*

Communications Series

ISBN	AUTHOR	TITLE
0-07-055327-0	Schlar	*Inside X.25: A Manager's Guide*
0-07-005075-9	Berson	*APPC: Introduction to LU6.2*
0-07-034242-3	Kessler	*ISDN: Concepts, Facilities, and Services*
0-07-071136-4	Wipfler	*Distributed Processing in CICS*
0-07-002394-8	Arnell, Davis	*Handbook of Effective Disaster/Recovery Planning*
0-07-009783-6	Cap Gemini America	*DB2 Applications Development Handbook*
0-07-009792-5	Cap Gemini America	*Computer Systems Conversion*

VAX/VMS

Concepts and Facilities

Jay Shah

McGraw-Hill, Inc.
New York St. Louis San Francisco Auckland Bogotá
Caracas Lisbon London Madrid Mexico Milan
Montreal New Delhi Paris San Juan Singapore
Sydney Tokyo Toronto

Library of Congress Cataloging-in-Publication Data

Shah, Jay.
  VAX/VMS: concepts and facilities / Jay Shah.
    p. cm.
  ISBN 0-07-056367-5
  1. VAX/VMS (Computer operating systems) I. Title.
  QA76.76.063S52   1991
  005.4'44—dc20   90-46316
  75433 CIP

Copyright © 1991 by McGraw-Hill, Inc. All rights reserved.
Except as permitted under the United States Copyright Act
of 1976, no part of this publication may be reproduced or distributed
in any form or by any means, or stored in a data base or
retrieval system, without the prior written permission of the publisher.

3 4 5 6 7 8 9 0 DOR DOR 9 6 5 4 3 2

ISBN 0-07-056367-5

*The sponsoring editor for this book was Theron Shreve, the editing
supervisor was Dennis Gleason, and the production supervisor was
Suzanne W. Babeuf. This book was set in Century Schoolbook by
McGraw-Hill's Professional Publishing composition unit.*

Printed and bound by Impresora Donneco Internacional S. A. de C. V.
a division of R. R. Donnelley & Sons Company.

Manufactured in Mexico

The following are trademarks of Digital Equipment Corporation: ALL-IN-1, DEC,
DEC/CMS, DEC/MMS, DECnet, DECwindows, DIGITAL, MASSBUS, MicroVAX, PDP, Q-
bus, ReGIS, ULTRIX, UNIBUS, VAX, VAXBI, VAXcluster, VAX RMS, VMS, VT, XMI.
IBM is a registered trademark of International Business Machines Corporation. X Window
System, Version II and its derivatives (X, X11, X Version 11, X Window system) are
trademarks of the Massachusetts Institute of Technology.

LIMITS OF LIABILITY AND DISCLAIMER OF WARRANTY The
author and publisher have exercised care in preparing this book and
the programs contained in it. They make no representation, how-
ever, that the programs are error-free or suitable for every application to which the reader may attempt to apply them. The author and
publisher make no warranty of any kind, expressed or implied, including the warranties of merchantability or fitness for a particular
purpose, with regard to these programs or the documentation or the-
ory contained in this book, all of which are provided "as is." The author and publisher shall not be liable for damage in connection with,
or arising out of the furnishing, performance, or use of these programs or the associated descriptions or discussions.
    Readers should test any program on their own systems and com-
pare results with those presented in this book. They should then con-
struct their own test programs to verify that they fully understand
the requisite calling conventions and data formats for each of the
programs. Then they should test the specific application thoroughly.

*Subscription information to BYTE Magazine: Call
1-800-257-9402 or write Circulation Dept., One Phoenix
Mill Lane, Peterborough, NH 03458.*

To my late father
Navnitlal Ambalal Shah
(1926–1975)

AUGUSTANA UNIVERSITY COLLEGE
LIBRARY

Contents

Preface

VAXes are perhaps the most versatile of all computers currently in production; the smallest ones cost about the same as an average-sized PC configuration, while the largest ones rival mainframes in performance. The unique feature of all VAXes is that the same operating system, VAX/VMS, can run on all the computers. In fact, the same set of distribution tapes can be used to load the operating system on any VAX. Usually, no changes are required to programs when they are moved from, say, a microVAX to a VAX 6000-400, though they may have to be recompiled and relinked if the operating system versions are different.

This book covers:

- VAX hardware
- VAX/VMS operating system features
- Software products
- Programming issues
- Systems management

Currently, a number of specialized books on VAX/VMS are available, but, in my opinion, no one book gives a comprehensive introduction to the VAX environment. The books are either introductory or, like the books on VAX MACRO, VAX utilities, and VAX BASIC, narrow in focus. This book will familiarize readers with jargon related to VAXes and what goes on at typical VAX installations. It will also explain programming features of VAX/VMS.

The book assumes that the reader has some computer background as a user or programmer. No attempt is made to explain terms which are common knowledge in the computer industry. Some of the basic material will be familiar to PC users, while mainframe users will find some of the operating system terminology easy to grasp. Readers can skim through the material they already know. Rather than providing a bibliography at the end of the book, each chapter has a reference section at the end. This makes it easier for the reader to locate documentation relevant to the chapter.

A number of demonstration programs are provided at appropriate places. Most of the programs are in C and COBOL, but it should be easy to convert these to any other language. All the programs have been tested to work as described (although they are not guaranteed).

Some of the features and commands described are available only to users having certain privileges. Even if some operations cannot be performed by naive users, the description gives an insight into how the system operates.

While a lot of issues have been discussed in this book, the book is by no means complete. The manufacturer's manuals should be consulted for details on the topics.

ACKNOWLEDGMENTS

I wish to thank Bindoo Patel and Alan Pendley with whom I have spent many days discussing issues of computer architecture. Geoff Greene and Jim Gursha critiqued a large portion of the manuscript. At Gujarat University in India, Kedar Bhatt and I developed courses on assembly language programming. I learned VAX/VMS internals then. My deep gratitude to Kedar and the University.

My guide for preparing the manuscript was Jay Ranade whose expertise helped determine the style and contents of the book. His encouragement and advice did much to improve my presentation of the material. The staff at McGraw-Hill shepherded the raw manuscript through the production stages. Theron Shreve and Nancy Sileo provided support and coordination through all the stages of book production. Thank you Jay, Theron, and Nancy.

Finally, thanks to my colleagues at Chase Manhattan Bank, Steve Flecha, Chia Hsu, Art (Buddy) Raynor, and Jim Rich, who have influenced the contents of the book.

Jay Shah

Introduction

VAX/VMS is Digital Equipment Corporation's (DEC's) operating system for its VAX range of computers. The name is an acronym for *virtual address extension/virtual memory system*. DEC was formed in 1957 and currently has its headquarters in Massachusetts. The VAX has its roots in the PDP-11 series of computers, which is fast becoming obsolete. The first VAX computer, VAX 11/780, was manufactured in 1977. This was followed by the 750, 730, and 785. These machines are no longer in production. Currently, VAXes are available in a variety of configurations including workstations like the VAXstation, microVAXes like the 3800, single processors like the 9000-210 and multiprocessors like the 6000-440, and VAXclusters. Table 1.1 gives a brief history of VAXes.

The VAX CPU has *16 general purpose data registers* each of 32 bits. The machine uses *32-bit addressing* with a virtual addressing range of 4 Gbytes. The CPU supports more than 400 instructions, including

TABLE 1.1   **Milestones in VAX Development**

Year	Milestone
1977	First VAX, the 11/780.
1983	VAXclusters announced. Ethernet support announced.
1984	VAX 8600 introduced.
1985	MicroVAX II introduced. The most powerful microcomputer ever.
1986	Local Area VAXcluster for Ethernet.
1987	MicroVAX 3000 series introduced.
1988	VAX 6000 series introduced. Some of these systems support multiprocessing with up to six processors per system. DECwindows, DEC's implementation of X-windows, announced.
1989	VAXstation 3100—desktop graphics workstations which also act as a platform for powerful DECwindows applications—introduced. VAX 9000 series introduced. First VAX series to have vector processing instructions.
1990	VAX 4000 series introduced. Fault-tolerant VAXes—VAXft 3000 series—introduced.

TABLE 1.2   Characteristics of Some VAX Systems

VAX system	CPU speed	Implementation technology	Maximum memory, Mbytes	Bus	Max. bus I/O throughput, Mbits/s
microVAX II	0.9	NMOS	16	Q-bus	3.3
VAXstation 3100	2.7	CMOS	32	SCSI	1.2
microVAX 3800	3.8	CMOS	64	Q-bus	3.3
VAX 6000-320	7.5	CMOS	256	VAXBI	60.0
VAX 8800	6.0	ECL	512	VAXBI	30.0
VAX 8978	48.0	ECL	4096	VAXBI	30.0
VAX 9000	30.0	ECL	4096	XMI	640.0

NOTES: CPU speed is relative to VAX 11/780. VAX 6000-320 is a dual-processor. VAX 8978 is an 8-node VAXcluster. Some of the VAXes achieve higher I/O rates by using multiple buses. The VAX 9000 speed is for a single-CPU version.

character string manipulation, packed decimal arithmetic, floating point arithmetic, and variable-length bit field instructions.

Peripheral devices and controllers are connected to the CPU by means of external buses. The major buses used on the VAXes are *Qbus, UNIBUS, VAXBI* and *XMI*. SCSI is also supported on some of the low-end VAXes. Qbus has a 16-bit data path and is used with the microVAXes and 4000 series VAXes; UNIBUS has a 16-bit data path and is used on some of the low-end 8000 series computers. UNIBUS is being phased out. VAXes in the 6000, 8800, and 8900 series use the VAXBI. VAXBI has a 32-bit data path. XMI is the newest and fastest bus. VAXes in the 6000 and 9000 series use this bus. Many of the VAXes support more than one bus. Table 1.2 summarizes system characteristics of some of the VAX types.

Figure 1.1 shows one of the many possible VAX configurations.

1.1   DECnet

One of the strengths of the VAX/VMS software is DECnet. DECnet is the networking component of VAXes for communications between VAXes (and other computers). For a programmer, files residing on devices attached to other VAXes on the network are similar to files on the programmer's system. Typical uses of a DECnet network are

- Copying files.

- Logging into other VAXes.

- Sharing of resources like files and fast line printers.

- Running distributed applications.

Ethernet technology, though not essential to run DECnet, is exten-

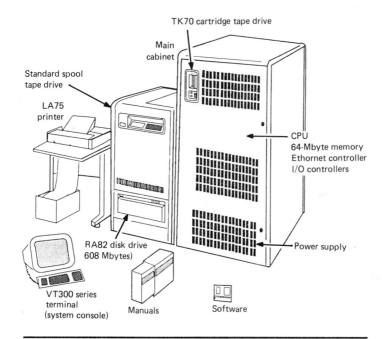

TK70 cartridge tape drive

Main cabinet

Standard spool tape drive

LA75 printer

CPU
64-Mbyte memory
Ethornet controller
I/O controllers

Power supply

RA82 disk drive
608 Mbytes)

VT300 series terminal
(system console)

Manuals

Software

Figure 1.1 A typical system: VAX 6000-420. (*Copyright ©
1990 Digital Equipment Corporation. All rights reserved.
Reprinted by permission.*)

sively utilized for networking. *Ethernet* is a bus with a rated bandwidth of 10 Mbits/s. VAXes in the same building are usually interconnected by Ethernet. Ethernet is also used to support terminal servers.
Terminal servers allow terminals to be logically connected to any
VAX on the network. Whereas Ethernet was designed for use in local
area networks (LANs), Ethernet bridges allow the Ethernet to be extended over long distances, even from one continent to another.

  Thinwire Ethernet is similar to standard Ethernet; the major difference is that the standard coaxial Ethernet cable is replaced by a thin-
ner version. Thinwire Ethernet hardware is more convenient to handle physically. Figure 1.2 shows an Ethernet network.

  VAXes can also be interconnected by point-to-point connections that
can be synchronous or asynchronous. These connections use the Digital Data Communications Protocol (DDCMP) under DECnet. Point-to-
point connections are normally used when VAXes are far apart or if
the connection is for a simple application where the installation of
Ethernet products is not cost-effective.

  DECNET also has SNA connectivity products, which allow VAXes
to communicate with IBM mainframes. Some of these products are
used for 3270 terminal emulation, APPC LU 6.2 task-to-task commu-

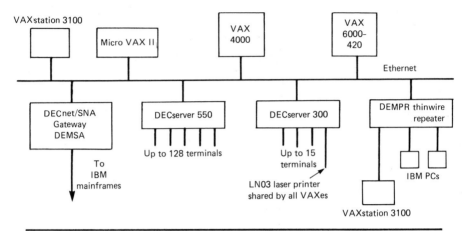

Figure 1.2   An Ethernet-based network.

nications, Remote Job Entry (RJE), and file transfer. DECnet also has support for X.25 connectivity, which allows VAXes to communicate with other computers on packet-switched networks like Telenet and Tymnet.

1.2 VAXclusters

A VAXcluster is a collection of VAXes running independently but sharing resources like tape and disk drives, printers, and batch job queues. A cluster is more tightly coupled than a network but more loosely coupled than a parallel processor. The cluster's shared communication path, called *computer interconnect* or CI, has a bus bandwidth of 70 Mbits/s. A typical cluster can match mainframe performance in most applications. Figure 1.3 shows a cluster block diagram.

   A cluster is more tightly coupled than a network, since devices can be shared, but it is more loosely coupled than a multiprocessor system, since each VAX in the cluster has an independent CPU and separate memory.

1.3 DIGITAL COMMAND LANGUAGE (DCL)

The user interface to VAX/VMS is the DCL. When a user logs in, a dollar sign prompt is issued by DCL:

   $

   DCL then waits for command input. DCL is a procedural language and an interpreter. Powerful programs (procedures) can be written using DCL. A sequence of commands can be stored in a file and executed at a later stage. DCL supports parameter substitution, commonly used

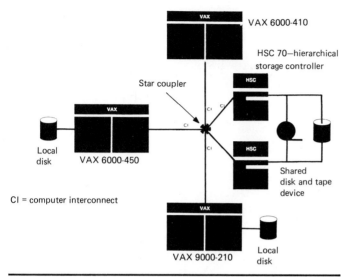

Figure 1.3   A typical VAXcluster configuration. (*Copy-right © 1986 Digital Equipment Corporation. All rights reserved. Reprinted by permission.*)

built-in functions, and conditional execution of commands. Here is an example of a DCL command:

```
$ BACKUP/VERIFY  DUA0:[TEST...]  MUA0:TEST.BCK/SAVE
```

Here is an example command file which compiles and links a COBOL program:

```
$! File: COBOLBUILD1.COM
$ COBOL PROGA.COB
$ LINK PROGA.OBJ
$ EXIT
```

Here is another example of a DCL command file. The command file compiles eight COBOL programs, PROG1.COB, PROG2.COB,...PROG8.COB, when executed by the command

```
$ @COBOL_BUILD
```

```
$! File: COBOL_BUILD.COM
$! Procedure to compile eight programs - PROG1 to PROG8
$ TEMP_VAR = 0            !variable to loop 8 times
$ compile:
$ COBOL PROG'TEMP_VAR'.COB
$ LINK PROG'TEMP_VAR'.OBJ
$ TEMP_VAR = TEMP_VAR + 1
$ IF TEMP_VAR .LT. 9 THEN $GOTO compile
$ EXIT
```

The chapter on DCL programming explains DCL in detail.

1.4 DECwindows

DECwindows is a windowing environment which runs on VAX-based graphics workstations. Decwindows is based on *The X-window system* developed at the Massachusetts Institute of Technology. It offers a graphics-oriented interaction with the VAX. DCL can be used in terminal emulation windows. Multiple windows allow multiple sessions to be displayed simultaneously.

X-windows may well become an industry standard for user interfaces. Currently, users accustomed to one vendor's products have to learn the new environment when moving over to another vendor's products. With X-windows this migration should become easy. To facilitate use of DECwindows, DEC has developed VAXstations which are suitable for windowing applications. Windowing applications are highly graphics-oriented, requiring parts of the screen to be painted very fast. VAXstations are suitable for this since the CPU is used mainly for handling the screen, although it can be used for running other applications. Basically, a VAXstation is a small VAX with a graphics terminal. The VAXstation normally connects to Ethernet and runs standard VAX/VMS. This book does not cover DECwindows in detail because of space limitations.

1.5 PROGRAM DEVELOPMENT

VAX/VMS and ULTRIX-32 are the major operating systems used on the VAX computers. Third-party Unix implementations are also used at many sites. ULTRIX-32 is DEC's implementation of Unix System V. In this book we will be looking only at VAX/VMS. Since VAX/VMS uses virtual memory management techniques, program size is usually not a limitation. Languages supported on the VAX/VMS include Ada, APL, BASIC, BLISS, C, COBOL, DIBOL, FORTRAN, LISP, VAX MACRO, OPS5, Pascal, PL/1, RPG II, SCAN, and VAX TPU. Of these, VAX TPU is the only language which comes bundled with the operating system. TPU (Text Processing Utility) is a programming language for manipulating textual data. Complex systems can be written in multiple languages with calls to programs written in other languages. The Run Time Library and System Services offer a collection of utility subroutines which can be called from programs.

Programs are created using an editor on the system. EVE (extensible VAX editor) is a popular editor. Other editors are EDT and LSE (language-sensitive editor). EDT was popular in the past but EVE is a more modern editor, so EDT is not discussed in this book.

A symbolic program debugger aids in program testing. The debugger displays multiple windows. Source code, program output, and user commands are displayed in separate windows. The debugger can be used for testing programs in any language. Conditional execution of statements and other features make the debugger a powerful programming tool.

The VAXset software engineering toolkit is a set of computer-aided software engineering (CASE) tools which aid in software project management. The toolkit consists of:

- *Code Management System* (CMS).   CMS manages source files for a project. It maintains a history of changes made to files by programmers.

- *Language Sensitive Editor* (LSE).   The LSE can be used to create or edit programs in any language. The editor provides cues on entering code which can be useful if you forget statement syntax. The programs can be compiled within the editor. Compilation errors can be displayed and the source program corrected from the editor.

- *Source Code Analyzer*(SCA).   SCA is a cross-referencing tool for analyzing usage of variables and routines. SCA can be used to search for variable declarations and usage in a set of source programs which constitute an executable image. The source program is displayed to show the exact occurrence of the variable.

- *Module Management System* (MMS).   MMS is used to build a system from an interdependent set of source programs (which constitute the system). Programs can be modified and then MMS can be used to generate the system. MMS checks revision dates on files and determines which parts of the system need to be compiled or rebuilt.

- *DEC Test Manager* (DTM).   DTM automates the testing of a software system to determine if the system runs as expected. DTM is a regression analysis tool. The programmer runs programs under DTM, which notes all input given by the programmer and all output generated by the application. Later on, when some programs are modified, DTM can be used to rerun the test to ensure that results are the same as those that were produced when the test was set up.

- *Performance and Coverage Analyzer* (PCA).   PCA shows how much time is spent by the CPU on each statement of a program during execution. It is an execution profiler which can be used to highlight bottlenecks in an application or to optimize programs.

Files used in programs can be sequential, relative, or indexed. The *record management services* (RMS) are used to manipulate files. RMS is normally available with the operating system. Many languages like COBOL automatically use RMS when files are handled within programs.

DECNET can be used to write distributed applications. Task-to-task communication is supported by DECNET.

1.6 LAYERED PRODUCTS

Most software products other than the operating system and DECNET are considered layered products. Some of the products are mentioned here but are not discussed any further in this book.

ALL-IN-1 is an integrated office automation package supporting word processing, graphics, spreadsheets, and electronic mail. Many of the subpackages used within ALL-IN-1 are also available separately. WPS-PLUS is a word processor. DECspell can be used to check and correct spellings. VAX Grammar Checker proofreads a document for grammatical correctness. VAX DECalc is a spreadsheet package. DECgraph can be used to prepare presentation graphs.

DEC offers a set of packages for application development:

- Two DBMSs are available from DEC. (1)VAX DBMS, which adheres to the Codasyl standard. It has a network architecture. (2)Rdb, which is a relational database management system. Rdb has an SQL (structured query language) interface.

- *Datatrieve* is a report writer and interpreter aiding fast program development at the expense of run time efficiency. It is good particularly for generating quick reports and graphical output.

- DECtp is a high-volume transaction processing system. It supports distributed processing and can be used for "mission critical" applications like electronic funds transfer where transaction integrity is required and failure of hardware components would be disastrous.

- *Applications control management system* (ACMS) is another transaction processing system which focuses on reduced application development time cycle.

Most end-user applications require forms to be displayed on screen and data to be accepted from fields within the form. While programmers can use standard input-output statements and perform data validation within programs, a number of packages are available for programming ease. *DECforms, terminal data management system* (TDMS), and *forms management system* (FMS) are used to design forms on screen. FMS is the oldest and currently the most commonly used screen design package. TDMS has most of the features of FMS; in addition, it can validate data without any programming. DECforms is the latest package conforming to ANSI/ISO FIMS (form interface management system). The DECform interface is being standardized by DEC for use with their DBMSs and other application development products.

VAX DOCUMENT is an electronic publishing package. Most of VAX documentation from DEC is created using this package. It is a good tool for producing in-house pamphlets, proposals, and other documents. It does not handle diagrams.

The DECtalk product consists of a hardware device and software programs. It can be used to create voice output and, when connected with a telephone system, it can recognize telephone key presses. In effect, an automated interactive telephone system can be designed.

VAX DEC/Shell is a Unix interface emulator. It is an alternative to the standard DCL interface.

1.7   SYSTEM MANAGEMENT

System management has different connotations for different people. Operator functions and network management are part of system management. Here are some typical system management tasks:

- Booting (starting up) and shutting down the system.

- Creating and modifying user accounts. The AUTHORIZE utility is used for this purpose.

- Performing disk backups. The BACKUP utility is used for this purpose.

- Monitoring system activity and tuning the system. Monitoring users, CPU, memory, disk usage, and network operations and processes. The MONITOR or the system performance analyzer (SPM) and the VAX performance advisor (VPA) can be used for this purpose.

- Generating accounting reports on resource usage by users. The ACCOUNTING utility can be used for this purpose.

- Installing and upgrading software products. VMSINSTAL can be used for this purpose.

- Customizing system command files and SYSGEN parameters. The AUTOGEN utility can be used to modify SYSGEN parameters.

1.8   CONVENTIONS

Certain conventions need to be mentioned here since they are pervasive throughout software products on VMS.

1.8.1   Prompts and qualifiers

Utilities and other software products issue a prompt consisting of a few characters followed by > . Examples are

UAF>	!issued by the AUTHORIZE utility
SYSGEN>	!issued by the SYSGEN utility
MAIL>	!issued by the MAIL utility
INSTALL>	!issued by the INSTALL utility

The HELP command can be entered to see how to use the utility. Almost all the software products have the HELP facility. Commands entered at the prompt are analyzed by the utility. Many utilities will accept commands stored in another file. To execute command files enter the file name preceded by the @ sign

```
INSTALL>  @INSCMD.COM
```

Control-Z is usually valid to exit from utilities.

Command qualifiers are specified after the command with the / sign. For example,

```
$ DIR/FULL
```

or

```
SYSGEN>  SHOW /DRIVER
```

Command and qualifier names can usually be shortened as long as they are unique. For example, the MOUNT command can be shortened to MOU but not to MO since there is another command which starts with MO, the MONITOR command.

1.8.2   Execution status

To abort any running application, the CTRL/Y key can be pressed. DCL will be ready to accept the next command. If CTRL/Y was pressed by mistake, the CONTINUE command can be issued to continue execution of the application.

When running any interactive application which does not display any data for a long time, the user at a terminal may want to be reassured that the application is running and not just "hung." Pressing CTRL/T causes a one-line status of CPU time, I/Os completed, and so on, to be displayed. The application continues normal execution. CTRL/T output is effective only if this command is issued before

```
$ SET CONTROL=T
```

1.8.3   Time format

Date and time have to be specified in many commands. The standard format is

dd-mmm-yyyy:hh:mm:ss.ss

Most of the fields are optional. Examples are

21-feb-1990:14:10

8:15   (8:15 am today)

31-dec-1990   (time is start of the day)

In most cases, the keywords YESTERDAY, TODAY, or TOMMOROW can also be specified. An example is

```
$ DIRECTORY /SINCE:YESTERDAY
```

1.9 VMS MANUALS

Basic documentation for VMS consists of the following kits:

- *Base set:* Overview of VMS, basic commands, system management and licence management.

- *General User Subkit:* VMS basics, DCL, editors and system messages.

- *System Management Subkit:* System maintenance, security, performance and networking.

- *Programming Subkit:* Programming utilitites (like debugger and linker), system routines, file system, system programming, device support and MACRO.

Other VMS documentation is on obsolete features and (new version) release notes. Each VAX has system-specific installation and operations manuals. Some other manuals are on RMS journaling, volume shadowing, parallel programming, and layered product development. Each software layered product has its own set of manuals, usually including a guide and a reference set. Hardware products also have separate manuals. A number of handbooks are also available.

1.10 FURTHER READING

Using VMS, Vol. 2A, General User Manuals.
Peters, J. F., and Holmay, P., *The VMS User's Guide*, Digital Press, Maynard, Mass., 1989.
VAX Professional Magazine (bi-monthly), Professional Press, Spring House, Pa.
Hubbard, J. R., *A Gentle Introduction to the VAX System*, TAB Professional and Reference Books, Blue Ridge Summit, Pa., 1987.
Malamud, Carl, *DEC Networks and Architectures*, McGraw-Hill, New York 1989.

Chapter

2

Getting Started on the System

VMS is a highly interactive operating system. Program development
functions, including compilations, are usually performed on-line. End-
user applications also run on-line with the user interface controlled by
one of the form management systems on VMS. Programs and commands can also be freely used in submitted batch files. Batch files are
typically used for end-of-day processing of on-line applications and
programs which run for a long time without any user interaction.

Terminal interaction is similar to that on PCs. Each character entered at the terminal is sent to the VAX, which in turn echoes it immediately, unlike mainframe terminals where characters are buffered
in the terminal until a function key is pressed. VT220 and VT320 are
the most common terminals. Many installations use third-party terminals which normally emulate VT series terminals. The user interface after log-in is also very much like that of most PCs. In fact, some
of the commands like DIRECTORY and TYPE are exactly the same in
their basic form. The system, though, is far more functional than a
PC, as will be seen in this book. This chapter introduces basic system
features for the novice user.

2.1   LOGGING IN

A user name and a password are required to gain access to the system.
These are supplied by the systems administrator. To log in interactively,
hit the Return key on the terminal. If the prompt local> is displayed,
then enter CONNECT nodename where node name is the name of the
system to log into. The Username: prompt should be displayed. Enter
your user name followed by the Return key. The next prompt will be
Password:. Enter your password. The password is not displayed. On successful log-in you should see the $ prompt. The prompt is issued by the
component of the operating system called *digital command language*

(DCL). DCL is your interface to the system. DCL commands can now be issued. All DCL commands are terminated with the Return key.

Terminal servers are described in the chapter on VAX/VMS hardware environment. Here is a sample log-in from a terminal connected to a terminal server.

```
Local> Connect  SCOOP

        Welcome to VAX/VMS V5.1-1

Username: SHAH
Password:
        Welcome to VAX/VMS version V5.1-1 on node SCOOP
        Last interactive login on Friday, 28-JUL-1989 12:51
        Last non-interactive login on Thursday, 27-JUL-1989 14:04
$
```

2.2 HELP

The HELP command is useful in order to see the list of commands which are recognized by DCL. HELP also displays usage information on the commands. Figure 2.1 shows an example of HELP usage.

2.3 DCL COMMANDS

DCL commands are terminated (and executed) by the Return key. Parameters for the command can be specified on the command line separated by spaces and/or tabs. If a required parameter is missing, DCL prompts for the parameter on the next line. For example, the TYPE command is used to display the contents of a file. It requires the file name as a parameter. To type the file MY.DOC, the command is

```
$ TYPE  MY.DOC
```

or

```
$ TYPE
_File: MY.DOC
```

The _indicates a continuation line. Most commands have qualifiers (also known as switches). Qualifiers specify options of the command. Qualifiers which apply to the command can be placed anywhere on the command line, qualifiers for particular parameters must follow the parameter. Qualifiers start with the slash character /. For example, all of the following commands will copy the file MY.DOC to the file YOUR.DOC and perform a read of the output record after each record is copied:

```
$ COPY/WRITE_CHECK  MY.DOC  YOUR.DOC
$ COPY  MY.DOC /WRITE_CHECK  YOUR.DOC
$ COPY  MY.DOC  YOUR.DOC/WRITE_CHECK
```

```
$ HELP

HELP

     The HELP command invokes the VAX-11 HELP Facility to display information
     about a VMS command or topic.  In response to the "Topic?" prompt, you can:

        Type the name of the command or topic for which you need help.

        Type PROCEDURES for information on commonly peformed tasks.

        Type HINTS if you are not sure of the name of the command or topic
        for which you need help.

        Type INSTRUCTIONS for more detailed instructions on how to use HELP.

        Type a question mark (?) to redisplay the most recently requested text.

        Press the RETURN key one or more times to exit from HELP.

     You can abbreviate any topic name, although ambiguous abbreviations result
     in all matches being displayed.


     Format:
     HELP [topic[subtopic]...]


     Additional information available:

ACCOUNTING ADVISE       ALLOCATE    ANALYZE     APPEND      Ascii       ASSIGN
ATTACH     BACKUP       CALL        CANCEL      CLOSE       Command_procedure
CONNECT    CONTINUE     CONVERT     COPY        CREATE      DEALLOCATE DEASSIGN
DEBUG      DECK         DEFINE      DELETE      DEPOSIT     DIFFERENCES
DIRECTORY  DISCONNECT DISMOUNT     DUMP        EDIT        EOD         EXAMINE
EXIT       Expressions              File_spec  GOSUB       GOTO        HELP
Hints      IF           INITIALIZE INQUIRE     Instructions            Lexicals
LIBRARY    LINK         LOGOUT      MAIL        MERGE       MESSAGE     MOUNT
New_Features_V44         Numbers    ON          OPEN        PERFORMANCE
PRINT      Privileges Procedures Protection PURGE          READ        RECALL
RENAME     REPLY        REQUEST     RETURN      RUN         RUNOFF      SEARCH
SET        SHOW         SNA_GM      SNA_Terminals           SORT        SPAWN
SPM        START        STOP        Strings     SUBMIT      Symbol_assignment
SYNCHRONIZE             THEN        Time        TYPE        UNLOCK      VPA
WAIT       WRITE

Topic? time

TIME

     Absolute time:

        dd-mmm-yyyy:hh:mm:ss.ss
        TODAY
```

Figure 2.1   Sample on-line HELP usage.

If a command takes a long time to execute, entering CTRL/T will
display a one-line status on the execution. Execution will not be interrupted. The status line displays the CPU time and I/Os performed.
These should keep increasing every time CTRL/T is entered. A command execution can be aborted by CTRL/Y. If CTRL/Y is entered by

```
          YESTERDAY
          TOMORROW

Delta time:

     dd-hh:mm:ss.ss

Combination time:

     An absolute time plus (+) or minus (-) a delta time.  Whenever a plus
     sign precedes the delta time value, the entire time specification must
     be enclosed in quotation marks.

     If a description states that a time can be expressed as an absolute time,
     a delta time, or a combination time, then you must specify a delta time
     as if it were part of a combination time.

Topic? wait

WAIT

     Puts your process into a wait state for the specified amount of time.

     Format
      WAIT time


     Additional information available:

     Parameters

WAIT Subtopic? para

WAIT

     Parameters

        time
        A time interval specified in the format hour:minute:second.hundredth,
        where hour is an integer in the range 0 through 59; minute is an
        integer in the range 0 through 59; second is an integer in the range 0
        through 59; hundredth (of a second) is an integer in the range 0
        through 99; the colons and period are required delimiters.  The
        format is hh:mm:ss.ss.

WAIT Subtopic? <RETURN>
Topic? <RETURN>
$
```

Figure 2.1   *(Continued)*

mistake, execution can be resumed by entering the CONTINUE command. Here is an example.

```
(Control-t display):
SCOOP::SHAH   15:07:38   VMSHELP    CPU=00:00:21.98   PF=4819   IO=236   MEM=623
```

The parameters displayed are node name, process name, time, image name, CPU time used by the process, page faults, I/O count, and working set size.

2.4   THE TERMINALS

DEC terminals use the ASCII character set for communication with the host. The terminal-to-host communications protocol is RS232 or RS423. The two major types of terminals are hard-copy terminals like the DECwriter III (LA120) and video terminals like the VT300 series. DECwindow terminals also offer a VT terminal emulator which functions essentially as the standard VT terminals. The VT300 series terminals supercede the older VT200 and VT100 series terminals. These terminals have a screen display of 80 or 132 columns of 25 lines. The twenty-fifth line is used for status displays. The top 24 lines scroll up when new lines are displayed at the bottom of the screen. Figure 2.2 shows the keyboard of a VT300 series terminal.

The keys are classified into four groups:

1. *Main keypad:* This is similar to the keyboard on most other computer terminals. Some keys need special mention:

CTRL	This key pressed with most other keys generates special codes. For example, pressing CTRL, keeping it pressed, and then pressing C generates the code 03. This two-key combination is written as CTRL/C.
LOCK	Switches between uppercase and lowercase character mode for the alphabetic keys. The lock indicator at the top right of the keyboard will be lit when the keyboard is in uppercase mode.
Compose character	This key is used to generate extended ASCII characters. Typically, the compose key is pressed followed by two other keys to generate a code. It is used mainly to generate foreign language characters.
< X]	This key is at the top right of the keyboard. It is the DELETE key, usually used to delete the last character entered.

Conventionally, some of the control keys have special meanings:

CTRL/C	Abort the current application and exit.
CTRL/Q	Continue a display stopped by CTRL/S. An XOFF character is sent to the system by the terminal.
CTRL/S	Stop all display to the terminal. An XON character is sent to the system by the terminal. This is useful to "freeze" the screen to check up what is displayed before allowing more information to be displayed. The HOLD-SCREEN key, F1, can also be used.
CTRL/T	Display a one-line summary of the process. For example, if you have issued the COPY command to copy a very large file,

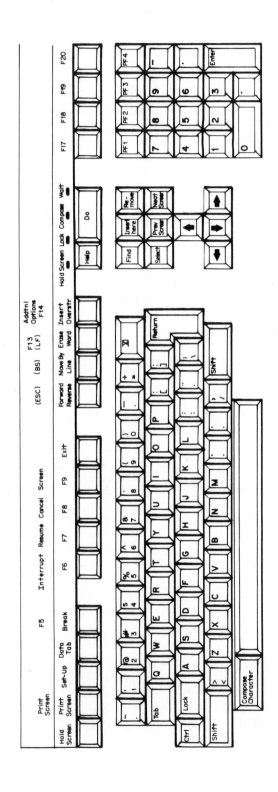

Figure 2.2 The VT series terminal keyboard.

CTRL/T can be used every few seconds to see the CPU time going up. If the CPU time is not going up, there may be a problem with the copy operation or the system.

CTRL/W   Refresh the screen if disturbed by, say, a power fluctuation.

CTRL/Y   Abort (interrupt) the current application and exit to DCL.

CTRL/Z   Exit from the current program.

2. *Editing keypad:* These keys are used by editors and screen-oriented forms and menus. The arrow keys are used by DCL also for command editing.

3. *Numeric keypad:* The keys PF1 to PF4 generate special codes. The other keys normally generate the codes displayed. Normally, the ENTER key is equivalent to the RETURN key. The numeric keypad can be programmed to transform into an application keypad. A different set of codes is generated when the keypad is in application mode. The keys are then interpreted in various ways depending on the application.

4. *Function keys:* There are 20 of these, F1 to F20. F1 is the HOLD-SCREEN key. It is used to stop or continue a display which is scrolling up on the screen. F2 dumps the screen image to the printer port of the terminal. It is used to generate hard copies of displays. F3 is used to enter the terminal SET-UP menu. The SET-UP menu allows you to change terminal characteristics like transmission speed and tab position settings. F4 is used to switch to the other session on dual session terminals like the VT330 and VT340. Note that the keys F1 to F4 do not send any codes to the computer. The F5 key generates the BREAK character, which is used by communications equipment. When the terminal is connected to terminal servers like the DECserver 200, 300, or 550, the BREAK key breaks the session temporarily and allows the terminal to issue DECserver commands. The session can be continued by the RESUME command issued to the DECserver.

The keys F6 to F20 generate codes which can be interpreted by the receiving application. Certain conventions are observed by most applications:

F6 is interpreted as CTRL/C.

F10 is interpreted as EXIT (or CTRL/Z).

F15 is used as a HELP key.

F16 (or DO) is used to temporarily change the mode of operation. For example, the EVE editor changes the mode from text entry to command entry when the key is pressed.

2.5 BASIC COMMANDS

All DCL command and qualifier names can be abbreviated to the first
four characters. Many commands and qualifiers can be abbreviated
further if the name does not conflict with the abbreviation of a different command or qualifier. A complete DCL command is entered as:

```
$ cmdname /cmdqual1/cmdqual2 ... para1/qual1/qual2 ... para2 ...
```

Qualifiers to a parameter or the command name can be specified in any
order following the parameter or the command name. Most command
name qualifiers can be specified anywhere on the command line.

2.5.1 TYPE

TYPE is used to display the contents of one or more files. For example,
to display files MY.DOC and PAYROLL.DATA, the command is

```
$ TYPE MY.DOC,PAYROLL.DATA
```

or

```
$ TY MY.DOC,PAYROLL.DATA
```

2.5.2 DIRECTORY

The DIRECTORY command is used to see the list of files in a directory on disk or tape. It displays the contents of the default directory on
the default disk. If a disk name and/or directory is specified as a parameter then the contents of that disk and/or directory is displayed.
For example, to display the contents of directory [TEST] on the default
disk the command is:

```
$ DIR  [TEST]
```

The /SIZE qualifier lists the size of the specified files and the /DATE
qualifier displays the creation dates of the files. For example,

```
$ DIR /SIZE /DATE  [BOOK]

Directory DUA5:[BOOK]

BOOK.INDEX;4     12    21-DEC-1988 04:22
SETHOST.LOG;2     7     3-MAY-1989 16:51
SETHOST.LOG;1    13     3-MAY-1989 16:43
START.DOC;3      17     3-MAY-1989 17:43
START.DOC;2      15     3-MAY-1989 17:32
START.DOC;1       2     3-MAY-1989 16:13
TMP.TMP;1         0     3-MAY-1989 17:44
Total of 6 files, 54 blocks.
```

Note that file names are sorted in alphabetic order. Also, file names contain a semicolon followed by a number called version. Typically, when a file is modified and written back by, say, the editor, a new version of the file is created. The new version is numbered one higher than the old one. Version numbers are described in more detail later in this chapter.

2.5.3 COPY

The command is used to make additional copies of files on disk or tape. For example, to copy MY.DOC to the directory [TEST] with a new name YOUR.DOC the command is

```
$ COPY  MY.DOC   [TEST]YOUR.DOC
```

2.5.4 RENAME

The command is used to change the names of existing files on disk. For example, to rename MY.DOC to JAY.DOC the command is

```
$ RENAME  MY.DOC  JAY.DOC
```

The RENAME command is useful to move a file from one directory to another. Move means to place the file in the new directory and remove it from the original directory. For example,

```
$ RENAME  [APPLE]MY.DOC  [NEWDIR]MY.DOC
```

MY.DOC is removed from the directory [APPLE] and placed in the directory [NEWDIR]. In fact, this feature can be used to move a complete directory and its sub-directories. For example, suppose the directory [BOOK] is under the directory [PETER] and now it is to be removed from [PETER] and placed under the directory [SHANKER.PROJECTS]. The command would be,

```
$ RENAME  [PETER]BOOK.DIR  [SHANKER.PROJECTS]BOOK.DIR
```

Now the directories and files which were under [PETER.BOOK] are accesses via the directory [SHANKER.PROJECTS.BOOK]. Files cannot be moved from one disk to another using this command. The COPY command followed by the DELETE command will have to used.

2.5.5 DELETE

The command is used to delete files. For example, the next command deletes version 2 of the file MY.DOC.

```
$ DELETE  MY.DOC;2
```

2.5.6 PURGE

Files on VAX/VMS have version numbers. When a file is edited, a new version of the file is created, but the old version still exists. For example, editing MY.DOC;8 (version 8 of MY.DOC) creates MY.DOC;9. If older versions are not deleted, many versions of files will exist on disk. Older versions should be periodically deleted to reduce cluttering of files and also to conserve disk space. The DELETE command can be used to delete files, but the PURGE command specifically deletes older versions of files. For example, to delete all except the latest version of the file MY.DOC, the command is

```
$ PURGE  MY.DOC
```

The /KEEP:n qualifier is useful to retain the last n versions of a file. To delete all but the latest three versions of MY.DOC the command is

```
$ PURGE/KEEP:3  MY.DOC
```

or even

```
$ PURGE  MY.DOC/KEEP:3
```

2.5.7 SET

This command is used to change various characteristics of the system or the current process. The SET PASSWORD command allows you to change your log-in password.

The SET TIME command is used to change the system date and time. The command requires you to have OPER and LOG_IO privileges. The format for specifying time is

dd-mmm-yyyy:hh:mm:ss.cc

where cc specifies hundredths of second. Most of the fields are optional. Date fields not specified are filled in from the current date, while time fields not specified are set to zero. Some examples follow:

```
$ SET TIME=7-SEP-1989:18:30:15.12
$ SET TIME=21-JAN-1992
$ SET TIME=18:30
```

SET DEFAULT is used to change your defaults disk drive and/or directory. The defaults are used when accessing files on disks. For example,

```
$ SET DEFAULT  DUB0:[TEST]
```

2.5.8 SHOW

The SHOW commands are used to display process or system characteristics. Commonly used SHOW commands are

$ SHOW DEFAULT   displays the default disk and directory used when accessing files.

$ SHOW MEMORY   displays system memory usage statistics.

$ SHOW NETWORK   displays names and node-numbers of computers which the VAX can communicate with. If the node is not a router, only the current node name and its router node name are displayed.

$ SHOW PROCESS   displays process name,terminal name, process identification, default disk and directory, User Identification Code (UIC) and process priority. Additionally, the /ALL qualifier displays process quotas, accounting information, dynamic memory usage, privileges, and rights identifiers.

$ SHOW SYSTEM   displays all processes running in the system along with their identification and resource usage information.

$ SHOW TIME   displays system data and time.

$ SHOW USERS   displays interactive users on the system (or cluster) along with their processes and terminal name.

2.5.9   PRINT

PRINT is used to queue files for printing. To print the files MY.DOC and YOUR.DOC, the command is

```
$ PRINT MY.DOC,YOUR.DOC
```

The command has a number of qualifiers:

/COPIES   number of printed copies of the file.

/DELETE   delete the file after printing.

/FLAG   print a banner page before printing the file.

/FORM   use a specified form (paper type) to print the file. The list of forms can be seen by SHOW QUEUE/FORM.

/HEADER   print a header line on every page of output. The header contains the file name and page number.

/PAGE   print specified pages of the file. For example, to print pages 5 through 20 the qualifier is /PAGE:(5,20).

/QUEUE   queue the file to a specified queue. Typically, each printer on the system will have one associated queue. To see the queues on the system the command is SHOW QUEUE. If this qualifier is not specified the file is sent to the queue SYS$PRINT.

For example,

```
$ PRINT  MY.DOC/COPIES=3/DELETE/FORM=LONG/QUEUE=LN03$PRINT
```

2.6 COMMAND EDITING

2.6.1 Command recall

DCL maintains a buffer for each terminal where it stores up to 20 previously entered commands. These commands can be recalled, edited, and reexecuted. To recall all the commands use

```
$ RECALL/ALL
```

To recall a particular command, say the fifth one, use

```
$ RECALL 5
```

The up and down arrow keys can also be used to scroll through the commands.

2.6.2 Editing the command line

Figure 2.3 lists the keys which are useful to edit the current or a recalled command line.

2.7 ERROR MESSAGES

VAX/VMS software adheres to a convention for displaying error messages. The operating system, compilers, utilities, and most other software display error messages in a uniform format. Here is an example of an error message when the TYPE command is not issued correctly:

```
$ TYPO  MY.DOC
%DCL-W-IVVERB, unrecognized command verb - check validity and spelling
\TYPO\
```

Key	Function
DELETE	Delete the last character entered
CTRL/A	Toggle between overstrike and insert modes. The mode applies to new characters entered on the command line.
Left arrow	Move cursor one character to the left.
CTRL/E	Move cursor to the end of line.
Right arrow	Move cursor one character to the right.
F12, CTRL/H, or BS	Move cursor to the beginning of line.
F13 or CTRL/J	Delete the word to the left of the cursor.
CTRL/U	Delete all characters to the left of cursor.

Figure 2.3 Command line editing keys.

The syntax for error messages is:

%FACILITY-L-IDENT, text

The fields are

FACILITY   The name of the program issuing the message.

L   Severity level of the message:
             S—success
             I—informational
             W—warning
             E—error
             F—fatal or severe error

IDENT   Abbreviated description.

text   Description in plain English.

Here is an example of the TYPE command specifying a file name
which does not exist on disk:

```
$ TYPE ME.DOC
%TYPE-W-SEARCHFAIL, error searching for SYS$SYSDEVICE:[SHAH]ME.DOC;
-RMS-E-FNF, file not found
```

2.8 DEVICES

Devices are usually attached to controllers which are circuit boards in
the CPU chassis (cabinet). A number of devices could be attached to
one controller. An example of a device name is DUB2:. A device is
identified as

DDCnnn:

where DD = is the generic device name (sometimes this has 3 characters).
      C = is the controller designation.
    nnn = is the specific device on the controller.

Corresponding to controllers, the operating system has software device drivers. For example, the KDB50 disk controller consists of two
boards which can be inserted in the backplane of a VAX 8700. This
controller can handle up to four RA series disk drives. The generic device name of the disks is DU. The software device driver is called
DUDRIVER. The controller is designated as A. The four disks will be
known as DUA0:, DUA1:, DUA2:, and DUA3:. If another controller is
added to the system, then it will be designated as B and the disks attached with this controller will be known as DUB0:, DUB1:, DUB2:

Device name	Device type	Typical devices
CS	Console floppy	RX02 floppy drive
DJ	Disks	RA60 removable disk
DU	Disks	RA90 fixed disk
LI	Line printer	LP25 300 lines per minute line-printer
LP	Line printer	LP29 2000 lines per minute line printer
LT	LAT devices (terminals over ethernet)	VT320 terminal or LN03 laser printer.
MU	Tapes	TA78 125 inch per second tape drive
MS	Tapes	TU81-PLUS streaming tape drive
MT	Tapes	TE16 tape drives
MB	Mailbox (software device)	MBA12:
NET	Network communications (software device)	NET4:
NL	NULL device (software device)	
OP	Operator console (software device)	
TT	Terminals	VT320 terminal
TX	Terminals	VT320 terminal
VT	Virtual terminal (software device)	VTA2:
XE	Ethernet	DEBNT controller for VAXBI bus. Connects to Ethernet cable
XQ	Ethernet	DELQA controller for Qbus bus. Connects to Ethernet cable.

Figure 2.4   Common devices on VAX/VMS.

and DUB3:. Figure 2.4 shows some devices and their mnemonic device names.

The system also supports software "devices." These have device drivers in the operating system but there is no hardware corresponding to them. An example is the mailbox device, MB, which is used for sending data from one process to another.

Device names on VAXcluster systems are preceded by the name of the computer on which the device resides and a $ sign. For example:

```
SCOOP$DUB6:   !VAXcluster device name for disk DUB6:
```

2.9   FILES

Here are some examples of file specifications:

```
SCOOP::DUA4:[TEST]PAYROLL.COB;27
SCOOP::PAYROLL.COB
DUA4:PAYROLL.COB
[TEST]PAYROLL.COB
PAYROLL.COB;-2
123_LONG_FILE_NAME.LONG_FILE_TYPE
```

Files can be created on disk or tape devices. The file specification syntax is

nodename::device:[directory]filename.filetype;version

Fields not specified assume default values. Default values depend on the command used to operate on the file. Generally, if version number is not specified, then the latest version is assumed. Node name is the computer on which the file resides. If it is not specified the node is assumed to be the VAX you are currently using.

Each process has a default device and directory. These are specified by the system manager in the user authorization file. When specifying file names, if the device and directory are not specified, the default values are assumed. To see the defaults use SHOW DEFAULT. To change the defaults use SET DEFAULT. For example,

```
$ SET DEFAULT  DJA2:[TEST.PROGRAMS]
```

Usually, filename and filetype have no default values. Each of these fields can be up to 39 characters long.

Version numbers start at 1 and can go up to 32,767. When not specified, it is assumed to be the latest version number. Version numbers is an extension of the .BAK method used on smaller computers for keeping previous versions of files. The latest version of the file can also be referenced as version 0. Versions can be specified going backward starting at the latest version by using a minus sign before the version. For example, if a file has 12 versions, then version −1 is the same as version 11.

Chapter 3, "Files and Directories," has more information.

2.9.1 Wildcards

Suppose you wish to create another copy of all the files in your directory which have a file type of COB. The next command copies all the COB files in your directory to the directory [BACKUP]:

```
$ COPY  *.COB  [BACKUP]*.*
```

The * is called a *wildcard*. It will match files with any file name and file type of COB. Wildcards are used to select a subset of files. The percent sign (%) is another wildcard. It matches any single character at the position specified. The ... wildcard is used to search for files in all subdirectories of the specified subdirectory. Usually, wildcards can be used wherever a file specification is required in DCL commands. Wildcards are not valid on node names and the percent wildcard is not valid on version numbers.

Examples of file specifications with wildcards follow:

PAYROLL.COB;*	All versions of PAYROLL.COB.
.;*	All files in the default device and directory.
PAY%.COB	Files having 4 characters in the file name with the first three characters PAY and file type as COB.
PAY*.COB	Files having first three characters as PAY in file name and file type as COB.
P*LL.COB	Files having file names starting with P and ending with LL and file type as COB.
[*]PAYROLL.COB	PAYROLL.COB files in all directories on the default disk.
[TEST...]PAYROLL.COB	PAYROLL.COB files in the [TEST] directory and all sub-directories of [TEST].

2.10   THE PROCESS

A *process* is the environment in which a program image executes. A number of processes are created when the system is brought up. Normally, the operating system creates a process for each user logged in. Processes can also be created by users. The operating system maintains a list of parameters which define the environment in which each process is running. The SHOW PROCESS command displays some of the process parameters. The /ALL qualifier displays a more complete list of parameters. Figure 2.5 shows a sample usage of the command.
The display consists of seven groups:

- Summary of process.

- Process quotas.

- Accounting information. This group displays a summary of resource usage.

- Privileges the process owns. Privileges are generally required to access resources not assigned to you. For example, the READALL privilege allows you to read files which are owned by other users. There are about 30 privileges which can be assigned to each user by the system administrator.

- Rights identifiers the process owns. These are privileges which allow you to access objects like files and memory sections which are protected by these rights.

- Summary of memory use by the process.

- Subprocesses created by the top-level process using the SPAWN command. These processes normally inherit the parent's process parameters. The ATTACH command can be used to attach the terminal to any one of these processes. In this case the process SCOTT

```
$ SHOW PROCESS /ALL

5-DEC-1989 12:44:33.42                   User: SCOTT
Pid: 0000023D   Proc. name: SCOTT_2      UIC: [BOOKS,SCOTT]
Priority:   4   Default file spec: DUA3:[SCOTT.MEMO]
Devices mounted: DUB6:

Process Quotas:
Account name: SCOTT
CPU limit:                      Infinite  Direct I/O limit:      20000
Buffered I/O byte count quota:    108880  Buffered I/O limit:    20000
Timer queue entry quota:            1000  Open file quota:         995
Paging file quota:                 17533  Subprocess quota:          9
Default page fault cluster:           64  AST limit:               198
Enqueue quota:                      1000  Shared file limit:       900
Max detached processes:                0  Max active jobs:           0

Accounting information:
Buffered I/O count:      138  Peak working set size:      388
Direct I/O count:          9  Peak virtual size:         2467
Page faults:             373  Mounted volumes:              0
Images activated:          1
Elapsed CPU time:      0 00:00:00.41
Connect time:          0 00:00:09.05

Process privileges:
CMKRNL          may change mode to kernel
DETACH          may create detached processes
ALTPRI          may set any priority value
OPER            operator privilege
EXQUOTA         may exceed quota
SYSGBL          may create system wide global sections
SHMEM           may create/delete objects in shared memory
SHARE           may assign channels to non-shared device
READALL         may read anything as the owner

Process rights identifiers:
 INTERACTIVE
 LOCAL
Process Dynamic Memory Area
    Current Size (bytes)        25600  Current Total Size (pages)   50
    Free Space (bytes)          21768  Space in Use (bytes)       3832
    Size of Largest Block       21712  Size of Smallest Block       16
    Number of Free Blocks           3  Free Blocks LEQU 32 Bytes     1
Processes in this tree:

SCOTT
  SCOTT_2 (*)
```

Figure 2.5 SHOW PROCESS output.

created the subprocess SCOTT_2. The symbol (*) indicates that SCOTT_2 is the current process.

2.11 OPERATING SYSTEM BASICS

When you log onto the system, a process is created which controls your terminal. The name of the process is the same as your username. More than one process in the system can have the same name but each process has a unique process identification number, or PID. The RUN/DETACH command can be used to create additional processes.

```
$ SHOW SYSTEM

VAX/VMS V5.1-1  on node SCOOP 4-DEC-1989 15:33:40.96   Uptime   5 19:18:05
   Pid   Process Name     State  Pri      I/O         CPU        Page flts Ph.Mem
00000081 SWAPPER          HIB    16        0   0 00:01:00.58        0      0
00000084 ERRFMT           HIB     8     5907   0 00:00:13.07       70    100
00000085 OPCOM            LEF     9     3060   0 00:00:08.29    11536    149
00000086 JOB_CONTROL      HIB     9     2983   0 00:00:06.24      129    260
00000087 VAXsim_Monitor   HIB     8     1560   0 00:00:03.46      345    204
00000088 NETACP           HIB    10    48295   0 00:12:36.72      401    301
00000089 EVL              HIB     6      293   0 00:00:00.90   123672     54  N
0000008A REMACP           HIB     9       63   0 00:00:00.11       77     53
0000008B SYMBIONT_0001    HIB     6       31   0 00:00:00.22      349    306
000001B2 _LTA63:          LEF     7     8486   0 00:02:16.65    77765   1000
000001B4 JANE             LEF     4   246446   0 00:39:15.96   568988    928
000001C1 SCOTT_1          CUR     4      148   0 00:00:00.41      355    370  S
000001C2 SCOTT            HIB     4    12018   0 00:00:26.42     4222   1271
```

Figure 2.6 SHOW SYSTEM output.

The process named JOB_CONTROL on many systems is a detached process which controls batch and print jobs. In fact, your process is a detached process created by the operating system when you log in.

The SHOW SYSTEM command displays the processes on the system. Figure 2.6 shows a sample usage of the command. The SHOW USER command displays users logged in from terminals. Figure 2.7 shows a sample usage of the command.

The SWAPPER process is created by the operating system. SWAPPER handles process swapping to and from disk when there are many processes on the system and not enough main memory or when restructuring processes in memory. ERRFMT formats and logs errors like device malfunctions. EVL (Event Logger) formats and logs network errors. NETACP handles file access on other computers on the network. REMACP controls user log-ins on this system from other systems on the network. VAXsim_monitor performs system integrity checks and reports degradation in system performance and devices. SYMBIONT processes send output from queues to printers connected to the system. OPCOM intercepts output for operators from the operating system and user processes. The output is sent to terminals designated as operator consoles and optionally logged to a disk file. The

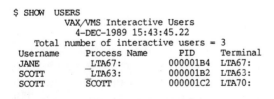

```
$ SHOW  USERS
            VAX/VMS Interactive Users
             4-DEC-1989 15:43:45.22
      Total number of interactive users = 3
   Username     Process Name     PID      Terminal
   JANE         _LTA67:       000001B4   LTA67:
   SCOTT        _LTA63:       000001B2   LTA63:
   SCOTT        SCOTT         000001C2   LTA70:
```

Figure 2.7 SHOW USERS output.

default disk log file is SYS$MANAGER:OPERATOR.LOG. The only other executable unit on the system is the operating system.

The two commands have given some other information. The system was up for more than five days. Process priority can be from 0 to 31. Lower-priority processes get CPU time only if higher priority processes do not require it. User processes usually execute at priority 4. CPU and I/O utilization are displayed for each process. The other columns are explained in later chapters. User SCOTT has logged into the system from two terminals. The first time a user logs in, the operating system creates a process with the username of the user. Further logins by the same user create processes with the name of the terminal from where the log-in is performed preceded by a underscore. The process with PID 000001C1 was created by the SPAWN command issued from the process SCOTT. The SPAWN command can be used to create a tree of subprocesses. The name of a spawned process is formed by using the process name of the top-level process followed by the underscore and a digit.

The SHOW MEMORY command displays a summary on system memory usage. Figure 2.8 shows a sample usage of the command.

The display indicates that about 69 percent (45,379/65,536) of main memory is unused. The process entry slots specify the number of processes that can be created on the system. The balance set slots specify the number of processes which can be in memory. If more processes than the maximum are created, some processes will be swapped out onto disk. Processes may also be swapped out if there is not enough

```
$ SHOW MEMORY
             System Memory Resources on  4-DEC-1989 16:32:39.67

Physical Memory Usage (pages):    Total      Free     In Use    Modified
   Main Memory (32.00Mb)          65536     45379      19891         266

Slot Usage (slots):               Total      Free    Resident     Swapped
   Process Entry Slots               70        44          26           0
   Balance Set Slots                 59        35          24           0

Fixed-Size Pool Areas (packets):  Total      Free     In Use        Size
   Small Packet (SRP) List          826        93         733          96
   I/O Request Packet (IRP) List    522       158         364         208
   Large Packet (LRP) List           60         0          60        1584

Dynamic Memory Usage (bytes):     Total      Free     In Use     Largest
   Nonpaged Dynamic Memory       3072000    722528    2349472      703248
   Paged Dynamic Memory           276992     59008     217984       55584

Paging File Usage (pages):                   Free     In Use       Total
   DISK$FEDBEDISK:[SYS0.SYSEXE]SWAPFILE.SYS  39536     10464       50000
   DISK$FEDBEDISK:[SYS0.SYSEXE]PAGEFILE.SYS  83338      6662       90000

Of the physical pages in use, 10620 pages are permanently allocated to VMS.
```

Figure 2.8   SHOW MEMORY output.

```
$ SHOW DEVICES
```

Device Name	Device Status	Error Count	Volume Label	Free Blocks	Trans Count	Mnt Cnt
DJA1:	Mounted	0	SYSDEVICE	23697	4	1
DUA3:	Mounted	0	DEVELOP	342270	112	1
DUB2:	Online	0				
DUB3:	Mounted	0	DEVELOP2	1057755	1	1

Device Name	Device Status	Error Count	Volume Label	Free Blocks	Trans Count	Mnt Cnt
MUA0:	Online	92				

Device Name	Device Status	Error Count
LTA0:	Offline	0
LTA23:	Online	0
OPA0:	Online	0
TXA7:	Online alloc	0

Device Name	Device Status	Error Count
LIA0:	Online alloc	0

Device Name	Device Status	Error Count
ETA0:	Online	0
PTA0:	Online	2
PUA0:	Online	1

Figure 2.9 SHOW DEVICES output.

```
$ SHOW DEVICE DUB3: /FULL
```

Disk DUB3:, device type RA82, is online, mounted, file-oriented device, shareable, available to cluster, error logging is enabled.

Error count	0	Operations completed	64603
Owner process	""	Owner UIC	[SYSTEM,TEST]
Owner process ID	00000000	Dev Prot	S:RWED,O:RWED,G:RWED,W:RWED
Reference count	1	Default buffer size	512
Total blocks	1216665	Sectors per track	57
Total cylinders	1423	Tracks per cylinder	15
Volume label	"DEVELOP2"	Relative volume number	0
Cluster size	3	Transaction count	1
Free blocks	1057755	Maximum files allowed	152083
Extend quantity	5	Mount count	1
Mount status	System	Cache name	"_DUA4:XQPCACHE"
Extent cache size	64	Maximum blocks in extent cache	105768
File ID cache size	64	Blocks currently in extent cache	50916
Quota cache size	0	Maximum buffers in FCP cache	273

Volume status: subject to mount verification, file high-water marking, write-through caching enabled.

Figure 2.10 SHOW DEVICES/FULL output.

```
$ SHOW  DEVICE  DUB3:  /FILES

Files accessed on device _DUB3: on  5-DEC-1989 12:35:37.46
Process name       PID     File name
                 00000000  [000000]INDEXF.SYS;1
SCOTT            000001B2  [SCOTT.DAT]TST_MESSAGES.DATA;1
SCOTT            000001B2  [SCOTT.DAT]SECURITY_FILE.DATA;1
SCOTT            000001B2  [SCOTT.TEST]POSITION_FILE.TEST;1
_LTA67:          000001B4  [JANE.DOC]MASTER_TABLE.DOCUMENT;1
```

Figure 2.11 SHOW DEVICES/FILES output.

physical memory to accommodate all the processes. The fixed-size pool area contains fixed-size slots of memory which are used when quick allocation and deallocation of small chunks of memory is required. Dynamic memory is where the processes and most of the operating system resides. Only a part of the operating system is in static memory. The paging files are used for swapped out processes and pages. These files must be created using the SYSGEN procedure and they must be large enough to accommodate any swapping and paging space requirements of the operating system.

The SHOW DEVICES command displays a summary of devices on the system as shown in Fig. 2.9. It is useful to find out which devices are mounted, free space on disks, which devices are allocated to processes, and the number of device malfunction errors on devices.

The error count gives the number of errors which have occurred while accessing the device. Error details can be displayed by creating an error report using the command ANALYZE/ERROR. Devices having the alloc status are for exclusive use of the process which has issued the ALLOCATE command for the device. The devices are grouped by disks, tapes, terminals, printers, and others. Further details on devices, like total space on a disk, can be displayed by using the /FULL qualifier. Figure 2.10 shows a sample usage of the command.

The /FILES qualifier is useful to find out all the files currently being accessed from a disk. Figure 2.11 shows a sample usage of the command.

The MONITOR utility is a useful tool to observe system behavior. It sends output to a file or displays it to your terminal updating the information at specified intervals (by default, every 3 seconds). Figure 2.12 shows some examples of MONITOR usage. The qualifiers are:

TOPCPU   lists the processes which are consuming the most CPU time.

TOPDIO   displays processes performing the most I/O mainly to disks and tapes.

TOPBIO   displays processes performing the most I/O mainly to terminals, printers, and over the network to other computers.

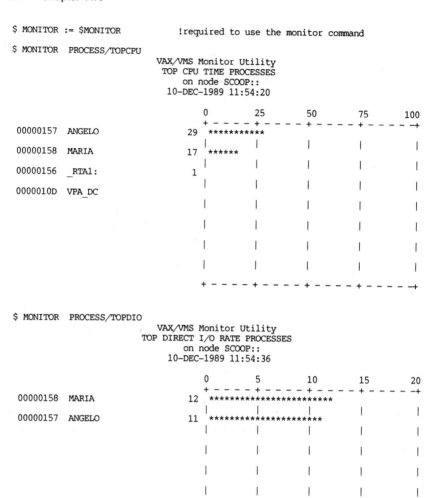

```
$ MONITOR := $MONITOR              !required to use the monitor command

$ MONITOR  PROCESS/TOPCPU
                          VAX/VMS Monitor Utility
                          TOP CPU TIME PROCESSES
                            on node SCOOP::
                          10-DEC-1989 11:54:20

                            0       25      50      75      100
                            + - - - + - - - + - - - + - - - -+
   00000157  ANGELO        29  ***********
                              |       |       |       |        |
   00000158  MARIA         17  ******
                              |       |       |       |        |
   00000156  _RTA1:         1
                              |       |       |       |        |
   0000010D  VPA_DC
                              |       |       |       |        |

                              |       |       |       |        |

                              |       |       |       |        |

                              |       |       |       |        |
                            + - - - + - - - + - - - + - - - -+


$ MONITOR  PROCESS/TOPDIO
                          VAX/VMS Monitor Utility
                        TOP DIRECT I/O RATE PROCESSES
                            on node SCOOP::
                          10-DEC-1989 11:54:36

                            0       5       10      15      20
                            + - - - + - - - + - - - + - - - -+
   00000158  MARIA         12  ************************
                              |       |       |       |        |
   00000157  ANGELO        11  ***********************
                              |       |       |       |        |

                              |       |       |       |        |

                              |       |       |       |        |

                              |       |       |       |        |

                              |       |       |       |        |
                            + - - - + - - - + - - - + - - - -+
```

Figure 2.12   MONITOR output.

2.12   FURTHER READING

Bynon, D. W., and Shannon, T. C., *Introduction to VAX/VMS*, 2d. ed., Professional Press, Spring House, Pa., 1987.

ERI Training with Jan Diamondstone, *Using VAX/VMS*, Prentice-Hall, Englewood Cliffs, N.J., 1988.

Sawey, R. M., and Stokes, T. T., *A Beginner's Guide to VAX/VMS Utilities & Applications*, Digital Press, Maynard, Mass., 1989.

DCL concepts, Vol. 3, VMS General User Manuals.

Using VMS, Vol. 2A, VMS General User Manuals.

MONITOR, Systems Management, Vol. 4, VMS General User Manuals.

```
$ MONITOR  PROCESS/TOPBIO
                        VAX/VMS Monitor Utility
                   TOP BUFFERED I/O RATE PROCESSES
                         on node SCOOP::
                       10-DEC-1989 11:54:54

                              0        5        10       15       20
                              + - - - - + - - - - + - - - - + - - - - -+
00000158  MARIA          12   ************************
                              |        |        |        |        |
00000146  _LTA12:          9  ******************
                              |        |        |        |        |
00000156  _RTA1:           8  ****************
                              |        |        |        |        |
00000157  ANGELO           2  ****
                              |        |        |        |        |
00000140  O115             1  **
                              |        |        |        |        |
00000106  JOB_CONTROL      1  **
                              |        |        |        |        |

                              |        |        |        |        |
                              + - - - - + - - - - + - - - - + - - - - -+
```

Figure 2.12   *(Continued)*

3

Files and Directories

Files can be created on disks and tapes. Examples of disk devices are the RA series drives, compact disk ROMs (CDROMs), floppy drives, and *electronic storage elements* (ESE-20); examples of tape devices are TU78 and TU81-PLUS standard tape drives, TK70 cartridge tape drives, and IBM 3480-compatible TA90 cartridge tape drive. Disks and tapes are known as volumes. Files on disks can have sequential, relative, or indexed organization, while tapes support sequential files only.

Each file on the disk is owned by one user. Normally, this user is the person who created the file. The owner can allow other users to access the file by specifying the type of protection for the file. Files reside within other files called *directories*. Directories can reside within other directories, effectively allowing users to maintain a set of logically related files separate from other files belonging to him or her. File size is limited by disk space or, if disk quotas are enabled, by disk quota. If a file is modified by, say, an editor, then a new version of the file is created. Older versions remain on disk until explicitly deleted by the DELETE or PURGE commands. Version numbers start at 1 and can go up to 32,767.

Because long file names can be easily forgotten, VMS has a wildcard facility which allows a set of files to be displayed (or accessed) based on match criteria. This chapter discusses these and other file management issues.

3.1 DISK FILES

Disks consist of logical blocks, each of 512 bytes. The first block on each disk, Block 0, is the *boot block*. It contains information for bringing up the operating system from that disk. If the disk does not contain the operating system, an error message is displayed on the console when attempting a boot. Block 1 is the home block. The home block contains the volume name, volume owner name, protection information, and a pointer

to the index file. The index file contains detailed information about all
the files and free space on the disk. The file structure on disks is known
as FILES-11 *on disk structure level 2* or FILES-11 ODS 2.

Every file on the disk resides in a directory. Directories are specified in
square brackets. The top-level directory of any disk volume is called the
master file directory (MFD) and is represented as [000000]. All the other
directories form a tree structure with [000000] as the root of the tree. Directories are files with file type of .DIR. An example is ANGELO.DIR.

The MFD [000000], contains files with file type .SYS, which contain
information on all the files on the volume. Usually, the MFD also contains files with file type .DIR, which are directory files for each user
who has access to the disk. Here is an example of a disk MFD. The
disk has two top-level user directories for ANGELO and MARIA.
Their directories are called *user file directories* (UFD). The three directory files, SYS0.DIR, SYSE.DIR, and SYSEXE.DIR and their
subdirectories contain systems software like the operating system
files, compilers, and utilities.

```
$ DIRECTORY/SIZE/DATE  DUB3:[000000]

Directory DUB3:[000000]

000000.DIR;1        4 15-JUN-1989 12:15
ANGELO.DIR;1       12  4-FEB-1989 11:35
BACKUP.SYS;1        0 15-JUN-1989 12:15
BADBLK.SYS;1        2 15-JUN-1989 12:15
BADLOG.SYS;1        0 15-JUN-1989 12:15
BITMAP.SYS;1      150 15-JUN-1989 12:15
CONTIN.SYS;1        0 15-JUN-1989 12:15
CORIMG.SYS;1        0 15-JUN-1989 12:15
INDEXF.SYS;1     4074 15-JUN-1988 12:15
SYS0.DIR;1          3 15-JUN-1989 12:15
SYSE.DIR;1          1 20-OCT-1988 11:45
SYSEXE.DIR;1        1 15-JUN-1989 12:25
MARIA.DIR;1        21  4-FEB-1989 11:35
VOLSET.SYS;1        0 15-JUN-1989 12:15
Total of 14 files, 4520 blocks.
```

You can see a list of files in Angelo's directory by using either of the
two commands:

```
$ DIRECTORY [ANGELO]
$ DIRECTORY [000000.ANGELO]
```

For example,

```
$ DIRECTORY  [ANGELO]

Directory DUB3:[ANGELO]

ASC.DAT;1      BAC.DIR;1      PROG.COB;3      PROG.EXE;1
PROG.OBJ;2

Total of 5 files.
```

The directory [ANGELO] is Angelo's top-level directory. He has a subdirectory, BAC.DIR, which in turn may contain files and directories. The files in this subdirectory can be listed by the command:

```
$ DIRECTORY  [ANGELO.BAC]
```

As can be seen, a complete directory is specified as:

[*top-level-directory.sub-directory.sub-directory...*]

There are two levels of subdirectories in [ANGELO.BAC]. Up to eight levels of subdirectories can be created. The terms directory and subdirectory are often used interchangeably since a directory is also a subdirectory of another directory. Only the MFD cannot be called a subdirectory since it is the root directory of the disk.

3.1.1 Wildcards with directory names

The * and % wildcards were introduced in Chapter 2. There are two more wildcards which can be used with directory names; ellipsis (...) and hyphen (-).

Ellipses are used to access all subdirectories below the one specified. Here are some examples:

```
$ DIRECTORY  [ANGELO...]
```

lists all files in all subdirectories under the directory [ANGELO].

```
$ DIRECTORY  [ANGELO.BAC...OLD]
```

lists all files in the subdirectory OLD.DIR, which is a subdirectory of the directory [ANGELO.BAC]. An example of the subdirectory listed is [ANGELO.BAC.TEST.DATA.OLD].

```
$ DIRECTORY  [...]
```

lists all files in all subdirectories under the current default directory. The default is displayed by the command SHOW DEFAULT.

The *hyphen wildcard* refers to the parent directory. Here are some examples:

```
$ DIRECTORY  [-]
```

lists all files in the directory above the current default subdirectory.

```
$ DIRECTORY  [-.TEST]
```

lists all files in the subdirectory [TEST] which is in the directory above the current default directory.

Here are some examples using a combination of wildcards:

$ DIRECTORY [*...]   All files in all directories and sub-
                                    directories on the default device.

$ DIRECTORY [...TEST...]   Files in all subdirectories under the
                                    subdirectory [TEST] which is a
                                    subdirectory under the current de-
                                    fault directory.

$ DIRECTORY DJA1:[*...]*.COB   All files with file type .COB in all
                                    subdirectories on disk DJA1:.

$ DIRECTORY [-...]   All files in all subdirectories under
                                    the parent directory of the current
                                    default directory.

$ DIRECTORY [.TEST.DATA]   Files in subdirectory [TEST.DATA].
                                    The subdirectory [TEST] is in the
                                    current default directory.

Normally, system disks and most large disks are mounted using the
command MOUNT/SYSTEM when the system is started. These disks
can be used by all users on the system provided they pass protection
checks. Disks mounted without the /SYSTEM qualifier are for private
use by one or more users.

3.2   TAPE FILES

Tapes are normally created using ANSI standard labels. To use a
tape, the tape drive must be allocated, initialized and mounted. At
many sites, the tape drives are in an area separate from users so an
operator may have to physically mount and dismount tapes for the users. Typical file manipulation commands are COPY and DIREC-
TORY. Files cannot be deleted. Here's an example of tape usage:

$ ALLOCATE MUA0:   Allocate the tape drive for exclusive use.

$ INITIALIZE MUA0: TEST01   Put an ANSI standard label on the tape.
                                    This step is omitted if the tape is not new.

$ MOUNT MUA0: TEST01   Mount the tape so that it is recognized by
                                    the operating system.

$ COPY MUA0:*.* DUB5:   Copy files from tape to disk.

$ DISMOUNT MUA0:   The tape can be removed from the drive.

If you do not know the tape label, use:

$ MOUNT/FOREIGN MUA0:   The label will be displayed.

  %MOUNT-I-MOUNTED, TEST01 mounted on _MUA0:

$ DISMOUNT/NOUNLOAD MUA0:   Software dismount. The tape is set to
                                    beginning-of-tape (BOT) mark so that the
                                    MOUNT command can be issued again
                                    with the volume name.

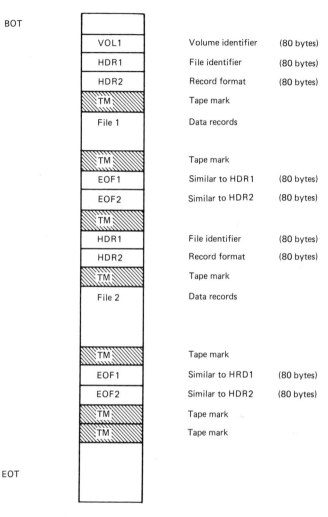

BOT

VOL1	Volume identifier (80 bytes)
HDR1	File identifier (80 bytes)
HDR2	Record format (80 bytes)
TM	Tape mark
File 1	Data records
TM	Tape mark
EOF1	Similar to HDR1 (80 bytes)
EOF2	Similar to HDR2 (80 bytes)
TM	
HDR1	File identifier (80 bytes)
HDR2	Record format (80 bytes)
TM	Tape mark
File 2	Data records
TM	Tape mark
EOF1	Similar to HRD1 (80 bytes)
EOF2	Similar to HDR2 (80 bytes)
TM	Tape mark
TM	Tape mark

EOT

HDR3 and HDR4 may also be present unless the tape is mounted with the command MOUNT/NOHDR3. These headers contain RMS attributes of the file. HDR3 and HDR4 should not be present if the tape is to be ported to other computers like IBM mainframes.

Figure 3.1 Structure of ANSI tape with two files.

Figure 3.1 shows the logical layout of a tape.

Some programs like BACKUP do not use ANSI standard processing for files although they create ANSI-labeled tapes. Instead, they use special formats mainly for faster processing. The tape will still be readable in block mode on tape drives of other types of computers. The DUMP command is useful to determine the structure of tape data. For example,

$ DUMP MUA0:   !Show tape marks like end Of File (EOF) and !data block
contents with their block sizes.

3.3 SOME USEFUL COMMANDS

$ SHOW DEVICES	Display devices on the system.
$ SHOW DEVICE DUB5:/FULL	Display volume information.
$ SHOW DEFAULT	Display default device and directory.
$ SET DEFAULT DUB5:[ANGELO.TEST]	Set defaults for file access.
$ CREATE/DIRECTORY [.TEST]	Create the subdirectory [TEST] in the current default directory.
$ DELETE TEST.DIR;1	Delete the directory [TEST] which is in the current directory.

3.4 USER IDENTIFICATION CODE (UIC)

Each user on the system has an UIC. A UIC consists of a group number and a member number. An example is [200,12]. Sometimes an alphabetic equivalent of the UIC is used by the system. An example is [SYSTEM,TEST]. A UIC is allocated by the system administrator when a new account is created. Each user has a unique UIC, but a number of users may have the same group number. Typically, users working on the same software project are assigned a common group number. UICs are used in the VMS protection scheme. For example, a file may be protected so that only users having group number 100 in their UICs can access the file.

3.5 VOLUME AND FILE PROTECTION

Volumes and files can be protected from access by unauthorized users. The protection is based on UIC. All users on the system are classified into four categories depending on their UIC:

SYSTEM   Users who have SETPRV privilege or a UIC group number between 1 and 10. The UIC group number range can be modified by SYSGEN described in the chapter on VMS utilities.

OWNER   The one user who created the file or initialized the volume.

GROUP   Users who have the same UIC group as the OWNER.

WORLD   All users including the one's in the other three categories.

3.5.1 Disk protection

Protection information is stored in the home block of each disk. Each disk can have the following protections for each category of user:

READ   allows read access to the files on the disk.

WRITE   allows file modification to existing files.

EXECUTE   allows file modification and creation of new files.

DELETE   allows files to be deleted on the disk.

For example, on disk DUB1:, SYSTEM and OWNER have READ, WRITE, EXECUTE, and DELETE access; GROUP has READ access, and WORLD has no access. This can be written as

```
S:RWED,O:RWED,G:R,W
```

The protection on the volume can be set by the SET VOLUME command. For example,

```
$ SET VOLUME DUB1: /PROTECTION=(S:RWED,O:RWED,G:R,W)
```

Volume protections can also be set when initializing the volumes. To see the owner and current protection set for the volume, the command is

```
$ SHOW  DEVICE DUB1: /FULL
```

So, if the owner is [100,5]:

- The user with UIC [100,20] is in the same group as the owner. He or she has read access.

- The user with UIC [1,44] is in the SYSTEM category. He or she has read, write, execute, and delete access to the disk.

- The user [40,23] is in the WORLD category, so he or she cannot access the disk.

3.5.2 Tape protection

Tapes can have two types of protections for each of the four user categories:

READ   allows read access to the tape.

WRITE   allows read and write access to the tape.

The protections can be set during initialization of the tape. For example,

```
$ INITIALIZE  MUA0:  TEST01 /PROTECTION=(S:RWE,O:RWED,G:RW,WO:R)
```

3.5.3 File protection

Files on disk can have protection similar to disk protection. Each file has an owner, the person who created the file. The command

DIRECTORY/OWNER lists files with their owner UICs. The command DIRECTORY/PROTECTION lists files with the protections for each of the four categories of users described above:

```
$ DIRECTORY/OWNER/PROTECTION

Directory DUB5:[TEST.TMP]

BAC.DIR;1        [24,1]     (RWE,RWE,RE,E)
FILES.DOC;15     [24,1]     (RWED,RWED,RE,)
START.DOC;63     [24,1]     (RWED,RWED,RE,)
START.DOCLNO;2   [24,1]     (RWED,RWED,RE,)

Total of 4 files.
```

The owner of all the files is [24,1] and the protections are listed for SYSTEM, OWNER, GROUP, and WORLD in that order. Note that WORLD has no access to the last three files.

File protections can be changed by the SET PROTECTION command. For example,

```
$ SET PROTECTION=(G:RWED,W:R)  *.DOC
```

The command grants all accesses to GROUP and read access to WORLD for all files with file type .DOC in the default directory. Protections for SYSTEM and OWNER are unchanged.

Access control lists (ACLs) allow files and volumes to be protected from an arbitrary set of users. ACLs supplement the UIC based protection schemes described above. They are described in the chapter on Systems Management.

3.6   FURTHER READING

Guide to Files and Devices, Vol. 2A, VMS General User Manuals.

Chapter

4

The EVE Editor

EVE, the extensible VAX editor, is now the standard text editor on VMS. The editor is actually a program written using the text processing utility (TPU). Users familiar with the older EDT editor should take the trouble to understand EVE. It will be worth the effort, since EVE has far greater functionality than EDT. Some of the highlights of EVE are

- *Multiple windows on screen:* Multiple files can be displayed and edited.
- *Keyboard macros:* Keys can be defined as a sequence of other keystrokes.
- *Programmable:* The TPU can be used to customize EVE to suit individual requirements and taste.
- *Journaling:* In case of a system failure, most of the editing done can be recovered later.
- *Place markers:* Positions in the files being edited can be marked by names. A previously marked position can be restored on the screen.
- *DCL commands can be issued from the editor:* Output is captured and displayed on the screen. The output can be edited.
- *Subprocess spawning:* Temporary exit to DCL to execute system commands is allowed.
- *Wildcards:* Wildcard (fuzzy) searches are supported.

4.1 GETTING STARTED

Before starting an editing session, the following keys on the keyboard should be identified: DO, HELP, FIND, PREV SCREEN, NEXT SCREEN, INSERT HERE, REMOVE, SELECT, UP-ARROW,

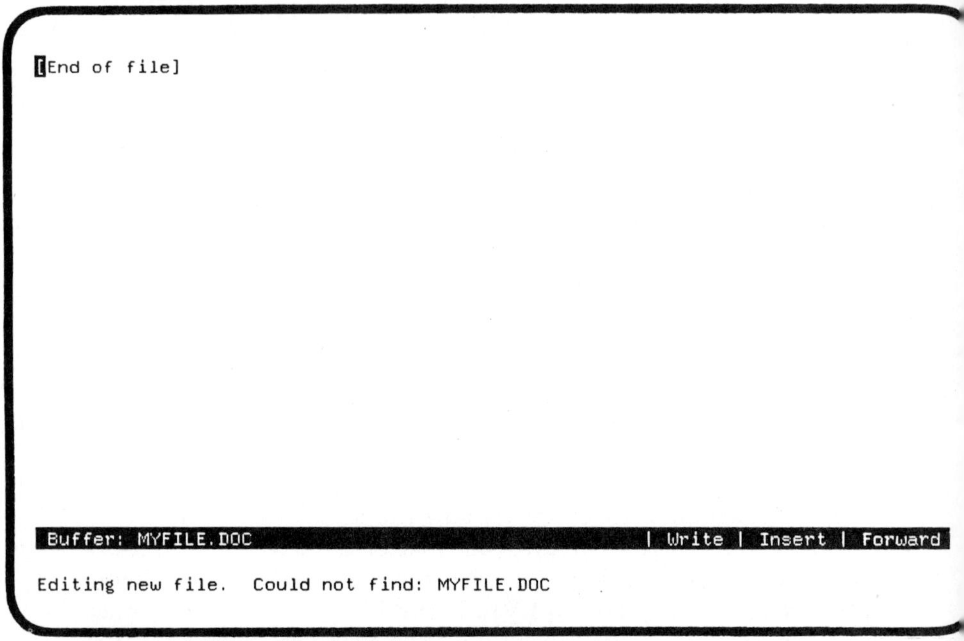

```
█End of file]




















 Buffer: MYFILE.DOC                                      | Write | Insert | Forward

Editing new file.   Could not find: MYFILE.DOC
```

Figure 4.1   EVE editor initial screen.

DOWN-ARROW, LEFT-ARROW, and RIGHT-ARROW. The older
VT100 terminals do not have some of these keys; in this case see the
HELP within the editor.

To edit the file MYFILE.DOC, the EVE editor can be run by the
command

$ `EDIT/TPU MYFILE.DOC`

If the file exists on disk, it is opened for editing and the first few lines
are displayed on the screen. The file is created in your current default
device and directory. If the file does not exist, a new file is created and
the screen looks as shown in Fig. 4.1.

To insert text in the file simply enter it on the keyboard. The up,
down, left and right arrow keys can be used to move through the file.
The DELETE key can be used to delete the character to the left of the
cursor. When text entry is complete, pressing the CTRL/Z key combination will save the file on disk and exit to DCL. EVE can be customized and enhanced using the TPU.

4.2   FUNCTION KEYS

Some of the keys are used as described in Fig. 4.2.

CUT and PASTE is the process of removing a block of text and placing it somewhere else. CUT and PASTE is achieved by the keys

Key	Use
HELP	Describes features of the editor.
DO	Allows commands to be entered.
FIND	Searches for text starting from the current position until the end of file.
SELECT	Starts selection of a block of text for various operations.
REMOVE	Used to remove a SELECTed block of text.
INSERT HERE	Inserts at the current position the block of text removed by a previous SELECT and REMOVE operation.
PREV SCREEN	Scrolls back one screen-full of the file.
NEXT SCREEN	Scrolls forward one screen-full of the file.
F14	Switches between insert and overstrike mode of text entry.
F11	Switches direction of search to forward or reverse for find and text replacement commands.
F10 or CTRL/Z	Saves the file and exits to DCL.
CTRL/E	Moves cursor to the end of current line.
CTRL/H	Moves cursor to the beginning of current line.
CTRL/V	Inserts non-printable characters in the file. The character has to be entered after this key.
CTRL/U	Deletes all characters from cursor to beginning of line.
CTRL/W	Repaints the screen.

NOTE: Some of the control keys, like CTRL/Y, are interpreted by the operating system.

Figure 4.2 Function keys.

SELECT and REMOVE (to cut text) and INSERT-HERE (to paste at current position). To delete a line, go to the beginning of the line, press SELECT, press DOWN-ARROW, and then press REMOVE.

4.3 THE DO KEY: ENTERING LINE-ORIENTED COMMANDS

The editor prompts for a command when the DO key is pressed. The command can be entered with parameters, if any. If parameters are not entered, the editor prompts for them. For example, to exit from the editing session without storing the changes on disk, the DO key is entered followed by the characters Q U I T and the RETURN key.

The DO commands are described next.

4.3.1 Text substitution

DO command: **REPLACE source replacement**

This replaces the source string by the replacement string after confirmation. The editor prompts if further replacements should be made or if all occurrences of source should be replaced. For example,

DO command: `REPLACE recieve receive`

4.3.2 Multiple files and buffers

The EVE editor creates an internal buffer when a file is opened. More than one file can be edited by reading in more files.

DO command: `GET FILE filename`

The name of each buffer is the same as the name of the file. To move from one buffer to another, effectively editing another file, the command is

DO command: `BUFFER buffername`

If buffername does not exist, then a new buffer is created. When exiting from the editor, all buffers are written out to the corresponding files. If a buffer was created (without an associated file), then the editor will prompt for a file name to write the buffer. The SHOW command displays information on all the buffers.

4.3.3 Multiple windows

Multiple windows can be created, and in effect, multiple files can be seen together. The editor can divide the screen into two halves and display a different buffer in each window. The same file can also be edited in two windows; this way two different parts of one file can be seen together.

DO command: `TWO WINDOWS`

Initially, when two windows are created, the same buffer is displayed in two windows. The BUFFER or GET FILE command can be used to display another buffer in the window where the cursor is. If the TWO WINDOWS command is issued again, the current window will split into two. So now there will be three windows on the screen. The cursor can be move from window to window by using the command

DO command: `NEXT WINDOW`

Figure 4.3 shows a screen with two windows with a different file in each window. To revert back to one window, the command is

DO command: `ONE WINDOW`

The one buffer which will then be displayed will be the one where the cursor was before the command was issued.

4.3.4 Place markers

The current text position can be marked by:

```
Dear Sir,

I am writing this letter to inform you of our software package
called the Super CPU Enhancer.

The Super CPU Enhancer reduces the execution time of each machine
language instruction by half, effectively doubling the CPU speed.



Buffer: MYFILE.DOC                           | Write | Insert | Forward
Dear Madam,

I am writing this letter to inform you of our software package
called the Super I/O Exerciser.

The Super I/O Exerciser is a powerful tool to monitor your I/O
and indicate if you need to purchase our I/O expansion kit.

We will be glad to send you the Super I/O Exerciser absolutely
free!!!
Buffer: SECONDFILE.DOC                       | Write | Insert | Forward
```

Figure 4.3 Two windows displayed by the EVE editor.

DO command: **MARK marker-name**

Marker-name is a string of ASCII characters. Different places can be marked by using different marker names for each position. Later, to go to any marked position use

DO command: **GO TO marker-name**

4.3.5 Keyboard macro

Most of the non-printable keys, like the control and function keys, can be defined as a sequence of other keys by the LEARN command. To define a key

Press the DO key,

Enter the command LEARN,

Enter any sequence of keys (except CTRL/R),

Enter CTRL/R,

Enter key to be defined.

For example, these key presses defines the key PF2 as "division":

DO key,

The characters L E A R N,

The RETURN key,

The characters d i v i s i o n

CTRL/R,

PF2 key.

After this, whenever PF2 is pressed, the word "division" is inserted in the text. The command supports nested key definition.

4.3.6 Other DO commands

The TOP command moves the cursor to the top of current file or buffer and BOTTOM command moves the cursor to the bottom. Any particular line in the buffer can be displayed directly by

DO command: **LINE line-number**

A system command can be executed by

DO command: **DCL dcl-command**

The command is executed in a subprocess of the current process. The output is displayed in a separate window and put in a buffer called DCL. The SPAWN command creates a subprocess in which a set of DCL commands can be executed. When the LOGOUT command is issued, the editing session is resumed.

4.4 JOURNALING

If the system fails while editing, most of the edits can be restored when the system is up again. To recover edits to the file MYFILE.DOC the command is

$ **EDIT/TPU/RECOVER MYFILE.DOC.**

The editor uses a journal file (with filetype .JNL) to intermittently store keystrokes entered. During recovery, these keystrokes are "replayed" by the editor. If after an edit session the exit from the editor is successful, the journal file is deleted.

4.5 EXTENDING EVE FUNCTIONALITY

This section describes advanced EVE features. EVE is implemented using the TPU utility. TPU is a complete programming language suitable for text processing. A TPU file normally has a file type of .TPU. When this file is compiled by TPU, an output file having a file type of .TPU$SECTION is created. This file can be specified with the /SECTION

qualifier on the $ EDIT/TPU command line. By default, the section file is
the EVE section file, SYS$LIBRARY:EVE$SECTION.TPU$SECTION.
EVE is compiled from a number of source .TPU programs. These programs are in SYS$EXAMPLES:. To extend EVE, the following steps
must be followed:

- Create a .TPU file with the new features. Familiarity with TPU is
  required.

- Create a MASTER and a VERSION files. These are required to extend TPU. See the example below.

- The file SYS$EXAMPLES:EVE$BUILD.TPU is specifically supplied to build TPU programs. Use this file to create a
  .TPU$SECTION file. Specify this file as a section file when using
  the editor. The original EVE functions plus the new features will be
  available during the edit session.

Here is an example. A new feature has to be added to the EVE editor. It is required that during the edit session, when the cursor is over
the name of a file, the editor should perform a GET on the file when
the PF3 key is pressed. Here is the TPU program to implement this.

```
! File: JAY_INIT.TPU
! This file demonstrates how EVE can be customized.
! The file offers one new feature during an EVE edit session:
!   If the cursor is on a filename, then pressing PF3 will cause TPU to get
!   that file in a buffer.
! This program also implements a help feature. PF2 can be pressed to display
! on-line help.
!
procedure jay_module_ident      ! Module version
return "V01.21";
endprocedure;
!
Procedure jay_module_init
!----------------------------
!Initialization routine, executed at start of edit session
!
! define PF2 and PF3
define_key("get_file", pf3, "read-in file shown at cursor position");
define_key("user_help", pf2, "help key");
!
!The next set of statements are for defining a help window which is displayed
!when the PF2 key is pressed.
!
help_win:=create_window(1,8,on);                 !define the help window size
!define text for the window status line
set (status_line,help_win,reverse,"Help of cutomized keys");
morehelp:=create_buffer("help-buf");             !a buffer for the help window
!the help buffer cannot be written to, is a system buffer and has no
!end-of-text marker
set(no_write,morehelp); set(system,morehelp); set(eob_text,morehelp,"");
!
main_buf:=current_buffer;
! write the help screen contents in the help buffer
position(morehelp);
```

```
copy_text("                         HELP"); Split_line;
copy_text("                         ===="); Split_line;
copy_text("PF3 - include file (name at cursor position)"); Split_line;
copy_text("PF2 - this help"); Split_line; Split_line;
copy_text("Press any key to continue:");

position(main_buf);
endprocedure;     !end of the initialization procedure

!Now the customized procedures
!-----------------------------

procedure get_file
!-----------------
! The procedure gets the file pointed to be the cursor.
!
 local file_string, word_string;
on_error
  If error = tpu$_parsefail then
   message('invalid filespec');
   return;
  endif;
endon_error;
word_string:=STR(eve$current_word);
file_string:=file_search(word_string); !File parse TPU built-in routine
if length(file_string) > 0 then
eve_get_file(file_string);
else
  message(fao('No such file'));
 endif;
endprocedure;

procedure user_help
!------------------
 local tmp;
 map (help_win,morehelp);
 update(help_win);
 tmp:=read_key;
 unmap(help_win);
endprocedure;
```

To compile this file, two more files are required, the MASTER and
the VERSION file. These files contain one line each:

```
$type jay_master.file
jay_init.tpu
$type jay_version.dat
V01.21
```

The command to create the entended EVE section file is:

```
$ edit/tpu/command=sys$examples:eve$build.tpu/nodisplay/-
noinitialization/output=jay jay
```

The command will combine the orginal EVE section file, the new TPU
file, jay.tpu, and create a section file jay.tpu$section. (Two other files,
jay.list and jay.init, will also be created).

To use EVE with the new features, enter the command:

```
$ EDIT/TPU/SECTION=userdisk:[shah]jay.tpu$section  MYPROG.COB
```

4.6 FURTHER READING

Guide to Text Processing, Vol. 5A, VMS General User Manuals.
VAXTPU Reference, Vol. 5B, VMS General User Manuals.

5

DCL Programming

Commands entered at the terminal are analyzed by the part of the operating system called the DCL interpreter. DCL is the most common command line interpreter (CLI); there are other CLIs like the Unix/SHELL interpreter. The DCL interpreter can also execute a file containing a list of commands. Such files are called indirect files or command files. Command files can also be used for programming at the command level. For example, the command file shown in Fig. 5.1 will compile and link nine COBOL programs; PROG0, PROG1, PROG2, ... PROG8.

To execute this command file, use

$ @COBOLCOMPILE

A few comments follow:

- By convention, command file names have a file type of .COM.

- DCL supports string and integer variables. These variables are called *symbols*. The symbol type is string or integer depending on the value assigned to it. For example,

```
TEMP_VAR = 5            !TEMP_VAR is an integer symbol.
```

```
$ TYPE COBOLCOMPILE.COM

$! Procedure to compile eight programs – PROG1 to PROG8
$ TEMP_VAR = 0          !variable to loop 8 times
$ compile:
$ COBOL PROG'TEMP_VAR'.COB
$ LINK PROG'TEMP_VAR'.OBJ
$ TEMP_VAR = TEMP_VAR + 1
$ IF TEMP_VAR .LT. 9 THEN $GOTO compile
$ EXIT
```

Figure 5.1 An example of a DCL command file.

```
TEMP_VAR = "TEST",    !TEMP_VAR is a string symbol.
```

Integer variables are stored in a longword so they have an accuracy of about 9 digits. Standard arithmetic can be performed with integers. Floating point and fractional numbers are not supported by DCL.

- An exclamation mark starts a comment on the line. The comment continues til the end of line. DCL ignores comments.

- Values of symbols can be substituted in a command line before the line is executed by enclosing the symbol within single quotes (apostrophes). For example, if TEMP_VAR has a value of 6, the next two commands are equivalent:

```
$ COBOL PROG'TEMP_VAR'
$ COBOL PROG6
```

- The IF or IF-THEN-ELSE statement can be used to conditionally execute commands. Structured programming constructs like FOR and WHILE loops and CASE and SWITCH statements are not supported directly.

- The GOTO statement transfers execution to the statement following the label specified. Label declarations have to be terminated with a colon(:).

- The $ sign is required before each command line.

- The EXIT statement terminates execution of the command file and DCL then accepts input from the terminal.

- The @FILENAME command entered at the terminal tells the DCL interpreter to execute commands specified in the file.

Another example of a DCL procedure is shown in Fig. 5.2.

5.1 TERMINAL I/O

The value of a symbol can be asked for from the terminal by the INQUIRE command. For example,

```
$!This command file displays 10 even numbers starting at 2
$ I = 1
$ LOOP:
$ WRITE SYS$OUTPUT I * 2
$ I = I + 1
$ IF I .GT. 10 THEN $EXIT
$ GOTO LOOP
```

Figure 5.2 An example of a DCL command file.

```
$ INQUIRE  TEMP_VAR  "Enter first program to be compiled"
```

The string is used as a prompt for the user to enter a value for
TEMP_VAR. The display would be:

```
Enter first program to be compiled:
```

Output can be sent to the terminal by the WRITE SYS$OUTPUT
command. For example,

```
$ WRITE  SYS$OUTPUT  "The value of symbol I is: ", I
```

The output could be:

```
The value of symbol I is: 23.
```

5.2 FILE I/O

Command procedures can open files and perform reads and writes on
them. For example,

```
$ OPEN/READ   INFILE   IN.DAT
$ OPEN/WRITE  OUTFILE  SUMMARY.REPORT
$ OPEN/APPEND OUTFILE  SUMMARY.REPORT
```

Here, INFILE and OUTFILE are internal logical names. Examples of
reads and writes are,

```
$ READ  INFILE  ONELINE
$ WRITE OUTFILE "Total records processed = ", I
```

Files should be closed before exiting the command file:

```
$ CLOSE   INFILE
$ CLOSE   OUTFILE
```

The qualifier /END_OF_FILE is used on READ statements to specify
a label where execution should continue if there is no more input in
the file.

Figure 5.3 show a program which reads an input file of integers, accepts a multiplication factor from the terminal, multiplies each integer by the factor, and writes the output to another file.

5.3 SYMBOLS

Symbols are variables for the DCL interpreter. There are two kinds of
symbols: *local* and *global*. When used in command files, local symbols
are deleted when the execution of the command file is over. Global
symbols retain their definition even when the command file execution
is over. Global symbols are defined with a double equal (= =) sign.
Some examples are:

```
$! File: MULTIPLY.COM
$! This program:
$!      reads a file, INPUT.DATA, which contains one integer per line,
$!      multiplies each integer by a constant value
$!      and writes the result, one integer per line, to a file OUTPUT.RESULT
$!
$  OPEN  INFILE  INPUT.DATA       !Read is the default OPEN mode.
$  OPEN/WRITE  OUTFILE  OUTPUT.RESULT
$!
$  INQUIRE  FACTOR  "Multiplication factor"
$!
$  LOOP:
$  READ/END_OF_FILE=INPUTOVER  INFILE  INP_INTEGER
$  OUT_INTEGER = INP_INTEGER * FACTOR
$  WRITE  OUTFILE  OUT_INTEGER
$  GOTO LOOP
$!
$  INPUTOVER:
$  CLOSE  INFILE
$  CLOSE  OUTFILE
$  EXIT
```

Figure 5.3   A DCL command file performing file I/O.

```
$ I = 55               !local integer symbol
$ J == 3 * (I + 44)    !global integer symbol, Value 297
$ S = "test"           !local string symbol
$ S == "test"          !global string symbol
```

Integer symbols can be assigned octal or hexadecimal values as in

```
$ L = %O25             !octal assignment, decimal value 21
$ K = %X33             !hexadecimal assignment, decimal value 51
```

If a symbol is defined in a command file and the symbol value is required even after the command file execution is over, the symbol should be defined as a global symbol.

A symbol name can have an asterisk in it. In this case, when the symbol is used, the name of the symbol can be shortened up to the characters before the asterisk. For example,

```
$ ALE*RT := @ALERTPROGRAM

$ ALERT   !These three statements run the command file ALERTPROGRAM.
$ ALER
$ ALE
```

Symbols have three major uses:

1. Symbol values can be substituted in command lines. For example, the next two lines in a command file will type the file MYFILE.DOC:

```
$ FILENAME := MYFILE.DOC
$ TYPE 'FILENAME'
```

2. Symbol values can be displayed.

3. Symbols can be used as commands. For example, the next two lines show how the symbol "SD" actually acts as a "SET DEFAULT" command:

```
$ SD == "SET DEFAULT"
$ SD DUA2:[TESTDIR]
```

This last feature is useful to create customized DCL commands and short forms of commonly used lengthy commands. Usually, a set of such symbols is defined by users in the file LOGIN.COM in their log-in directory. The file LOGIN.COM is executed automatically by the system every time a user logs in, so the symbols will always be available. The symbols should be defined as global symbols so that they remain defined even when LOGIN.COM finishes execution.

5.3.1 String symbols

String symbols can be defined in a number of ways as shown in these examples:

```
$ S = "TEST STRING"        !local string symbol
$ S := TEST STRING         !same as the previous one.
$ S == "TEST STRING"       !global string symbol
$ S : == TEST STRING       !same as the previous one.
```

String symbols can be added (concatenated) as in:

```
$ S1 = "String1"
$ S2 = "string2"
$ S3 = S1 + "and" + S3 !S3 is "String1 and string2"
```

Substrings of a symbol can be extracted using the function F$EXTRACT. For example,

```
$ S1 = "123456789"
$ SUBSTRING1 = F$EXTRACT(2,4,SUBSTRING1)  !2 is offset, 4 is length
$! SUBSTRING1 contains "3456"
```

In the next two command lines, the GOTO is executed if the first four characters of the current process name is "SHAH":

```
$ user = f$getjpi("","USERNAME")
$ if f$extract(0,4,user) .eqs. "SHAH" then $GOTO KILLPROCESS
```

Parts of a string can be removed, as in:

```
$ S1 := "123P4567"
$ S2 :== S1 - "P"
$! S2 contains "1234567"
```

A symbol value can be substituted within a string by preceding the symbol with two apostrophes and terminating it with a single apostrophe. For example,

```
$ I  =  23
$ S1 := Test
$ S3  =  "I='I'"            !S3 becomes "I=23"
$ S3  =  "I='I', S1='s1'"   !S3 becomes "I=23, S1=Test"
```

Contrast symbols with logical names are described in Chapter 7.

5.4 LEXICAL FUNCTIONS

Let us say that the current time and date are to be displayed on the terminal from the command file. DCL does not support calls to system libraries and services. Instead, a number of functions are available for retrieving system information and for various other operations. These are called *lexical functions*. The date and time can be displayed by the lexical function F$TIME.

```
$ SYSTIME = F$TIME() !symbol SYSTIME contains current date and time
$ WRITE SYS$OUTPUT SYSTIME
```

All lexical function names start with F$. There are about 33 such functions. The function names are followed by zero or more parameters enclosed in parentheses. Parentheses are required even if there are no parameters as in the case of the function F$TIME. Lexical functions are also known as lexicals.

Consider another lexical function: F$SEARCH. It can be used to search for a set of files on disk. The program if Fig. 5.4 displays the names of all files in the directory [SOURCE] which have a file type of .COB.

When the F$SEARCH function is first used, it returns the first file matching the file specification given as the first parameter. On subsequent use of the function one more file matching the specification is returned. The process continues until no more files match the specification. Then an empty string is returned. The second parameter, which is 4 in this case, is called a *stream identifier*. The command file can contain multiple use of the function each matching a different file specification. Each of these searches is identified by a different stream identifier. The stream identifier is an integer or an integer expression.

Figure 5.5 is an example of a command file which shows all the files in the current directory and all subdirectories below. The F$PARSE

```
$ COBFILES:
$ COBFILE = F$SEARCH("[SOURCE]*.COB",4)
$ IF  COBFILE .EQS. ""  THEN  $EXIT
$ WRITE  SYS$OUTPUT  COBFILE
$ GOTO COBFILES
```

Figure 5.4 A DCL command file using a lexical function.

```
$! This is file TREE.COM
$! Display all files in the current directory and all sub-directories.
$! The tree structure of the directories is displayed by indentation.
$! Level is the symbol which indicates how deep the current sub-directory
$! is. It is also used as a stream identifier for the F$SEARCH lexical
$! function which searches for all files in the current sub-directory.
$! Indent is the symbol for displaying a number of spaces before each
$! filename is displayed. The number of spaces depends on the current
$! subdirectory level. The symbols dir1, dir2 ... store the sub-directory
$! names at each level.
$
$ level=1                 !current directory is considered at level 1
$ dir1=f$directory()      !this lexical function returns the current directory
$ currentdir=f$directory()
$ indent=""               !initially, no indentation when file names are
$                         !displayed.
$ write sys$output -
        "Tree structure of current directory and sub-directories."
$ write sys$output " "
$
$ONEFILE:
$ currentfile=f$search(currentdir+"*.*;*",level)
$ IF currentfile .eqs. ""
$    THEN
$        !no more files, go back up to the parent directory if present.
$        IF level .eq. 1
$            THEN
$                exit
$            ELSE
$                level = level - 1
$                indent = indent - "   "
$                currentdir = dir'level'
$        ENDIF
$    ELSE
$        !if this is a directory go down one level else print this filename
$        filetype = f$parse(currentfile,,,"type")
$        IF filetype .eqs.  ".DIR"
$            THEN
$                !Step down the subdirectory
$                filname = f$parse(currentfile,,,"name")
$                dir'level' = currentdir !Store the current directory. It
$                                        !will be used when stepping up
$                                        !directories.
$                currentdir = currentdir - "]" + "." + filname + "]"
$                level = level + 1
$                indent = indent + "   "
$            ELSE
$                WRITE SYS$OUTPUT indent,currentfile
$        ENDIF
$    ENDIF
$ GOTO ONEFILE
```

Figure 5.5   A DCL command file to display a directory tree structure.

lexical function returns the part of the file specified; in this case the file type (like .COB) and the file name are extracted from the complete file specification. The program should be carefully understood, because it is typical of the many command files on the system.

Figure 5.6 shows the output from the execution of the program in Fig. 5.5.

The command HELP LEXICALS shows how each function can be used. Some of the information these lexicals provide is process infor-

AUGUSTANA UNIVERSITY COLLEGE
LIBRARY

```
Tree structure of current directory and sub-directories.
DUA3:[ARNOLD]MAIN.DOC;1
DUA3:[ARNOLD]TEST.COB;2
  DUA3:[ARNOLD.TEST]CUSTOMER.COB;2
  DUA3:[ARNOLD.TEST]NEWPROG.COB;4
    DUA3:[ARNOLD.TEST.OUTPUT]CUSTOMER.REPORT;12
DUA3:[ARNOLD]USER.PRT;3
  DUA3:[ARNOLD.VERIFY]OUT.PRT;5
DUA3:[ARNOLD]WORK.DONE;21
```

Figure 5.6   Tree structure of a directory.

mation like quotas and actual usage of resources, device information like disk space used, file attributes like file size and translated forms of logical names.

5.5   COMMAND FILE TESTING AND DEBUGGING

The SET VERIFY command in a command file displays each command as it is executed. When a command file is working properly this command can be commented out. The SET NOVERIFY command disables display of commands during execution. These commands can be used to selectively verify execution of parts of the file.

Symbol values can be displayed by using the command "SHOW SYMBOL symbolname". For example,

```
$ SHOW SYMBOL TEMP_VAR
```

or

```
$ SHOW SYMBOL * !Display all the symbols
```

5.6   ERROR HANDLING

Normally, during command file execution, if a command does not execute successfully, the execution is terminated with an error message. It may be necessary to execute further commands even if some commands fail. This can be achieved by placing the command SET NOON at the top of the command file. Then if commands fail, an error message is displayed and execution continues. The SET ON command enables termination on error.

The ON command specifies an error trap routine which can handle error processing in case commands fail to execute successfully. The $STATUS symbol contains the integer code which specifies the status of execution of each command. For successful execution of a command, the value of the symbol is 1, otherwise it will contain another value.

AUGUSTANA UNIVERSITY COLLEGE
LIBRARY

Note that its value will be set by the system after every command except a few like IF (so that its value can be tested by the IF statement). The program in Fig. 5.7 types the file FIRST.TEST if present else it will type the file SECOND.TEST. The lexical function F$MESSAGE displays an explanation text corresponding to the integer status code specified as a parameter.

The ON command has three forms: ON WARNING, ON ERROR, and ON SEVERE_ERROR. The error types are in increasing order of severity. A trap for WARNING errors also traps the other two more severe errors, while a trap for ERROR traps for SEVERE_ERROR also.

To write an error trap routine, first determine the errors which can occur when the command file executes. Decide on which of and how these errors should be handled; then code the error trap routine. In the error trap routine, errors not handled by the routine are displayed for some other action by the user at the terminal.

5.7 PARAMETERS ON THE COMMAND LINE

Up to eight parameters can be specified on the command line as in:

```
$ @COMPILE PROG2 /DEBUG
```

The parameters are equated to symbols P1 and P2 by the system as

```
$ P1 = PROG2
$ P2 = /DEBUG
```

These symbols can be used to control execution of the command file. Here is a command file which will compile the C program specified as

```
$! typical error handling
$! type file FIRST.TEST if present. If there is even a WARNING error then
$! type SECOND.TEST.
$
$ ON WARNING THEN $GOTO SECONDFILE
$ TYPE FIRST.TEST
$ WRITE SYS$OUTPUT "Successful display of the first file"
$ EXIT
$
$ SECONDFILE:
$ TMP_STATUS = $STATUS
$ ON WARNING THEN $EXIT
$ WRITE SYS$OUTPUT "Problem when typing FIRST.TEST"
$ WRITE SYS$OUTPUT F$MESSAGE(TMP_STATUS)
$ TYPE SECOND.TEST
$ WRITE SYS$OUTPUT "Successful display of the second file"
$ EXIT
```

Figure 5.7 Error processing in a DCL command file.

parameters. The second parameter specifies whether the compilation will be with the debugging option of the compiler.

```
$! This is file COMPILE.COM
$! An example of running this command file is
$! $ @compile  prog2  /debug
$! Note that the second parameter is optional.
$! The file compiles the "c" program specified on the command line.
$! The second parameter is applied as a qualifier to the compiler and linker.
$!
$
$ CC 'P2' 'P1'          !in the example, this command executes as
                        ! $ CC /DEBUG PROG2
$ LINK 'P2' 'P1'        !in the example, this command executes as
                        ! $ LINK /DEBUG PROG2
$!
```

5.8   NESTING COMMAND FILES

A command file can "call" another command file. When the execution of the called command file is over, execution resumes at the next statement of the previous command file. For example,

```
$!This command file calls PROCESSTEST.COM
$ COBOL TEST
$ LINK TEST
$ @PROCESSTEST          !Nested call to another command file
$ WRITE SYS$OUTPUT "Test successful"
```

5.9   SYSTEM COMMAND FILES

VAX/VMS system software makes extensive use of command files for system functions. You can read these files to see the full power of DCL programs. Some files have to be customized for individual installations. The files are:

SYS$MANAGER:LTLOAD.COM	Starts LAT on the node. This will allow connections from terminal servers like DECSERVER 500 to the VAX.
SYS$MANAGER:STARTNET.COM	Starts DECNET on the current node. Use SYS$MANAGER:NETCONFIG.COM to define the current node in the network database. Usually done only once, when the system is created.
SYS$MANAGER:SYLOGIN.COM	This file executes for every user just after a successful log in. Symbols which are to be used by everyone on the system can be defined here.

SYS$MANAGER:SYSHUTDWN.COM   This file executes when the system is being shut down. It can be used to perform cleanup operations required by applications. The system is shut down by entering the command @SYS$SYSTEM:SHUTDOWN.

SYS$MANAGER:SYSTARTUP_V5.COM   This file is executed when system is booted. It has to be customized by the system manager to contain system startup commands to mount system disks, start DECNET, start applications, start the batch, print queue manager, and so on.

SYS$SYSTEM:SHUTDOWN.COM   This command file should be executed to shut down the system. It executes the file SYS$MANAGER:SYSHUTDWN.COM and performs winding-down operations like sending a shut-down message to all users logged in, dismounting disks and stopping the queue manager, and error logger processes.

SYS$UPDATE:AUTOGEN.COM   This procedure is used to modify SYSGEN parameters. New SYSGEN parameters should be placed in SYS$SYSTEM:MODPARAMS.DAT before executing this procedure.

SYS$UPDATE:STABACKIT.COM   Used to create a tape or disk which can be then used to boot the standalone BACKUP program. Standalone backups can be used to back up or restore disks without having to load the complete operating system.

SYS$UPDATE:VMSINSTAL.COM   This is the standard procedure for installing or upgrading software products.

SYS$UPDATE:VMSLICENSE.COM   A user-friendly procedure for registering software licenses.

5.10 FURTHER READING

Using DCL, Vol. 3, VMS General User Manuals.
DCL Dictionary, Vol. 4, VMS General User Manuals.
Anagnostopoulos, P. C., *VAX/VMS: Writing Real Programs in DCL*, Digital Press, Maynard, Mass., 1989.

6

Utility Commands

Standard VAX/VMS comes bundled with a set of commands which can be classified as utilities. These are:

SEARCH	Searches for strings in specified files.
DIFFERENCES	Shows the difference between the contents of two files.
DUMP	Shows the raw data in a file or tape.
MAIL	Communications facility for users.
PHONE	Interactive communications facility for users.
SORT	Sort-merge utility.

The BACKUP utility is described in the chapter on System Management.

6.1 SEARCH

The two files shown here were used in the examples in this section:

```
This file is SEARCH_TEST.DOC
This a file for testing the search utility.
It contains the words "many" and "some" a number
of times.

Many programs can be stored in one directory.
Suppose these are COBOL programs.
Some times you may forget the name of the program
but you know that the program contains a variable
called generate_list. You can use the search utility
to search all the COBOL programs and report the
filenames of programs containing the variable
generate_list. The file names will be listed with
some of the lines in the file.

The search utility can be asked to search all the
files or some files in a directory by using wildcards.
The search utility is very useful but many VAX users
do not know about it.
```

```
This file is DIFF_TEST.DOC.
This a file for testing the search utility.
It contains the words "many" and "some" a number
of times.

Suppose you made some modifications to a program
and created a new version of the program file.
Later you wish to see the differences between
the old and the new program. There are many ways
to do this but the simplest is to use the
DIFFERENCE utility.
```

The SEARCH command searches for lines in specified files which contain the specified string (or strings). For example, the next command displays the file names in the default directory and lines of files containing the string "many":

```
$ SEARCH  *  *   many

******************************
MYDISK:[SHAH.TMP]DIFF_TEST.DOC;2

It contains the words "many" and "some" a number
the old and the new program. There are many ways

******************************
MYDISK:[SHAH.TMP]SEARCH_TEST.DOC;2

It contains the words "many" and "some" a number
Many programs can be stored in one directory.
The search utility is very useful but many VAX users
```

Search strings should be specified in quotes if they contain blanks and tabs:

```
$ SEARCH  *.*   "ascii number"
```

The next command searches for all lines containing "many" or "some":

```
$ SEARCH  *.*   many,some

******************************
MYDISK:[SHAH.TMP]DIFF_TEST.DOC;2

It contains the words "many" and "some" a number
Suppose you made some modifications to a program
the old and the new program. There are many ways

******************************
MYDISK:[SHAH.TMP]SEARCH_TEST.DOC;2

It contains the words "many" and "some" a number
Many programs can be stored in one directory.
Some times you may forget the name of the program
some of the lines in the file.
files or some files in a directory by using wildcards.
The search utility is very useful but many VAX users
```

Multiple files can be specified separated by commas:

```
$ SEARCH  util.doc , test.doc  many , some
```

SEARCH has some useful qualifiers:

/MATCH

/EXACT

/FORMAT

/STATISTICS

/WINDOWS

The /MATCH qualifier allows AND, OR, NOR and NAND of search strings. The next command searches for lines containing "many" and "some" both on the same line

```
$ SEARCH/MATCH = AND  *.*  many,some
```

During searches, uppercase and lowercase characters are considered equivalent unless the /NOEXACT qualifier is used:

```
$ SEARCH/EXACT  *.*  Many ! Search for "Many". "many" will not
                           match.
```

The /FORMAT = DUMP qualifier puts nonprintable characters in a printable mnemonic form. The qualifier is useful for scanning nontext files.

/STATISTICS gives a summary information on the search.

```
$ SEARCH/STATISTICS  *.*  many , some

*******************************
MYDISK:[SHAH.TMP]DIFF_TEST.DOC;2

It contains the words "many" and "some" a number
Suppose you made some modifications to a program
the old and the new program. There are many ways

*******************************
MYDISK:[SHAH.TMP]SEARCH_TEST.DOC;2

It contains the words "many" and "some" a number
Many programs can be stored in one directory.
Some times you may forget the name of the program
some of the lines in the file.
files or some files in a directory by using wildcards.
The search utility is very useful but many VAX users

Files searched:              2      Buffered I/O count:       6
Records searched:           31      Direct I/O count:         3
Characters searched:      1077      Page faults:             35
Records matched:             9      Elapsed CPU time:  0 00:00:00.06
Lines printed:              17      Elapsed time:      0 00:00:00.14
```

/WINDOWS displays a number of lines above and below the line which has a matching string. This is useful to determine the context of the search string:

```
$ SEARCH  *.*  many/window = 4
```

6.2 DIFFERENCES

The difference utility is used to compare the contents of two files. Normally the files will be normal ASCII rather than binary. Here are two files which are used in the examples which follow.

```
This is file DIFF1.DOC.
This a file for testing the DIFFERENCE utility.
It contains the words "many" and "some" a number
of times.

Suppose you made some modifications to a program
and created a new version of the program file.
You may wish to see the differences between
the old and the new program. There are many ways
to do this but the simplest is to use the
DIFFERENCE utility.


This is file DIFF2.DOC.
This a file for testing the DIFFERENCE utility.

Suppose you made some modifications to a program
and created a new version of the program file.
Later on you may wish to see the differences between
the old and the new program. There are many ways
to do this but the simplest is to use the
DIFFERENCE utility.
```

Here is an example showing how to use the utility:

```
$ DIFFERENCES  DIFF1.DOC  DIFF2.DOC

************
File DUA4:[TECH4.PGM.MEMO.BK.CHAP.UTIL.TMP]DIFF1.DOC;1
    3    It contains the words "many" and "some" a number
    4    of times.
    5
******
File DUA4:[TECH4.PGM.MEMO.BK.CHAP.UTIL.TMP]DIFF2.DOC;1
    3
************
************
File DUA4:[TECH4.PGM.MEMO.BK.CHAP.UTIL.TMP]DIFF1.DOC;1
    8    You may wish to see the differences between
    9    the old and the new program. There are many ways
******
File DUA4:[TECH4.PGM.MEMO.BK.CHAP.UTIL.TMP]DIFF2.DOC;1
    6    Later on you may wish to see the differences between
    7    the old and the new program. There are many ways
************

Number of difference sections found: 2
Number of difference records found: 3

DIFFERENCES /IGNORE=( )/MERGED=1-
    DUA4:[TECH4.PGM.MEMO.BK.CHAP.UTIL.TMP]DIFF1.DOC;1-
    DUA4:[TECH4.PGM.MEMO.BK.CHAP.UTIL.TMP]DIFF2.DOC;1
```

Each set of difference are displayed between two lines with 10 asterisks. The lines different in the two files are displayed separated by 6 asterisks. One extra line is displayed so that the context in the file can be easily determined.

Blank lines can be ignored by using /IGNORE = BLANK_LINES as

```
$ DIFFERENCES/IGNORE=BLANK_LINES  DIFF1.DOC  DIFF2.DOC

************
File DUA4:[TECH4.PGM.MEMO.BK.CHAP.UTIL.TMP]DIFF1.DOC;1
     3    It contains the words "many" and "some" a number
     4    of times.
     6    Suppose you made some modifications to a program
     7    and created a new version of the program file.
     8    You may wish to see the differences between
     9    the old and the new program. There are many ways
******
File DUA4:[TECH4.PGM.MEMO.BK.CHAP.UTIL.TMP]DIFF2.DOC;1
     4    Suppose you made some modifications to a program
     5    and created a new version of the program file.
     6    Later on you may wish to see the differences between
     7    the old and the new program. There are many ways
************

Number of difference sections found: 1
Number of difference records found: 5

DIFFERENCES /IGNORE=(BLANK_LINES)/MERGED=1-
    DUA4:[TECH4.PGM.MEMO.BK.CHAP.UTIL.TMP]DIFF1.DOC;1-
    DUA4:[TECH4.PGM.MEMO.BK.CHAP.UTIL.TMP]DIFF2.DOC;1
```

The utility can be used to compare two versions of the same file. This feature is particularly useful when a new version of a program does not work while the old version was working (What did I add to the program?).

6.3 DUMP

The command is useful to print out the binary values of data in a file or tape. It is particulary useful for tapes which cannot be easily mounted for read access. The tape can be mounted with, say, MOUNT MUA0:/FOR, and then the the next command can be used to dump its contents

```
$DUMP  MUA0:
```

The output will display tape header, tape marks, and contents of each block. The utility can also be useful to dump the binary contents of a disk file. Files can be dumped as 512-byte blocks or by logical records in the file. Starting and ending records can also be specified to dump selected portions of the file.

This command has the following qualifiers:

/ascii	|
/decimal	|Specifies display data representation.
/hex	|By default hex and ascii values are displayed.
/octal	|
/byte	|
/longword	|Specifies grouping for the displayed data.
/word	|
/record	Specifies logical record display.
/block	Specifies display of blocks of the file. Optionally the starting record or block number and the ending or count of the number of records or blocks can be specified. Below are examples of DUMP statements.

```
DUMP/RECORD=(START:3,END:5)  customer.dat
DUMP/RECORD=(START:3,COUNT:3)  customer.dat
```

Here is a sample dump:

```
$ DUMP/RECORD=(START:2,COUNT=3) customer.fdl

Dump of file SYS$SYSDEVICE:[TESTING.DATA]CUSTOMER.FDL;2
on 17-FEB-1989 17:47:10.26
File ID (6510,3,0)   End of file block 2 / Allocated 2

Record number 2 (00000002), 48 (0030) bytes

 39312D42 45462D36 31220954 4E454449 IDENT."16-FEB-19 000000
 41562020 2037333A 36323A37 31203938 89 17:26:37   VA 000010
 22726F74 69644520 4C444620 31312D58 X-11 FDL Editor" 000020

Record number 3 (00000003), 6 (0006) bytes

                    4D45 54535953 SYSTEM......... 000000

Record number 4 (00000004), 17 (0011) bytes

 4D562F58 41560909 09454352 554F5309 .SOURCE...VAX/VM 000000
                                  53 S.............. 000010
```

The DUMP utility is also described in the chapter on RMS.

6.4   MAIL

The MAIL utility is useful for sending messages to other users. The users could be on other computers on a DECNET network. The utility is entered by the command

```
$ MAIL
```

The SEND command of the utility asks for a username. Then the text to be sent to the other user has to be entered. The message is terminated by a CTRL/Z. The message will be sent to the mail file of the receiving user. If the user is logged on the system, his terminal will display a line like:

```
New mail on node SCOOP from SCOOP::SHAH
```

If the receiver is not logged into the system , when he or she logs on a message like

```
You have 2 new Mail messages.
```

will be received.

To read mail from another user, enter the MAIL utility and enter the RETURN key at the MAIL> prompt (The READ command can also be entered). Continue pressing the return key until all new mail has been read.

Here is a sample usage of MAIL:

```
MAIL> send
To:     BHATT
Subj:   Can you help me with a COBOL program link?
[EOB]
*i
            I am facing a problem with one of my programs which is
            accessing a sharable library. Can you give me a call to
            discuss this?

            jay X5456

[EOB]
*exit

MAIL> exit
```

Note that MAIL uses the EDT editor by default. If you wish to use another editor, say, TPU (EVE), then use

```
MAIL> SET EDITOR TPU
```

The setting will be in effect until changed again.

Mail can also be sent using just one DCL command line as in

```
$ MAIL /SUBJECT="Need your help on a link" PROBLEM.DOC BHATT
```

where PROBLEM.DOC is the file containing the mail message.

You can extract a message to a file for printing or for some other purpose by reading the message and the entering, say,

```
MAIL> EXTRACT MAIL.DOC
```

where MAIL.DOC is the file where the message will be stored.

The SEARCH command can be used to search for a string in all the mail messages in the current folder

```
MAIL> SEARCH "MYPROG"  !Show first message in current folder
containing "myprog" in it.
```

To send mail to a user on another node, precede the user name by node name:

```
MAIL> send
To: SCOOP::BHATT
```

To exit mail just enter CTRL/Z.

6.4.1   Replying to messages

The REPLY command can be entered while reading a message. It sets up the receiver's name and subject; you have to enter the reply text:

```
MAIL> REPLY
```

6.4.2   Setting mail characteristics

Some of the mail characteristics can be personalized by each user. For example, a short message can be displayed at the receiver's terminal by setting the PERSONAL_NAME parameter

```
MAIL> SET  PERSONAL_NAME  "Jay Shah at X5456"
```

Then, when mail is sent to another user, he or she will see a message like

```
New mail on node SCOOP from SCOOP::SHAH "Jay Shah at X5456"
```

The WASTEBASKET folder contains deleted messages and it is purged when you exit from MAIL. You may want to keep all your old messages. The next command will do it

```
MAIL> SET  NOAUTO_PURGE
```

Later, if the WASTEBASKET folder needs to be cleaned, the command is

```
MAIL> PURGE  !Purge WASTEBASKET (not to be confused with ''$
PURGE'')
```

The editor to be used for entering messages can be changed by

```
MAIL> SET  EDITOR  TPU  !Use the EVE editor.
```

You can keep a copy of every message you mail by

```
MAIL> SET  COPY_SELF  SEND
```

6.4.3   Sending mail to multiple users

Mail can be sent to multiple users by specifying the user names separated by commas

```
MAIL>  send
To: BHATT,MURPHY
```

A file containing user names can also be used. The file is then specified preceded by an @:

```
MAIL>  send
To: @LIST.MAI

$ TYPE LIST.MAI

BHATT
MURPHY
CRANE
```

The list of user names in the file is known as a *distribution list.*

6.4.4 Folders

Each user has a file, MAIL.MAI, in their log-in directory. Mail is stored in this file. The file consists of folders, and folders contain mail messages. Folders can be thought of as subdirectories within MAIL.MAI. To see a list of folders the command is

```
MAIL>  DIR/FOLDERS
```

You can create your own folders. The MAIL utility uses three folders:

MAIL   Contains messages which have been read.

NEWMAIL   New messages are stored here.

WASTEBASKET   Messages which have been deleted are stored here.

When a message arrives, it is stored in the NEWMAIL folder. Once you read the message it is stored in the MAIL folder. When a message is being read, the DELETE command can be given to send it to the WASTEBASKET folder. The WASTEBASKET folder is purged when you exit from the MAIL utility.

To see messages in the current folder use:

```
$ mail
MAIL>  directory
                                                         MAIL
   # From            Date          Subject

   1 TOPVAX::SHAH2   23-JAN-1990   Do you have a dictionary?
   2 TOPVAX::SHAH2   23-JAN-1990   Can you help me with a COBOL
                                   compilation
   3 TOPVAX::SHAH2   18-FEB-1990   NETWORK COPY
MAIL>
```

To select another folder use a command like:

```
MAIL> SELECT  WASTEBASKET
```

To read a particular message just enter the message number

```
MAIL> 5   !read message 5
```

To delete a particular message, give the message number as in

```
MAIL> DELETE  10   !delete message number 10
```

If a message is being read, it can be deleted by

```
MAIL> DELETE   !delete current message
```

6.5 PHONE

This utility is used to communicate interactively with another user on the current node or another node. To start a conversation with user BHATT, use

```
$ PHONE  BHATT
```

The other user must be logged into the system. BHATT's terminal will display a message like

```
SCOOP::SHAH is phoning you on SCOOP:: (11:42:01)
```

The message will be displayed at 10-second intervals on BHATT's terminal until he or she answers by entering PHONE with the ANSWER parameter

```
$ PHONE  ANSWER
```

Your and BHATT's terminal will be divided into two regions; in one you will see text entered by you, and in the other, text entered by BHATT. See Fig. 6.1. After the conversation, enter 'bye' and then CTRL/Z twice. To call someone on another node use a command like

```
$ PHONE  TOPVAX::BHATT
```

6.6 SORT/MERGE

The SORT utility can be used to sort (and merge) files of any type: sequential, relative or indexed. Consider an input file TEST.INP which is to be sorted:

```
                    ┌─────────────────────────────┐
                    │   VAX/VMS Phone Facility     │           13-OCT-1989
  ┌──────────────── └─────────────────────────────┘
  │ %
  │
  │ ─────────────────────────────────────────────────────────────────────────────
  │                             TRIM01::TECH4
  │ Hi. Want to join me for lunch at YIP's ?
  │
  │
  │
  │
  │
  │ ─────────────────────────────────────────────────────────────────────────────
  │                             TRIM01::BHATT
  │ I would love to. What time?█              ●
  │
  │
  │
  │
  │ ─────────────────────────────────────────────────────────────────────────────
  └────────
```

Figure 6.1   A PHONE screen.

```
$ TYPE TEST.INP
ABC 21345 4323
HIJ 65766 7677
KLM 12654 3232
ZZZ 92127 4876
AAA 54566 7123
PQR 02123 6543
TUV 43234 0123
EFG 32343 2365
IJK 32343 2365
JKL 02123 3232
```

To sort the file on the first set of numbers use

```
$ SORT /KEY=(POSITION=5,SIZE=5)  TEST.INP  TEST.SORT1
```

```
$TYPE TEST.SORT1
PQR 02123 6543
JKL 02123 3232
KLM 12654 3232
ABC 21345 4323
EFG 32343 2365
IJK 32343 2365
TUV 43234 0123
AAA 54566 7123
HIJ 65766 7677
ZZZ 92127 4876
```

To sort the file on two keys , the primary key being the first number and the secondary key the second number in each record, use:

```
$ SORT /KEY=(POSITION=5,SIZE=5) /KEY=(POSITION=11,SIZE=4)
TEST.INP  TEST.SORT2

$TYPE  TEST.SORT2
JKL 02123 3232
PQR 02123 6543
KLM 12654 3232
ABC 21345 4323
EFG 32343 2365
IJK 32343 2365
TUV 43234 0123
AAA 54566 7123
HIJ 65766 7677
ZZZ 92127 4876
```

Up to 255 sort keys can be specified. The input file can be of any organization (sequential, realtive, or indexed), the output file will be of the same organization. If large files are to be sorted, SORT will create temporary work files on the disk SYS$SCRATCH.

To merge files, the command is similar to SORT except that multiple input files (up to 10) are specified

```
$ MERGE /KEY=(POSITION=5,SIZE=5) /KEY=(POSITION=11,SIZE=4)-
TEST.SORT2,TMP.SORT3  TEST.MERGE1
```

Note that the input files specified to the merge must be individually sorted on the keys specified.

6.6.1 Key data types

The sort keys specified in the above commands were ASCII characters. Keys can be of other data types like packed decimal. The key type can be specified as in

```
$ SORT /KEY=(POSITION=3,SIZE=5,PACKED_DECIMAL)  TMP.INP  TMP.SORT1
```

The key data types are

- CHARACTER (default)
- BINARY (signed)
- BINARY,UNSIGNED
- F_FLOATING
- DECIMAL
- DECIMAL,LEADING_SIGN

6.7 FURTHER READING

Utilities, Vol. 2B, VMS Programming Manuals.

Using VMS, Vol. 2B, General User Manuals.

Anagnostopoulos, P. G., "MODL, the Manager for Organized Distribution Lists," *VAX Professional Magazine*, February 1990, pp. 11–15.

7

Logical Names

A *logical name* is a "variable" whose value is a string of characters. The value of a logical name is also known as the equivalent name or the translated name. For example, the next command defines the logical name MYDISK as DUB2:

```
$ DEFINE MYDISK DUB2:
```

The ASSIGN command can also be used, but its syntax differs from the DEFINE command. Logical names can be displayed by

```
$ SHOW LOGICAL MYDISK
"MYDISK" = "DUB2:" (LNM$PROCESS_TABLE)
```

or

```
$ SHOW LOGICAL *  !Display all defined logicals
```

To delete a logical name use

```
$ DEASSIGN MYDISK
```

Logical names are sometimes referred to as *logicals*.

7.1 USES OF LOGICAL NAMES

7.1.1 Device independence

In all file specifications, if the device name is actually a logical name, then the operating system substitutes it with the value of the translated logical name. For example, the file specification MYDISK:FILE1.DAT is translated as DUB2:FILE1.DAT (using the logical name defined above). If at some later stage, my files are moved to disk DJA3:, command files and other programs referencing my files can still do so if the value of the logical name MYDISK is reassigned as:

```
$ DEFINE  MYDISK  DJA3:
```

7.1.2 Using directories as devices

Consider the logical name assignment

```
$ DEFINE TEST MYDISK:[SHAH.MYTEST]
```

Here, the logical name TEST refers to a directory. TEST can then be used as a "device." So the next set of commands are equivalent

```
$ DIR  TEST:*.DAT
$ DIR  MYDISK:[SHAH.MYTEST]*.DAT
$ DIR  DJA3:[SHAH.MYTEST]*.DAT
```

7.1.3 Search lists

A logical can be assigned a list of values. For example,

```
$ DEFINE SLIST MYDISK:[SHAH.MYTEST], MYDISK:[SHAH.DEBUG],
MYDISK:[TMP.TEST]
```

The list can be used to search through all the directories:

```
$ DIR SLIST:*.COM


Directory MYDISK:[SHAH.MYTEST]

DELQUERY.COM;5           1   30-OCT-1987 12:58:01.00
DIRSEARCH.COM;5          2   29-DEC-1987 12:51:20.00
DOWN.COM;4               1   27-OCT-1988 14:43:48.56

Total of 3 files, 4 blocks.

Directory MYDISK:[TMP.MYTEST]

MOU.COM;2                1   1-JUN-1989 10:48:00.50
MYMAILEDIT.COM;2         2   4-JAN-1989 13:44:33.11

Total of 2 files, 3  blocks.

Grand total of 2 directories, 5  files, 7  blocks.
```

Note that there are no .COM files in [SHAH.DEBUG]. The search list feature can be used for maintaining one logical "device" which is actually a set of subdirectories. Search lists can be used to make one logical device out of a number of devices and directories as

```
$ DEFINE  MYDEV  DUB3:, DJA1:, MYDISK:[SHAH]
```

7.1.4 Interprocess communications with logical names

Logical names defined at group and system level are described later in this chapter. Since these logical names are "visible" to other processes on the system, they can be used to communicate data between processes. See the chapter on Advanced Programming to use this feature.

7.2 LOGICAL NAMES AND SYMBOLS COMPARED

Logical names are somewhat similar to symbols. The major differences are:

- Arithmetic and string manipulation can be directly performed on symbols but not on logical names.
- Symbols are available only to the process declaring them. Logical names can be "seen" by other processes if defined at the group or system level.
- Symbols act as commands as in

```
$ SD   : = =  SET  DEFAULT
$ SD   [SHAH.DEBUG]
```

Logical names cannot be used as commands.

- If a symbol is used as a command and there is a corresponding logical name also, then the symbol is translated before the logical name.
- Device names in file specifications can be logical names but not symbols.

7.3 LOGICAL NAME TABLES

Logical names for each user are stored in four basic tables:

- *Process table:*   Contains logical names which can be used by the one process which is the user's process.
- *Job table:*   Contains logical names which can be used by the user's main process and spawned processes.
- *Group table:*   Contains logical names which can be used by all processes in the same UIC group.
- *System table:*   Contains logical names which can be used by all processes on the system.

Other tables can also be created though we will not discuss that here. When a logical name is to be translated, the operating system searches these tables for the logical name in the order shown above. To see all the logical names which are accessible to you, use

```
$ SHOW LOGICAL *

(LNM$PROCESS_TABLE)

  "MYDISK" = "DUB2:"
  "SHAHSYS" = "SYS$MANAGER"
          = "SYS$SYSTEM"
          = "SYS$LIBRARY"
  "SYS$COMMAND" = "_LTA11:"
  "SYS$DISK" [exec] = "SYS$SYSDEVICE:"
  "SYS$ERROR" = "_LTA11:"
  "SYS$INPUT" [exec] = "_LTA11:"
  "SYS$OUTPUT" [exec] = "_LTA11:"
  "TT" = "LTA11:"

(LNM$JOB_80E99870)

  "SYS$LOGIN" = "SYS$SYSDEVICE:[TECH4]"
  "SYS$LOGIN_DEVICE" = "SYS$SYSDEVICE:"
  "SYS$SCRATCH" = "SYS$SYSDEVICE:[TECH4]"

(LNM$GROUP_000031)
  "TEST_FILE" = "[MYTEST]EMPLOYEE.DAT;5"

(LNM$SYSTEM_TABLE)

  "LMF$LICENSE" = "SYS$COMMON:[SYSEXE]LMF$LICENSE.LDB"
  "MOM$LOAD" = "MOM$SYSTEM:"
  "MOM$SYSTEM" = "SYS$SYSROOT:[MOM$SYSTEM]"
  "SYS$ANNOUNCE" = ".Welcome to VAX/VMS V5.1-1   "
  "SYS$DISK" = "DUB6:"
  "SYS$ERRORLOG" = "SYS$SYSROOT:[SYSERR]"
  "SYS$EXAMPLES" = "SYS$SYSROOT:[SYSHLP.EXAMPLES]"
  "SYS$HELP" = "SYS$SYSROOT:[SYSHLP]"
  "SYS$LIBRARY" = "SYS$SYSROOT:[SYSLIB]"
  "SYS$MANAGER" = "SYS$SYSROOT:[SYSMGR]"
  "SYS$MESSAGE" = "SYS$SYSROOT:[SYSMSG]"
  "SYS$NODE" = "SCOOP5::"
  "SYS$SHARE" = "SYS$SYSROOT:[SYSLIB]"
  "SYS$SYSDEVICE" = "DUB6:"
  "SYS$SYSROOT" = "DUB6:[SYS0.]"
             = "SYS$COMMON:"
  "SYS$SYSTEM" = "SYS$SYSROOT:[SYSEXE]"
  "SYS$UPDATE" = "SYS$SYSROOT:[SYSUPD]"
```

Notes on the output:

- The logical names in the four tables are displayed separately.
- The group table name shows that the UIC group of the process is 31.
- Some of the logical names have multiple values. These are search lists.

Examples shown are SHAHSYS and SYS$SYSROOT.

- All the logical names in the system table and most of the logical names in the other tables are defined by the system or some other products. Most of the system-defined logical names translate to directories on the system disk (SYS$SYSDEVICE). These directories store system files.

- Some of the logical names are defined in terms of other logical names. For example, SYS$LIBRARY is defined using SYS$SYSROOT.

- Some logical names are defined twice, once in "super" mode and again in "exec" mode. An example is SYS$INPUT. Depending on the mode of CPU during translation (SUPERVISOR or EXECUTIVE), one of the two names is used for translation. For example, for DCL commands, the super logical name will be used while the operating system is running in executive mode, and if it needs to translate a logical name for the process, then it would use the "exec" version of the logical name. The other logical names are used in all modes. Actually logical names can be in each one of the four CPU modes: Kernel, Executive, Supervisory and User.

Logical names can be inserted (or replaced) in any table by

```
$ DEFINE/PROCESS MYDISK DUB2: !Same as "$ DEFINE MYDISK DUB2:"
$ DEFINE/JOB MYDISK DUB2:
$ DEFINE/GROUP MYDISK DUB2:
$ DEFINE/SYSTEM MYDISK DUB2:
```

Group and system privileges will be required to enter logical names in the group and system logical tables.

7.4 SOME COMMON LOGICAL NAMES

The system logical table contains a set of logical names which can be used by everyone on the system. For example, the logical SYS$OUTPUT is normally assigned to your terminal. The system sends output to SYS$OUTPUT which normally translates to your terminal. You can change the assignment of this logical name to send output to a file:

```
$ DEFINE/USER SYS$OUTPUT TMP.TMP    !Redefine the logical. /USER means
                                    !the definition stays only for the
                                    !next command.

$ DIR                               !DIRECTORY output goes to the file
                                    !TMP.TMP. Type out the file.

$ DIR                               !The output now goes to your terminal
                                    !since SYS$OUTPUT was redefined
                                    !temporarily for one command only.
```

Some of the common logical names are described here:

```
( LNM$PROCESS_TABLE )

    "SYS$COMMAND" = "_LTA3:"                    !System accepts terminal input
                                                !from here.
    "SYS$ERROR" = "_LTA3:"                      !Error messages from the
                                                !system are displayed here.
    "SYS$INPUT" = "_LTA3:"                      !System accepts input from here.
    "SYS$OUTPUT" [super] = "_LTA3:"             !System sends output here.
    "TT" = "LTA3:"                              !This is the process's
                                                !terminal.

( LNM$JOB_80E72360 )

    "SYS$LOGIN" = "SYS$SYSDEVICE:[TECH4]" !Login directory of process (user)

( LNM$GROUP_000001 )

( LNM$SYSTEM_TABLE )

    "SYS$COMMON" = "DUB6:[SYS0.SYSCOMMON.]"     !System directory.
    "SYS$DISK" = "DUB6:"                        !System disk.
    "SYS$EXAMPLES" = "SYS$SYSROOT:[SYSHLP.EXAMPLES]"
                                                !Sample programs of various
                                                !products.
    "SYS$HELP" = "SYS$SYSROOT:[SYSHLP]"         !All kind of help files.
    "SYS$LIBRARY" = "SYS$SYSROOT:[SYSLIB]"      !Object libraries, sharable
                                                !images and, generally, files
                                                !shared by users
    "SYS$MANAGER" = "SYS$SYSROOT:[SYSMGR]"      !System manager's directory.
                                                !Contains command files to
                                                !start queues, network and
                                                !so on.
    "SYS$MESSAGE" = "SYS$SYSROOT:[SYSMSG]"      !Error message files
    "SYS$NODE" = "SCOOP5::"                     !Node name on DECNET
    "SYS$SHARE" = "SYS$SYSROOT:[SYSLIB]"        !Same as SYS$LIBRARY:
    "SYS$SYSROOT" = "DUB6:[SYS0.]"              !Root directory for most
                = "SYS$COMMON:"                 !System files
    "SYS$SYSTEM" = "SYS$SYSROOT:[SYSEXE]"       !Mainly system executable
                                                !images like DCL and compilers,
                                                !and device drivers.
    "SYS$UPDATE" = "SYS$SYSROOT:[SYSUPD]"       !Command files to install
                                                !new software, software
                                                !licenses, update SYSGEN
                                                !parameters and so on.
```

The system refers to files on the disk using logical names for the root directory. The main reason is to maintain device and directory independence. For example, most system commands like COPY, COBOL (compilation), and BACKUP cause an image from the directory SYS$SYSTEM to be executed in your process. SYS$SYSTEM is defined using SYS$SYSROOT as the root directory. SYS$SYSROOT in turn is defined using a "real" root directory (DUB6:[SYS0.]) and SYS$COMMON. (SYS$SYSROOT is actually defined as a search list.) This method is used so that in case the system is moved to another disk, only the logical names referring to the physical disk (which is DUB6: in this case) need to be changed to point to the new disk; all the programs and operating system references to SYS$SYSROOT, SYS$SYSTEM, and so on, need not be changed.

7.5   SYSTEM DISK FOR VAXclusters

You will note that all system references to directories are below the root directory DUB6:[SYS0]. In fact you can build another operating system on the same disk by keeping files for this operating system below the root directory DUB6:[SYS1]. If the disk is shared by two VAXes, one VAX can be booted with the operating system in [SYS0...] and the other VAX with the operating system in [SYS1...]. These two operating system will not interfere with each other's files on disk provided all references are through the logical names on the respective VAXes. This feature is exploited by VAXclusters to share the system disk and yet maintain independence of each CPU on the cluster.

7.6   USING LOGICAL NAMES IN COMMAND PROCEDURES AND PROGRAMS

In DCL command files, the value of a logical name can be assigned to a symbol by the lexical function F$TRNLNM (translate logical name):

```
$ VAL = F$TRNLNM("SYS$SYSDEVICE")   ! Symbol VAL = DUA0:
```

The lexical function has many forms. See HELP on the function by using:

```
$ HELP  LEXICAL  F$TRNLNM
```

To create logical names in DCL command files use the DEFINE command shown in the examples above.

Logical names can be created, deleted, and translated from programs. There are three system service calls for this purpose; $CRELNM, $DELLNM and $TRNLNM. The chapter on program development explains how to use system services.

One of the key reasons for using logical names for files in a program is that the logical name is translated at run time so that the files can reside on any disk or in any directory as long as the logical names used in the program are defined at the DCL level before the program is run.

7.7   FURTHER READING

Guide to Using VMS, Vol. 2A, General User Manuals.

8

Program Development

Program sources are created using editors like EDT, EVE, and LSE. Compilation of the program creates an object module with file type of .OBJ. Linking this object module by itself or with other object modules creates an executable image with file type of .EXE. These images are executed by the RUN command. This chapter uses COBOL to demonstrate program development features, but the process for other languages is very similar; wherever the word COBOL is mentioned in a command, it can be substituted by the name of other languages— FORTRAN, PASCAL, CC (for C language), BASIC and so on.

A COBOL program is used in this chapter. This program can be understood by programmers of any language. Please study the program before reading the chapter. Here are the basic steps in getting a program to run:

```
$ EDIT/EVE  TEST.COB  !create the file
```

Here is a sample program.

```
Identification division.
Program-id.     sample.
Date-written.   dec/89.

* The program:
*       reads an input file with each record containing a number followed
*                                       by textual information,
*       multiplies the input number by a constant number accepted from
*                       the terminal,
*       writes the new number and the text to the output file for each record.

Environment division.
* Declaration of files and program variables

 Input-output section.
 File-Control.
        select  test-in   assign to "[test.input]inp.data".
        select  test-out  assign  to "duc4:[test.output]out.data".
```

```
Data division.
 File section.
 fd   test-in.
 01   test-in-rec.
         03 inp-number          pic 9(4).
         03 inp-text            pic x(53).
 fd   test-out.
 01   test-out-rec.
         03 out-number          pic 9(4).
         03 out-text            pic x(53).

Working-storage Section.
 77  mult-factor                pic 9(4) usage comp.

Procedure Division.
* Program execution starts here.
10-open.
         open input test-in. open output test-out.
         display "Enter multiplication factor: " with no advancing.
         accept mult-factor with conversion.
20-read-file.
         read test-in at end go to 30-close.
         compute out-number = inp-number * mult-factor.
         move inp-text to out-text.
         write test-out-rec.
         go to 20-read-file.
30-close.
         close test-in, test-out.
         stop run.
```

The program can be compiled by

```
$ COBOL   TEST.COB
```

Error messages, if any, will be listed on the terminal. The output is a file TEST.OBJ. The object file has to be linked to create the executable image

```
$ LINK   TEST.OBJ
```

The output is TEST.EXE. This file can be executed by the RUN command:

```
$ RUN   TEST.EXE
Enter multiplication factor: 2
$
```

Actually, the file types .COB, .OBJ, and .EXE are optional in these commands.

Compiler qualifiers

Each language has its own set of compilation switches (qualifiers). Qualifiers are specified after the command as:

```
$ COBOL/LIST/FIPS   TEST.COB
```

Qualifiers common to most languages are

/LIST	Produces a listing file containing compilation errors, cross reference and so on.
/DEBUG	Inserts debugger in the object module. The debugger is described later.
/CROSS_REFERENCE	Generates a cross reference of symbols and writes it in the listing file.
/DIAGNOSTICS	Creates a special file with file type of .DIA for use by the language sensitive editor.
/MACHINE_CODE	Generates assembly language code which is shown in the listing file. The code shows what the machine executes for each of the source language statements.

Refer to the individual language manuals for qualifiers specific to particular languages. Figure 8.1 is an example of COBOL compilation created by the following commands

```
$ COBOL/LIST/CROSS_REFERENCE TEST
$ TYPE TEST.LIS
```

8.1 LINK

The linker automatically searches two system library files for unresolved symbol (and subroutine) references after all the files in the LINK command have been processes. These libraries are SYS$SYSTEM:IMAGLIB.OLB and SYS$SYSTEM:STARLET.OLB. The system services and run time library (RTL) routines are in these files.

The LINK command has these commonly used qualifers:

/CROSS_REFERENCE	Generates a cross reference of symbols and writes it in the linker listing file (file type .MAP). The cross reference lists symbol references across separately compiled programs and also shows the position of the symbol in memory when the program is executed.
/DEBUG	Inserts debugging code in the executable image. Normally, to use the debugger, this qualifier is required with the compilation and linking commands
/MAP	Creates memory allocation listing which shows symbols and program sections.
/LIBRARY	Searches the library for unresolved symbol references. This qualifier is placed after an object library file name.
/OPTIONS	Some parameters cannot be placed on the LINK command line. An example is a shareable library.

```
 1        Identification division.
 2        Program-id. sample.
 3        Date-written.    dec/89.
 4
 5    *   The program:
 6    *     reads an input file with each record containing a number followed
 7    *                                        by textual information,
 8    *     multiplies the input number by a constant number accepted from
 9    *                                        the terminal,
10    *     writes the number and the text to the output file.
11
12        Environment division.
13        Input-output section.
14        File-Control.
15            select  test-in   assign to "inp.data".
16            select  test-out  assign  to "dua4:[tech4.tmp]out.data".
17        Data division.
18        File section.
19        fd  test-in.
20        01  test-in-rec.
21            03 inp-number            pic 9(4).
22            03 inp-text              pic x(53).
23        fd  test-out.
24        01  test-out-rec.
25            03 out-number            pic 9(4).
26            03 out-text              pic x(53).
27
28        Working-storage Section.
29        77  mult-factor             pic 9(4) usage comp.
30
31        Procedure Division.
32        10-open.
33            open input test-in. open output test-out.
34            display "Enter multiplication factor:" with no advancing.
35            accept mult-factor with conversion.
36        20-read-file.
37            read test-in at end go to 30-close.
38            compute out-number = inp-number * mult-factor.
39            move inp-text to out-text.
40            write test-out-rec.
41            go to 20-read-file.
42        30-close.
43            close test-in, test-out.
44            stop run.
```

Figure 8.1 An example compilation in COBOL.

```
SAMPLE                                         6-Jun-1989 12:01:07    VAX COBOL V3.2-42           Page   2
Cross Reference in Alphabetical Order          5-Jun-1989 16:30:05    DUA4:[TECH4.TMP]TEST.COB;15 (1)

10-OPEN           32#
20-READ-FILE      36#   41
30-CLOSE          42#   37
INP-NUMBER        21#   38
INP-TEXT          22#   39
MULT-FACTOR       29#   35        38
OUT-NUMBER        25#   38*
OUT-TEXT          26#   39*
SAMPLE             2#
TEST-IN           15#   19#   33
TEST-IN-REC       20#         37
TEST-OUT          16#   23#   33
TEST-OUT-REC      24#   40         43
```

Figure 8.1 (*Continued*)

SAMPLE
Compilation Summary

6-Jun-1989 12:01:07   VAX COBOL V3.2-42
5-Jun-1989 16:30:05   DUA4:[TECH4.TMP]TEST.COB;15 (1)

PROGRAM SECTIONS

Name	Bytes	Attributes							
0 $CODE	447	PIC	CON	REL	LCL	SHR	EXE	RD	NOWRT Align(2)
1 $LOCAL	1172	PIC	CON	REL	LCL	NOSHR	NOEXE	RD	WRT Align(2)
2 $PDATA	764	PIC	CON	REL	LCL	SHR	NOEXE	RD	NOWRT Align(2)
3 COB$NAMES	24	PIC	CON	REL	LCL	SHR	NOEXE	RD	NOWRT Align(2)
4 COB$NAMES	20	PIC	CON	REL	LCL	SHR	NOEXE	RD	NOWRT Align(2)

DIAGNOSTICS

Informational: 1 (suppressed by command qualifier)

COMMAND QUALIFIERS

COBOL /LIST/CROSS_REFERENCE TEST

/NOCOPY_LIST /NOMACHINE_CODE /CROSS_REFERENCE=ALPHABETICAL
/NOANSI_FORMAT /NOSEQUENCE_CHECK /NOMAP
/NOTRUNCATE /NOAUDIT /NOCONDITIONALS
/CHECK=(NOPERFORM,NOBOUNDS) /DEBUG=(NOSYMBOLS,TRACEBACK)
/WARNINGS=(NOSTANDARD,OTHER,NOINFORMATION)
/STANDARD=(NOSYNTAX,NOPDP11) /NOFIPS

STATISTICS

Run Time: 0.37 seconds
Elapsed Time: 1.31 seconds
Page Faults: 160
Dynamic Memory: 414 pages

Figure 8.1 (Continued)

These parameters have to be put in an options file and the file has to be specified on the link command line followed by the /OPTIONS qualifier.

/SHAREABLE

This qualifier can be placed after the LINK command or after a file name in the /OPTIONS file. If placed after the LINK command, the output created is a shared image. If placed in the /OPTIONS file following a file name, the file is an input shared image.

Figure 8.2 is an example of a LINK map file created by the following commands

```
$ LINK/MAP/CROSS_REFERENCE TEST
$ TYPE TEST.MAP
```

8.2 SHAREABLE LIBRARIES AND C LANGUAGE PROGRAMS

Most C programs use the shareable library SYS$SHARE: VAXCRTL.EXE. The following commands compile and link C programs:

```
$CC TEST
$LINK TEST,SYS$INPUT/OPTIONS
sys$share:vaxcrtl/share
```

The commands can be used as a template to use shareable libraries in other languages.

8.3 THE DEBUGGER

VAX/VMS has a powerful symbolic debugger which can be very useful during program testing. Some of the features are

- It is common for all the VMS languages though some commands are language specific.
- Program debugging is at source language level.
- It has standard features like single stepping, tracing and breakpointing, and examining and modifying values of program variables.
- Watching a variable for a change in value during program execution and conditional execution of commands by use of IF, FOR, REPEAT, and WHILE statements.
- Any editor can be invoked from the debugger to modify the source program during the debug session.

```
                          6-JUN-1989 12:05        VAX-11 Linker V05-02                    Page  1

                      +------------------------+
                      + Object Module Synopsis !
                      +------------------------+

Module Name   Ident      Bytes   File                              Creation Date   Creator
-----------   -----      -----   ----                              -------------   -------
SAMPLE        0           2427   DUA4:[TECH4.TMP]TEST.OBJ;13        6-Jun-1989 12:01   VAX COBOL V3.2-42
COB$RMS_BLOCKS X-1          100   SYS$COMMON:[SYSLIB]STARLET.OLB;1   8-APR-1988 01:32   VAX-11 Bliss-32 V4.2-761
SYS$P1_VECTOR X-4            0   SYS$COMMON:[SYSLIB]STARLET.OLB;1   8-APR-1988 04:20   VAX MACRO V5.0-8
COBRTL_       V05-000        0   SYS$COMMON:[SYSLIB]COBRTL.EXE;1    8-APR-1988 04:58   VAX-11 Linker V04-92
LIBRTL2       V05-000        0   SYS$COMMON:[SYSLIB]LIBRTL2.EXE;1   8-APR-1988 04:54   VAX-11 Linker V04-92

                      +--------------------------+
                      ! Program Section Synopsis !
                      +--------------------------+

Psect Name           Module Name   Base       End        Length           Align     Attributes
----------           -----------   ----       ---        ------           -----     ----------
$PDATA                             00000200   000004FB   000002FC (  764.) LONG 2   PIC,USR,CON,REL,LCL,  SHR,NOEXE,  RD,NOWRT,NOVEC
                     SAMPLE        00000200   000004FB   000002FC (  764.) LONG 2
COB$NAMES_____2                  000004FC   00000513   00000018 (   24.) LONG 2   PIC,USR,CON,REL,LCL,  SHR,NOEXE,  RD,NOWRT,NOVEC
                     SAMPLE        000004FC   00000513   00000018 (   24.) LONG 2
COB$NAMES_____4                  00000514   00000527   00000014 (   20.) LONG 2   PIC,USR,CON,REL,LCL,  SHR,NOEXE,  RD,NOWRT,NOVEC
                     SAMPLE        00000514   00000527   00000014 (   20.) LONG 2
$LOCAL                            00000600   00000AF7   000004F8 ( 1272.) LONG 2   PIC,USR,CON,REL,LCL,LCL,NOSHR,NOEXE,  RD,  WRT,NOVEC
                     SAMPLE        00000600   00000A93   00000494 ( 1172.) LONG 2
                     COB$RMS_BLOCKS 00000A94   00000AF7   00000064 (  100.) LONG 2
$CODE                             00000C00   00000DBE   000001BF (  447.) LONG 2   PIC,USR,CON,REL,LCL,  SHR,  EXE,  RD,NOWRT,NOVEC
                     SAMPLE        00000C00   00000DBE   000001BF (  447.) LONG 2
```

Figure 8.2 An example LINK map file.

```
                                         +-----------------------------+
                                         ! Symbol Cross Reference !
                                         +-----------------------------+

Symbol            Value        Defined By         Referenced By ...
------            -----        ----------         -------------
COB$AB_NAM        00000A98-R   COB$RMS_BLOCKS     SAMPLE
COB$ACC_SCR       00000E4C-RX  COBRTL             SAMPLE
COB$DISP_NO_ADV   00000E50-RX  COBRTL             SAMPLE
COB$HANDLER       00000E58-RX  COBRTL             SAMPLE
COB$IOEXCEPTION   00000E48-RX  COBRTL             SAMPLE
COB$POS_ACCEPT    00000E54-RX  COBRTL             SAMPLE
LIB$AB_CVTPT_U    00000E68-RX  LIBRTL2            SAMPLE
LIB$AB_CVTTP_U    00000E64-RX  LIBRTL2            SAMPLE
SAMPLE_           00000C00-R   SAMPLE
SYS$CLOSE         7FFEE1B8     SYS$P1_VECTOR      SAMPLE
SYS$CONNECT       7FFEE1C0     SYS$P1_VECTOR      SAMPLE
SYS$CREATE        7FFEE1C8     SYS$P1_VECTOR      SAMPLE
SYS$EXIT          7FFEDF40     SYS$P1_VECTOR      SAMPLE
SYS$GET           7FFEE180     SYS$P1_VECTOR      SAMPLE
SYS$IMGSTA        7FFEDF68     SYS$P1_VECTOR
SYS$OPEN          7FFEE208     SYS$P1_VECTOR      SAMPLE
SYS$PUT           7FFEE188     SYS$P1_VECTOR      SAMPLE


DUA4:[TECH4.TMP]TEST.EXE;11              6-JUN-1989 12:05      VAX-11 Linker V05-02      Page   2

Symbol            Value        Defined By         Referenced By ...
------            -----        ----------         -------------


Key for special characters above:
+-----------------+
! *  - Undefined  !
! U  - Universal  !
! R  - Relocatable!
! X  - External   !
! WK - Weak       !
+-----------------+
```

Figure 8.2 (*Continued*)

```
+------------------+
! Image Synopsis !
+------------------+
```

```
Virtual memory allocated:                             00000200 00000FFF 00000E00 (3584. bytes, 7. pages)
Stack size:                                           20. pages
Image header virtual block limits:                    1. (        1. block)
Image binary virtual block limits:                    2. (  8. (  7. blocks)
Image name and identification:                        TEST 0
Number of files:                                      6.
Number of modules:                                    6.
Number of program sections:                           11.
Number of global symbols:                             366.
Number of cross references:                           32.
Number of image sections:                             15.
User transfer address:                                00000C00
Debugger transfer address:                            7FFEDF68
Number of code references to shareable images:        7.
Image type:                                           EXECUTABLE.
Map format:                                           DEFAULT WITH CROSS REFERENCE in file DUA4:[TECH4.TMP]TEST.MAP;1
Estimated map length:                                 42. blocks
```

```
+----------------------+
! Link Run Statistics !
+----------------------+
```

Performance Indicators	Page Faults	CPU Time	Elapsed Time
Command processing:	57	00:00:00.04	00:00:00.06
Pass 1:	232	00:00:00.40	00:00:01.81
Allocation/Relocation:	19	00:00:00.04	00:00:00.17
Pass 2:	197	00:00:00.23	00:00:01.16
Map data after object module synopsis:	8	00:00:00.04	00:00:00.04
Symbol table output:	2	00:00:00.00	00:00:00.07
Total run values:	515	00:00:00.75	00:00:03.31

Using a working set limited to 10000 pages and 82 pages of data storage (excluding image)

Total number object records read (both passes): 122
of which 23 were in libraries and 3 were DEBUG data records containing 66 bytes
59 bytes of DEBUG data were written, starting at VBN 9 with 1 blocks allocated

Number of modules extracted explicitly   = 0
     with 2 extracted to resolve undefined symbols

0 library searches were for symbols not in the library searched

A total of 0 global symbol table records was written

LINK/MAP/CROSS_REFERENCE TEST

Figure 8.8 (Continued)

The COBOL program shown above will be used to illustrate the debugger functions. It can be understood by programmers of other languages so be familiar with it. To debug a program, it has to be compiled and linked with the /DEBUG qualifier.

```
$ COBOL/DEBUG/LIST  TEST
$ LINK/DEBUG  TEST
```

The /LIST qualifier should be used for the compilation because the line numbers refered to in the debugger are in the listing file. Keep a printout of this listing file handy when debugging. If the compilation command (like for the C compiler) has a /NOOPTIMIZE qualifier, then it must be used. When the program is run, the debugger prompt, DBG, will be issued. Commands can be then issued to the debugger. To simply run the program to completion use the GO command:

```
$ RUN TEST
        VAX DEBUG Version V5.1-01

%DEBUG-I-INITIAL, language is COBOL, module set to SAMPLE
DBG> GO
Enter multiplication factor: 2

%DEBUG-I-EXITSTATUS, is '%SYSTEM-S-NORMAL, normal successful completion'
DBG> EXIT
$
```

Of course, normally programs will have problems and the debugger will be used to resolve them. While the debugger will work in the line-oriented mode, the screen oriented mode is more convenient. Use

```
DBG>  SET MODE SCREEN ; SET STEP NOSOURCE
```

There are actually two commands; the second command does not display source lines as the debugger output when stepping through a program. This is because the source lines are displayed on the screen anyway. The screen is divided horizontally into three windows; the top window displays the source statements as they are being executed, the middle window displays output from the debugger, and the bottom window is for your input and input error messages. Initially the screen does not display source lines; the STEP command should be issued to step to the start of the executable part of the program:

```
DBG>  STEP
```

Figure 8.3 shows how the screen after this command is executed. Note the arrow at the left on the top window. It points to the next statement that will be executed. The keypad at the right of the keyboard implements some of the commonly used commands. For example, the command to enter screen mode which was entered above can

```
- SRC: module SAMPLE -scroll-source-----------------------------------------------
     28: Working-storage Section.
     29:  77  mult-factor          pic 9(4) usage comp.
     30:
     31: Procedure Division.
     32: 10-open.
 ->  33:          open input test-in. open output test-out.
     34:          display "Enter multiplication factor: " with no advancing.
     35:          accept mult-factor with conversion.
     36: 20-read-file.
     37:          read test-in at end go to 30-close.
     38:          compute out-number = inp-number * mult-factor.
- OUT -output------------------------------------------------------------------
stepped to SAMPLE\10-OPEN\%LINE 33




- PROMPT -error-program-prompt-----------------------------------------------

DBG> STEP
DBG> █
```

Figure 8.3 A DEBUG screen.

be executed by just entering the PF3 key. Use the PF2 (help) key to see the definitions of the keypad keys.

As with most VMS software, the HELP command shows how to use the debugger.

8.3.1 Basic debugging commands

Variable values can be examined by:

```
DBG> EXAMINE mult-factor
```

Variable values can be changed by:

```
DBG> DEPOSIT mult-factor=5
DBG> DEPOSIT out-number=inp-number * mult-factor + 1
```

The STEP command executes one source line (a line may have multiple statements in which case all the statements will be executed). The STEP n command executes n lines of statements

```
DBG> STEP
DBG> STEP 5
```

The SET TRACE/LINE command displays the line numbers of program lines as they are executed. Usually it is followed by the STEP n or GO command to see the flow of program execution. The trace also shows the flow of execution through system and system-shareable library routines. This display is usually not required and can be disabled by the command

```
DBG> SET TRACE/LINE/NOSYSTEM/NOSHARE
```

Trace can be disabled by

```
DBG> CANCEL TRACE/ALL
```

The SET BREAK command sets break points at specified lines, labels, or subroutines. If during program execution (say, by the GO command) the break point location is encountered, the program stops execution, displays the location of the break point and returns control to you for further action. Variables can be examined or changed or other debugger commands can be issued before allowing execution to continue:

```
DBG> SET BREAK 20-READ-FILE    !For break at a label or subroutine
DBG> SET BREAK %LINE 37        !For break at a source program
line
```

Multiple break points can be set by using the command more than once. The SHOW BREAK command displays all the break points. Break points can be canceled by

```
DBG> CANCEL BREAK 20-READ-FILE
DBG> CANCEL BREAK/ALL          !Cancel all break points set.
```

The SET WATCH command monitors the variable mentioned in the command and breaks execution when the value of the variable changes:

```
DBG> SET WATCH mult-factor
```

In this case, program execution stops when a value is entered for the variable mult-factor. Program execution can be resumed by the GO or STEP commands.

Multiple watch variables can be set. The SHOW WATCH command displays all the variables being watched and "watches" can be disabled by the CANCEL WATCH command.

8.3.2 Other features

The SEARCH command is used to search for a string of characters in the program. This debugger SEARCH command should not be confused with the DCL $ SEARCH command. The line containing the string is displayed along with the line number. Range of lines to search can be specified; by default the search starts at the top of the program. All occurrences of the string can be displayed by the /ALL qualifier. Examples follow

```
DBG> SEARCH "mult-factor"      !Search from top of program

DBG> SEARCH/NEXT               !Search for the next occurence
                               !of the string "mult-factor".
```

```
DBG>  SEARCH  20:9999  "mult-factor"      !Search from line 20 till end
                                          !of program (or line 9999 if the
                                          !program has more lines).

DBG>  SEARCH/ALL  0:9999  "mult-factor"   !Search and display all lines
                                          !containing the string speci-
                                          fied.
```

Normally, the top window displays the line which will be executed next and the lines around this line. To display another part of the program use

```
DBG>  EXAMINE/SOURCE  %LINE  40    !center source window display
                                   around this line
```

The keypad keys "8" and "2" (KP8 and KP2) can be used to scroll up and down through the source program.

8.3.4 Conditional execution of debugging commands

The IF, FOR, REPEAT, and WHILE conditional statements turns the debugger into a programming language! Here are examples of these commands:

```
DBG>  IF mult-factor = 0 THEN (DEPOSIT mult-factor=5; GO)
DBG>  FOR I = 1 TO 10 DO (DEPOSIT mult-factor=I; EXAMINE
          mult-factor)
DBG>  REPEAT 25 DO (EXAMINE inp-number; STEP)
DBG>  WHILE inp-number not = 323 DO (EXAMINE inp-number; STEP 3)
```

The boolean expressions should be valid in the language being used, in this case COBOL. The commands SET BREAK, SET TRACE, and SET WATCH can be conditionally executed and special action can be specified when the command is executed:

```
DBG>  SET TRACE/NOSYSTEM/NOSHARE/LINE WHEN (mult-factor not = 0)
              !If the GO command is issued after this command,
              !the program will be traced after the value of
              mult-factor
              !is entered as a non-zero value.
DBG>  SET BREAK 20-READ-FILE DO (EXAMINE inp-number,out-number; GO)
              !If the GO command is issued after this command,
              !the program will display the value of inp-number and
              !out-number every time the label 20-READ-FILE is
              encountered.
DBG>  SET WATCH out-number WHEN (inp-number > 200) DO (EXAMINE
              inp-number;GO)
              !When inp-number is > 200, break when the value of
              out-number
              !is modified, display value of inp-number and
              out-number
              !(Out-number is automatically displaed by the WATCH),
              !and continue execution.
```

Debugger commands can be stored in files and executed from the debugger using the @ sign

```
DBG> @INIT.DBG
```

Many languages make extensive use of subprograms or modules (like functions in C, subroutines in FORTRAN, and procedures in Pascal). Since variable names and other names may be the same in different modules, the names may have to be qualified, as in

```
DBG> EXAMINE  sort-subroutine  est-var
```

Here, the command refers to the variable test-var in the subroutine called sort-subroutine is. Use SHOW MODULE to see the modules in the program.

Variable values within structures can be displayed using the standard language syntax as:

```
DBG> EXAMINE  SCHOOL.STUDENT    !In PASCAL
```

To see symbol (variable) information, use

```
DBG> SHOW  SYMBOL *                !Display all known symbols
DBG> SHOW  SYMBOL/TYPE  test-in-rec  !Display symbol type and size
type SAMPLE™EST-IN-REC
    record type (anonymous, 2 components), size: 57 bytes
data SAMPLE™EST-IN-REC
    record type (anonymous, 2 components), size: 57 bytes
```

The source program can be edited from the debugger by

```
DBG> SET EDITOR EDIT/TPU   !You can specify other editors here
DBG> EDIT                  !Spawn process to edit source file,
                            return
                           !to debugger on exit
```

8.4 SYSTEM SERVICES AND RUN TIME LIBRARIES (RTLs)

VMS has a set of *library routines* like the $GETTIM routine, which returns the current date and time. These can be "called" from any language by passing appropriate parameters. These routines are stored in two object library files (SYS$SHARE:IMAGELIB.OLB and SYS$SHARE:STARLET.OLB) which are automatically accesed by the LINK command. So to use these routines, no special parameters are required during compilation and linking. The following commands can be used to see a brief description of these routines:

```
$ HELP SYSTEMSERVICES
$ HELP RTL
```

Each call returns a longword integer status. This status should be checked after every call in case the called routine did not execute properly.

Here is a simple program which displays the system data and time. Two calls are made to the system, $GETTIM and $ASCTIM. $GETTIM gets the the current time from the system in binary form of 8 bytes. The $ASCTIM routine converts this internal form of time to a ASCII-displayable form. The program is shown in COBOL and in C. It should be easy to convert it to other languages.

```
$ TYPE TIME.COB

Identification Division.
  Program-id.   Sys-calls.

* The program illustrates use of system services and Run Time Library (RTL)
* calls. The $GETTIM system service is used to get the current (date and)
* time from the system into the variable timbuf-internal. This time is a
* 64-bit internal representation. The $ASCTIM system service is called
* to convert this time to a printable ascii form.
* In CALL statements, "using by value" is equivalent to "using" since
* parameters are passed by value as default.

Environment Division.
Data Division.
Working-storage Section.
* Variables for time-date conversions from internal to ASCII form.

    01  timbuf-internal     pic x(8).
    01  timlength           pic s9(4) comp value 8.
    01  timbuf-ascii        pic x(30).
    01  timcvtflg           pic s9(9) comp value 0.
    01  call-status         pic s9(9) comp.
Procedure Division.
10-start.
        call "sys$gettim" using by reference timbuf-internal
                                giving call-status.
        if call-status is failure then call "sys$exit" using call-status.

        call "sys$asctim" using by reference timlength,
                                by descriptor timbuf-ascii,
                                by reference timbuf-internal,
                                timcvtflg
                                giving call-status.
        if call-status is failure then call "sys$exit" using
                                by value call-status.

        display timbuf-ascii.
```

```
$ TYPE TIME.C

main( )
{
#include stdio
#include descrip
#include ssdef

        unsigned char timbuf_internal[8],timbuf_ascii[30];
        int  timcvtflg = 0, status;
        struct
        {                                        /*string descriptor*/
        unsigned short  timlength;
        unsigned char   datatype;
        unsigned char   descriptor_class;
        char            *address;
        }    timbuf_ascii_descriptor =
                { 30, DSC$K_DTYPE_T, DSC$K_CLASS_S, timbuf_ascii};

        status = sys$gettim(&timbuf_internal);
        if (status!=SS$_NORMAL) exit(status);

        status = sys$asctim(    &timbuf_ascii_descriptor.timlength,
                                &timbuf_ascii_descriptor,
                                &timbuf_internal,
                                timcvtflg
                           );
        if (status!=SS$_NORMAL) exit(status);

        printf("%s",timbuf_ascii);
};
```

To run these programs the steps are:

```
$ !Cobol program
$ COBOL time
$ LINK time
$ RUN time
  7-DEC-1989 11:30:12.04


$ !The C program
$ CC time
$ LINK TIME,sys$input/options
sys$share:vaxcrtl/share
$ RUN time
  7-DEC-1989 11:30:30.60
```

The most important issue is determining how to pass the parameters required for each call and how to set up data structures for them in the language you are using. The HELP command shows the parameters required for each call:

$ HELP SYSTEM_SERVICES $ASCTIM

SYSTEM_SERVICES

  $ASCTIM

      The Convert Binary Time to ASCII String service converts an absolute
      or delta time from 64-bit system time format to an ASCII string.

      Format:

          SYS$ASCTIM [timlen] ,timbuf ,[timadr] ,[cvtflg]

      Arguments:

    timlen

    VMS usage: word_unsigned
    type: word (unsigned)
    access: write only
    mechanism: by reference

    Length (in bytes) of the ASCII string returned by $ASCTIM.   The
    timlen argument is the address of a word containing this length.

    timbuf

    VMS usage: time_name
    type: character-coded text string
    access: write only
    mechanism: by descriptor--fixed
    length string descriptor

    Buffer into which $ASCTIM writes the ASCII string.   The timbuf
    argument is the address of a character string descriptor pointing to
    the buffer.

    timadr

    VMS usage: date_time
    type: quadword (unsigned)
    access: read only
    mechanism: by reference

    Time value that $ASCTIM is to convert. The timadr argument is the
    address of this 64-bit time value. A positive time value represents
    an absolute time. A negative time value represents a delta time.
    If a delta time is specified, it must be less than 10,000 days.

    cvtflg

    VMS usage: longword_unsigned
    type: longword (unsigned)

    access: read only
    mechanism: by value

    Conversion indicator specifying which date and time fields $ASCTIM
    should return.   The cvtflg argument is a longword value, which is
    interpreted as Boolean. A value of 1 specifies that $ASCTIM should
    return only the hour, minute, second, and hundredth of second
    fields. A value of 0 (the default) specifies that $ASCTIM should
    return the full date and time.

Since a number of languages and other products are supported on VAX/VMS, a standard means of communications has to be defined for programs calling programs in other modules or the operating system. This standard is the *VAX Calling Standard*. Most programmers need not be aware of the standard because they use CALL statements which follow the syntax for the language they use. The standard is relevant when using, say, multiple languages.

CALL statements in high-level languages and other programming products generate (or should generate, if you are developing layered products) machine code meeting the following conditions:

- Parameters are passed as an argument list. The argument list can be in memory or on the stack. Figure 8.4 shows the format of the argument list.

- While parameter types can be mutually understood by the calling and called programs, VMS has a set of data types which should be used if applicable. For example, there is a parameter type for strings. A string descriptor and the string data can be declared by using the specified format.

- The called procedure can return a condition code. The code is placed in register R0. If the code has 64-bits then register R1 can also be used.

Programs calling system services and RTL routines adhere to the VAX Calling Standard. The next section shows how the calling standard is used within high level languages.

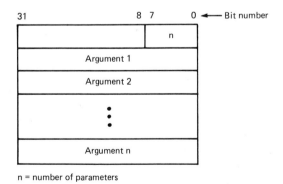

n = number of parameters

Figure 8.4   VAX Calling Standard: A Call argument list.

8.4.1.1 Call Parameters

There are three basic parameter passing mechanisms: by value, by reference and by descriptor. By value is obvious. By reference means the address of the memory location containing the parameter is passed. By descriptor means the address of the descriptor of the parameter is passed.

Descriptors are usually used when passing string values. The descriptor gives the length of the string passed. Descriptors can be for various data types like arrays of integers or date and time but string descriptors are the most common. A string descriptor has 8 bytes as shown here.

Length	an unsigned word (2 bytes, length of string)
Data type	an unsigned byte (value = 14 for text strings)
Class	an unsigned byte (value = 1 for text strings)
Address	an unsigned longword (4 bytes, address of string)

Programmers using COBOL or most of the other languages are lucky; the language sets up string descriptors when declaring a string or array of characters. Here is how three different parameters are declared and passed to a routine.

```
*parameter passing in COBOL
working-storage section.
* parameter1 is a 2 byte integer.
* parameter2 is a string descriptor for a string of length 30.
* parameter3 is a 4 byte integer.

    01  parameter1              pic 9(4) comp value 8.
    01  parameter2              pic x(30).
    01  parameter3              pic 9(9) comp value 0.
    01  call-status             pic s9(9) comp.

procedure division.
* calling a system routine. parameter1 is passed by reference, parameter2
* is a string descriptor passed by reference, parameter3 is passed by value.

        call "sys$routine" using
                          by reference parameter1,
                          by reference parameter2,
                          parameter3
                          giving call-status.
        if call-status is failure then call "sys$exit" using
                          by value call-status.
```

Programmers using C have to make their own string descriptors:

```
/* Parameter passing in C */

/* parameter1 is a 2-byte integer passed by reference.
 * parameter2 is a descriptor (for a 30 character string) and it
 * is passed by reference.
 * parameter3 is a 4-byte integer passed by value.
 */
        unsigned short parameter1;
        unsigned char str[30];
        struct
        {                          /*string descriptor*/
        unsigned short  length;
        unsigned char   datatype;
        unsigned char   descriptor_class;
        char            *str_address;
        } parameter2 = { 30, 14, 1, str};
        unsigned int parameter3

main()
{
        status = sys$routine( &parameter1, &parameter2, parameter3);
        if (status!=SS$_NORMAL) exit(status);
};
```

8.5 FURTHER READING

Introduction, Vol. 1, VMS Programming Manuals.
VMS Programming Manuals.

9

RMS—Record Management Services

VAX/VMS supports three major types of disk files: *sequential, relative,* and *indexed* (ISAM). Tape files can be sequential only. These files and records in these files are manipulated using the Record Management Services (RMS for short). Since RMS is integrated with the operating system, no commands have to be issued to use it. RMS can be used over DECNET to manipulate files on other nodes by specifying the node name in the file specifications.

Logically, files consist of a sequence of blocks on disk. Physically, these blocks may be scattered on the disk. Information about block usage in maintained in two files, INDEXF.SYS and BITMAP.SYS. These files are in directory [000000] on each disk. The block size (also known as sector size) on disk is 512 bytes. The record size can be defined to be variable or fixed when the file is created. For practical applications, files can be arbitrarily large provided there is adequate free disk space.

Records in sequential files can be accessed sequentially from the beginning of the file. Once a record is skipped over, it can be accessed only by scanning the file from the first record. Records are created at the end of the file and cannot be deleted. Records can be updated as long as the new record's size does not exceed the size of the existing record.

Relative files, also known as random files, have fixed-size record cells. When the file is created, the cells may be defined to contain fixed or variable-length records. Records can be accessed in any order. So record number 50 can be accessed followed by record 10 and then record 65. Records can be inserted, deleted or updated at any cell position.

Records in indexed files have keys. Records can be accessed randomly by specifying the key of the record. Records can also be accessed sequentially sorted by keys. Keys are defined by their position and length in the record. For example, an indexed file can have records each having 120 bytes and two keys, the first key of length 7 starting at position 5 and the second key of length 25 at position 50. An indexed file has at least one key called the primary key. The file can have up to 254 additional keys called alternate keys. Indexed files have two logical areas; one contains the data records and the other contains keys and data record pointers. The keys are stored sorted as a B-tree data structure. Actually, if an index file has more than one key then a separate area can be created for each key.

To see file attributes of an existing file the command is

```
$ DIR/FULL  filename
```

For example,

```
$ DIR/FULL customer.dat

Directory SYS$SYSDEVICE:[SHAH.SUB.MEMO.BOOK]

CUSTOMER.DAT;15              File ID:   (1526,286,0)
Size:            15/15       Owner:     [200,12]
Created:   10-JUL-1988 15:20  Revised:  10-JUL-1988 15:21 (1)
Expires:   <None specified>  Backup:    <No backup done>
File organization:  Indexed, Prolog: 3, Using 2 keys
File attributes:    Allocation: 15, Extend: 0, Maximum bucket size: 2
                    Global buffer count: 0, No version limit
Record format:      Fixed length 55 byte records
Record attributes:  Carriage return carriage control
Journaling enabled: None
File protection:    System:RWED, Owner:RWED, Group:RE, World:
Access Cntrl List:  None

Total of 1 file, 15/15 blocks.
```

The file is CUSTOMER.DAT version 15. The used size is 15 blocks and the actual allocated size is 15 blocks also. The file type is indexed and has two keys. The record attribute parameter specifies that RMS will append a carriage return (and line feed) after every record when the file is typed.

9.1   RECORD FORMATS

RMS supports four record formats:

1. *Fixed length:*   All records have the same length. The record length is stored in the file header.

2. *Variable length:*   Records have variable lengths. Each record is preceded by a 2-byte header specifying the length of the record.

3. *VFC:*   These are variable with fixed length control records. Each record has a variable data area with a fixed control field in the front. The control field can be used as a "hidden" field for storing information pertaining to the record.

4. *Stream:*   Records are variable length delimited by a terminator. The terminator is usually a carriage return, line-feed or a carriage return and a line-feed (specified as Stream_CR, Stream_LF or Stream).

While the maximum record size depends on file attributes, RMS supports a size of at least 16,000 bytes for any format. Relative and indexed files support variable-length records, but the maximum record size must be specified for relative files when the file is created. Since relative files have fixed record cells, space is not conserved by storing records of sizes less than the maximum. Figure 9.1 shows various record formats.

Usually, fixed record format incurs the least processing overhead. Variable record formats also do not have a high overhead but 2 bytes per record are used up to store the count of characters in the record. Figure 9.2 shows some file characteristics.

9.2   INITIAL ALLOCATION

RMS allocates disk blocks dynamically as new records are added to files. This incurs the overhead of scanning for free blocks on disks. This overhead can be eliminated if disk blocks are allocated to the file when it is created. Also, if disk blocks are allocated dynamically, there is a chance of the disk running out of free blocks. If the number of records to be stored is known when the file is created, then preallocating the required number of blocks ensures that the disk will not run out of space when creating records in the file. If more blocks are required when writing to the file at a later stage, RMS allocates them dynamically.

9.3   EXTEND SIZE

When a record is being added to a file and there are no more blocks in the file, RMS allocates just enough blocks from the disk's free block list to fit the new record. This allocation overhead can be reduced by

• 28-byte fixed-length records (fix: 28)

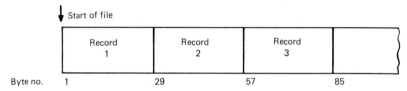

Byte no.   1   29   57   85

• Variable-length records (VAR)

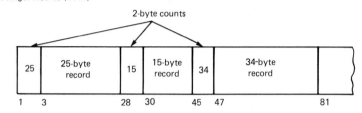

Byte no.   1   3   28   30   45   47   81

• Stream records (STM)

Byte no.   1   21   23   49   51   85   87

• Variable with fixed control field records (VFC). Fixed control field = 6 bytes.

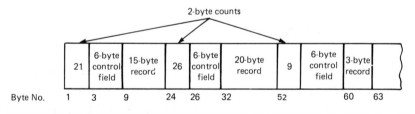

Byte No.   1   3   9   24   26   32   52   60   63

Figure 9.1   RMS record formats.

allocating more blocks at a time than required for storing the record. That way when additional records are created, RMS does not have to allocate new blocks for every record created. The number of new blocks allocated at a shot is called the *extend size*. The extend size can be specified when the file is created.

For example, if a file has fixed-size records each 1000 bytes and the extend size is 7, then when the first record is created RMS allocates 7 blocks (7 × 512 = 3584 bytes) to the file. No blocks are allocated when

File organization	Record format	Maximum record size	Random access support
Sequential	FIX	32,767	No
	VAR	32,767	No
	VFC	32,767-FSZ	No
	STM	32,767	No
Sequential(tape)	VAR	9,995	No
Relative	FIX	32,225	Yes
	VAR	32,253	Yes
	VFC	32,253-FSZ	Yes
Indexed	FIX	32,224	Yes
	VAR	32,224	Yes

NOTE: FIX = fixed-length records; VAR = variable-length records; STM = stream records (including STM_CR and STM_LF); VFC = variable length with fixed control field records; FSZ = fixed control field size of VFC records.

Figure 9.2 File characteristics

the next two records are created. A set of 7 blocks will be allocated when the fourth record is created.

Large extend sizes may cause the last extend of the file to be mostly empty. The default extend quantity is defined when the disk is initialized. This can be overridden during the disk mount. For example,

```
$MOUNT /EXTENSION=10 DUA0: VMSUSER
```

sets an extend size of 10 blocks for disk DUA0. To see the disk's extend size use the command:

```
$SHOW DEVICE DUA0: /FULL
```

9.4 DISK CLUSTER SIZE

The free/allocated information of every block on the disk is maintained in a table file called BITMAP.SYS. One entry would normally be required for each block. To reduce the size of this table, the minimum allocation quantity is a disk cluster (not to be confused with a VAXcluster), which is defined as one or more consecutive blocks. So if the cluster size parameter is 4, then the size of the cluster allocation table would be one-fourth the size of a similar table maintaining block allocation information. When a file requires more blocks, RMS determines how many blocks the file should have as determined by the extend size parameter. Just enough clusters are allocated to fit the blocks to be allocated. In addition to fragmentation due to overallocation of blocks in the last extend of the file, there is further disk fragmentation due to overallocation of blocks in the last cluster of the file. As a trade-off, RMS speed increases. The cluster size parameter can be displayed by

```
$SHOW DEVICE DUA0:/FULL
```

9.5   BUCKETS

A *bucket* is a sequence of blocks used by RMS for each transfer from disk to memory and memory to disk. If the bucket size of a file is defined as 5 during file creation and a block is required to be read by RMS, then RMS will read the complete bucket containing the block. Reading five blocks at a time is faster than reading five blocks one block at at a time. Large bucket sizes are useful for sequential access in relative or indexed files since then the probability is high that the next record to be accessed has already been read in memory. More physical memory is used as file buffers for larger buckets. Records cannot span across buckets. If records will be accessed in random mode rather than sequentially, large bucket sizes may in fact slow down RMS. Bucket sizes can be up to 32 blocks in RMS. A default bucket size of 0 will cause the bucket size to be just large enough to hold one record.

9.6   SPANNING

If a file contains records of size 500 bytes, the first record will fit in the first block allocated to the file while the second record will span over from the first block to the second. In fact, most records in the file will span blocks so that most reads and writes involve two blocks. To avoid this, the file can be defined to have no-spanning of records, which means records cannot continue across blocks and that maximum record size is limited to 512 bytes. (Actually 510 bytes for VARIABLE record length files, since 2 bytes are used for storing the size of each record. Also, some more bytes may be used up in index files for index information). When a record is being created in a no-spanning file and the record cannot fit in the remaining space in the last block of the file, that space will be wasted and the record will be stored in the beginning of the next block. No-spanning reduces file I/O at the expense of unutilized fragments in the file. See Figure 9.3.

9.7   FILE SHARING AND RECORD LOCKING

Many on-line applications require a number of programs to share the same set of disk files. The first program opening a file can allow

200-byte fixed-length records

- No block spanning file

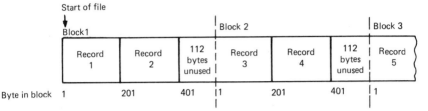

- Block spanning file

Block 1 | Block 2 , | Block 3

| Record 1 | Record 2 | Record 3 | Record 4 | Record 5 | Record 6 |

Byte in block   1   201   401 | 89   289   489 |

Figure 9.3   Record spanning.

No access

Read access or

Read and write access

to other programs attempting to open the file.

When two programs share a file, there is a possibility of both of them attempting to update a particular record simultaneously. RMS supports two methods for record locking to avoid contention:

Automatic record locking

Manual record locking

In the case of automatic record locking, RMS handles record locking on behalf of the program accessing the file. If the file is opened for read access, then other programs are allowed read access to any record. If the file is opened for write or update, other programs cannot access records being read by the first program. This is the default locking method.

If the first program opening a file declares manual record locking, then the programs explicitly lock and unlock records. Multiple records from the same file can be locked using this method. Any record can be locked so that other programs cannot access the record at all or can access it for reading only.

9.8 INDEXED FILES

Here are some terms used in the context of indexed files.

9.8.1 Duplicate keys

When an indexed file is created, the DUPLICATE KEY option can be specified for any key. Records with the same key value can be inserted in a file only if the DUPLICATE KEY option is specified for that key number. When accessing these records, only the first record can be retrieved by giving the key value. The other records have to be accessed sequentially.

9.8.2 Changeable keys

When the CHANGEABLE KEY option is specified for alternate keys, existing records can be updated with new values for these alternate keys and RMS will update the alternate indexes accordingly. An update which changes the primary key has to be implemented as a DELETE followed by an INSERT of the record.

9.8.3 Areas

By default, data and keys are intermingled in the data blocks of the index file. For better performance they can be placed in separate areas within the same file. An *area* is simply a internal logical partition of the file for better performance when searching for keys. In fact each key group (specified by key number) can be placed in separate areas. Separate areas can be specified when creating files using the EDIT/FDL utility.

9.8.4 Bucket size

A bucket is an integer multiple of 512-byte blocks. Each area in an area consists of a set of buckets. When records are inserted, keys are in key buckets. When a bucket is filled up and a new key has to be inserted in the bucket, the bucket is split and the depth of the tree structure increases by 1. This reduces CPU performance. Larger bucket sizes should be specified when the file is created. The trade-off is that when keys are searched in buckets, whole buckets are brought in memory and this in turn deteriorates performance if bucket sizes are large. Generally, bucket sizes should be increased if index depth levels exceed 1.

9.8.5 Fill factor

Usually, a number of records are inserted initially when index files are created. Records are then inserted randomly in the future. If key buckets are packed (with a fill factor of 100 percent) by the initial record load, there will be many bucket splits when records are inserted randomly later. This causes a deterioration in performance. If a lower fill factor (say 50 percent) is specified when the file is created, the initial record load will fill buckets only to the level specified. Later, when records are inserted randomly, the free space in the buckets is used to store key information, reducing the amount of bucket splits. The trade-off for a lower fill factor is that more disk space is required for the initial loading of the file.

Figure 9.4 show how to access RMS INDEXED files in COBOL.

9.9 RMS WITH C AND MACRO

In COBOL, BASIC, and FORTRAN and most other high-level languages, the languages have standard constructs for accessing RMS files. C has some constructs built in the language, but these do not support many of the RMS features. For example, C has no means of accessing indexed files; VAX/VMS system service routines have to be used for this purpose. MACRO-32 uses a set of macros defined in SYS$LIBRARY:STARLET.MLB. This file is scanned during assembly of programs.

9.9.1 RMS data structures

RMS associates four data structures with every file:

1. *FAB (file access block):*   Contains file information like file organization.

2. *RAB (record access block):*   Contains record level information such as record number for relative files.

3. *XAB (extended access block):*   Contains additional information such as key length and position for indexed files.

4. *NAM (name block):*   Optional block for storing complete file name specification when the FAB contains incomplete (wildcard) information. For example, the file specification in FAB may not contain version number (latest version assumed), but RMS will store it in the NAM block when the file is opened.

```
IDENTIFICATION DIVISION.
PROGRAM-ID. INDEXIO.
* The program opens and populates an indexed file with two keys.
* The compilation commands are:
*       $ COBOL INDEXIO
*       $ LINK INDEXIO

ENVIRONMENT DIVISION.
INPUT-OUTPUT SECTION.
FILE-CONTROL.
     SELECT CIF-FILE ASSIGN TO "CUSTOMER.DAT"
        ORGANIZATION IS INDEXED
        ACCESS MODE IS DYNAMIC
        RECORD KEY IS DDA-NUMBER
        ALTERNATE RECORD KEY IS SWIFT-ADDRESS WITH DUPLICATES.
DATA DIVISION.
FILE SECTION.
FD  CIF-FILE.
01  CUSTOMER-INFORMATION.
    02  DDA-NUMBER            PIC X(9).
    02  CUSTOMER-ADDRESS      PIC X(35).
    02  SWIFT-ADDRESS         PIC X(11).

PROCEDURE DIVISION.
START-PROGRAM.
    OPEN OUTPUT CIF-FILE.
    DISPLAY "Creating and populating the CIF indexed file".
    DISPLAY "Enter OVER for DDA-NUMBER to terminate".
    PERFORM UNTIL DDA-NUMBER = "OVER"
       DISPLAY "Enter DDA number: " WITH NO ADVANCING
       ACCEPT DDA-NUMBER WITH CONVERSION
       IF DDA-NUMBER NOT = "OVER" THEN
          DISPLAY "Enter SWIFT address: " WITH NO ADVANCING
          ACCEPT SWIFT-ADDRESS
          DISPLAY "Enter customer address: " WITH NO ADVANCING
          ACCEPT CUSTOMER-ADDRESS
          WRITE CUSTOMER-INFORMATION INVALID KEY
             PERFORM
             DISPLAY "Problem during write,  RMS STATUS = "
                 RMS-STS OF CIF-FILE WITH CONVERSION
             STOP RUN
             END-PERFORM
          END-IF
       END-PERFORM.
    STOP RUN.
```

Figure 9.4 COBOL program accessing a RMS INDEXED file.

Opening a file requires creation of these data structures, storing the file and record attributes in them, and issuing the RMS OPEN call. In C the four data structures are defined by RMS.H. The basic C RMS calls for file operations are sys$create, sys$open, sys$close and sys$erase. These calls take the address of FAB as the only parameter and return RMS STATUS. The basic record operation calls are sysget, sysput, sys$update and sys$delete. These calls take the address of RAB as the only parameter and return RMS STATUS.

Since the four data structures contain a lot of fields, RMS.H provides prototypes for initializing them with default values. For example, the prototype to initialize the FAB data structure is cc$rms_fab.

The file RMS.H is in the SYS$LIBRARY: directory. The fields of the four data blocks are described in the files NAM.H, FAB.H, RAB.H, and XAB.H within the directory SYS$LIBRARY:.

Figure 9.5 is an example in C to create an indexed file and write one record in it. The optional NAM block is not used.

```
/*      INDEXIO.C
 *      Program opens and populates a RMS indexed file.
 *      The compilation commands are:
 *              $ cc indexio
 *              $ link indexio,sys$input:/option
 *              sys$share:vaxcrtl.exe/share
 */
#include rms
#include stdio
#include ssdef
struct FAB fab;
struct RAB rab;
struct XABKEY primary_key,alternate_key;
int rms_status;

struct {                                /*Indexed file record layout*/
        char dda_number[9];
        char customer_address[35];
        char swift_address[11];
        } cif_record;

main()
{

char input_buffer[512];                     /*for terminal input*/

initialize("CUSTOMER.DAT");

                                            /*open file and
                                            set up fab,rab,xab*/
rms_status = sys$create(&fab);              /*create the file*/
if (rms_status != RMS$_NORMAL)
    {
    printf("file: CUSTOMER.DAT create error\n");
    exit(rms_status);
    };
rms_status = sys$connect(&rab);            /*associate fab and rab*/
if (rms_status != RMS$_NORMAL)
    {
    printf("file: CUSTOMER.DAT open error\n");
    exit(rms_status);
    };

/* get input from user and write records to file*/
printf("Creating and populating indexed file\n");
for (;;)                                    /*forever*/
    {
    printf("Enter dda number (OVER to terminate): ");
    gets(&input_buffer);
    if (strcmp("OVER",input_buffer) == 0) exit();
    strncpy(cif_record.dda_number,input_buffer,
            sizeof cif_record.dda_number);

    printf("Enter customer address: ");
```

Figure 9.5   Index file I/O from the C language.

```
        gets(&input_buffer);
        strncpy(cif_record.customer_address,input_buffer,
                sizeof cif_record.customer_address);

        printf("Enter SWIFT address: ");
        gets(&input_buffer);
        strncpy(cif_record.swift_address,input_buffer,
                sizeof cif_record.swift_address);


        rab.rab$b_rac = RAB$C_KEY;              /*these are required*/
        rab.rab$l_rbf = &cif_record;            /*for every write   */
        rab.rab$w_rsz = sizeof cif_record;

        rms_status = sys$put(&rab);             /*write record to file*/
        if (rms_status != RMS$_NORMAL &&
            rms_status != RMS$_OK_DUP)
            {
            printf("file: CUSTOMER.DAT write error\n");
            exit(rms_status);
            };
        }; /*for loop end*/
} /*end of main*/



initialize(file_name)
        char *file_name;
/* This routine is required to initialize the fab,rab and xab data
 * structures.
 */
{
        fab = cc$rms_fab;                       /*default initializations*/
        fab.fab$b_fac = FAB$M_DEL |             /*record operations to be*/
                        FAB$M_GET |             /*performed: delete,read*/
                        FAB$M_PUT |             /*write and update */
                        FAB$M_UPD;
        fab.fab$l_fna = file_name;
        fab.fab$b_org = FAB$C_IDX;

                                                /*file organization indexed*/
        fab.fab$b_fns = strlen(file_name);
        fab.fab$l_xab = &primary_key;           /*pointer to first xab*/

        rab = cc$rms_rab;                       /*initialize rab*/
        rab.rab$l_fab = &fab;                   /*rab points to fab*/
                                                /*of the indexed file*/

        primary_key = cc$rms_xabkey;            /*first xab is for*/
                                                /*primary key*/
        primary_key.xab$w_pos0 = 0;             /*key position in record*/
        primary_key.xab$b_ref = 0;              /*this is primary key*/
        primary_key.xab$b_siz0 = sizeof cif_record.dda_number;
                                                /*key size*/
        primary_key.xab$l_nxt = &alternate_key;


                                                /*pointer to second xab*/

        alternate_key = cc$rms_xabkey;
                                                /*initialize second xab
                                                  which is for the
                                                  secondary key*/
        alternate_key.xab$b_flg = XAB$M_DUP;
                                                /*allow duplicate keys*/
        alternate_key.xab$w_pos0 =
                (char *) &cif_record.swift_address
                -(char *) &cif_record;          /*position of this key*/
        alternate_key.xab$b_ref = 1;            /*this is key 1*/
        alternate_key.xab$b_siz0 =
                sizeof cif_record.swift_address; /*key size*/
}; /*end of initialize*/
```

Figure 9.5 (*Continued*)

9.10   RMS UTILITIES

The utilities FDL, CONVERT, and DUMP aid in the maintenance of RMS files. FDL is the *file definition language* facility. It is used to create specifications for RMS files and create the RMS files. CONVERT is used to copy records from one file to another of any organization. It can also be used to restructure files; say, change the position of keys. The records will change to reflect the organization of the output file. DUMP is used to display file contents in ASCII, decimal, hexadecimal, and octal representations.

9.10.1   FDL

While the OPEN statement in the VAX languages allows any existing file to be opened for update; not all RMS parameters can be specified when creating a file. The FDL facility can be used to create files with most RMS parameter specification and the file can then be opened for update by programs.

The FDL facility is also useful for modifying RMS parameters for existing files. For example, a file contains 82-byte records and a new field of 6 bytes is to be added at the end of each record. An FDL file containing the RMS parameters of the original data file is created using the ANALYZE/RMS/FDL command. The FDL file is edited to reflect the new record length of 88 bytes. This can be done using any text editor or the EDIT/FDL command. The new data file is created using the CREATE/FDL command. Records from the old file are copied to the new file using the CONVERT command. The new records can be padded with blanks to the right by using the /PAD qualifier with the CONVERT command.

The FDL facility can be accessed by three commands:

1. *EDIT/FDL:*   Used to create a definition file containing specifications for RMS data files.

2. *CREATE/FDL:*   Used to create an empty data file from a previously created specifications file.

3. *ANALYZE/RMS/FDL:*   Used to create a specifications file using the RMS parameters of an existing data file.

9.10.1.1   EDIT/FDL

The syntax for the command is

```
$ EDIT/FDL  fdl-file-spec
```

The command can be used to create a new FDL file or edit an existing one. Questions are asked depending on the response to previous questions. Here is an example for creating an indexed file with fixed-length records of size 180 bytes and one key starting at position 4 (fifth byte of the record) and length 9 bytes. Default values are specified for most answers. A question mark response to any question elicits help on that question. Figure 9.6 shows an example usage of the FDL utility.

```
$ edit/fdl customer.fdl

                   Parsing Definition File
SYS$SYSDEVICE:[TECH4]CUSTOMER.FDL; will be created.

(Add Delete Exit Help Invoke Modify Quit Set View)
Main Editor Function          (Keyword)[Help] : I

(Add_Key Delete_Key Indexed Optimize
 Relative Sequential Touchup)
Editing Script Title          (Keyword)[-]    : I

Target disk volume Cluster Size (1-1Giga)[3]   :
Number of Keys to Define        (1-255)[1]     :

(Line Fill Key Record Init Add)
Graph type to display         (Keyword)[Line] :

Number of Records that will be Initially Loaded
into the File                 (0-1Giga)[-]   : 100

(Fast_Convert NoFast_Convert RMS_Puts)
Initial File Load Method      (Keyword)[Fast] : ?

Fast_Convert:    using the VAX-11 Convert/Fast_Load option
NoFast_Convert: using the VAX-11 Convert/NoFast_Load option
RMS_Puts:        writing to a file from a High Level Language

(Fast_Convert NoFast_Convert RMS_Puts)
Initial File Load Method      (Keyword)[Fast] :

Number of Additional Records to be Added After
the Initial File Load         (0-1Giga)[0]   :
Key  0 Load Fill Percent      (50-100)[100]  : 50
(Fixed Variable)
Record Format                 (Keyword)[Var] : FIX
Record Size                   (1-32231)[-]   : 180

(Bin2  Bin4  Bin8  Int2  Int4  Int8 Decimal String
 Dbin2 Dbin4 Dbin8 Dint2 Dint4 Dint8 Ddecimal Dstring)
Key  0 Data Type              (Keyword)[Str] :

Key  0 Segmentation desired   (Yes/No)[No]   :
Key  0 Length                 (1-180)[-]     : 4
Key  0 Position               (0-176)[0]     : 9
Key  0 Duplicates allowed     (Yes/No)[No]   :
File Prolog Version           (0-3)[3]       :
Data Key Compression desired  (Yes/No)[Yes]  :
Data Record Compression desired (Yes/No)[Yes] :
Index Compression desired     (Yes/No)[Yes]  :

        *|
        9|
```

Figure 9.6 Creating an INDEXED file with the FDL utility.

```
          8|
Index     7|
          6|
Depth     5|
          4|
          3|
          2|  2
          1|    1 1 1 1 1 1 1 1 1 1 1 1 1 1 1 1 1 1 1 1 1 1 1 1 1 1 1 1 1 1 1
          +- + - - - + - - - - + - - - - + - - - - + - - - - + - - - - + - +
          1      5     10       15       20       25       30  32
                   Bucket Size (number of blocks)
```

Prolog Version   3 KT–Key 0 Type   String EM–Emphasis Flatter (3)
DK–Dup Key 0 Values   No KL–Key 0 Length   4 KP–Key 0 Position   9
RC–Data Record Comp   0% KC–Data Key Comp   0% IC–Index Record Comp   0%
BF–Bucket Fill   100% RF–Record Format Fixed RS–Record Size   180
LM–Load Method   Fast Conv IL–Initial Load   100 AR–Added Records   0
(Type "FD" to Finish Design)
Which File Parameter   (Mnemonic)[refresh]   : FD

Text for FDL Title Section   (1–126 chars)[null]:
Test for learning the FDL facility
Data File file–spec   (1–126 chars)[null]:
customer.dat
(Carriage Return FORTRAN None Print)
Carriage Control   (Keyword)[Carr] :

Emphasis Used In Defining Default: (Flatter files   )
Suggested Bucket Sizes: (3   3   12)
Number of Levels in Index: (1   1   1)
Number of Buckets in Index: (1   1   1)
Pages Required to Cache Index: (3   3   12)
Processing Used to Search Index: (126 126   510)

Key 0 Bucket Size   (1–63)[3]   :
Key 0 Name   (1–32 chars)[null]:
Account number
Global Buffers desired   (Yes/No)[No]   :
The Depth of Key 0 is Estimated to be No Greater
than 1 Index levels, which is 2 Total levels.

Press RETURN to continue (^Z for Main Menu)
(Add Delete Exit Help Invoke Modify Quit Set View)
Main Editor Function   (Keyword)[Help] : exit

SYS$SYSDEVICE:[TECH4]CUSTOMER.FDL;1   44 lines

Figure 9.6 *(Continued)*

Following are some comments about the program in Fig. 9.6.

- Each question shows the possible responses in parenthesis. Default values are specified in square brackets. A dash for the default value means the value has no defaults and must be specified.

- The index depth graph shows the depth of key indexes of the B-tree structure for the number of initial load records specified and various bucket sizes. If the graph shows a depth greater than 4 for the bucket size specified then the bucket size should be increased.

- Key load fill percents should be less than 100 if records will be added randomly in the future. If initially the file will be empty and all records will be added randomly in the future then this parameter is insignificant.

The definition file created, customer.fdl, is a text file. Minor changed can be made to it using a text editor like EVE. The recommended procedure for modifying the file is to use EDIT/FDL and selecting the MODIFY option from the main menu. The file is shown in Fig. 9.7.

```
$ TYPE customer.fdl

TITLE    "Test for learning the FDL facility"

IDENT    "16-FEB-1989 17:26:37    VAX-11 FDL Editor"

SYSTEM
         SOURCE                      VAX/VMS

FILE
         NAME                        "customer.dat"
         ORGANIZATION                indexed

RECORD
         CARRIAGE_CONTROL            carriage_return
         FORMAT                      fixed
         SIZE                        180

AREA 0
         ALLOCATION                  48
         BEST_TRY_CONTIGUOUS         yes
         BUCKET_SIZE                 3
         EXTENSION                   12

AREA 1
         ALLOCATION                  3
         BEST_TRY_CONTIGUOUS         yes
         BUCKET_SIZE                 3
         EXTENSION                   3

KEY 0
         CHANGES                     no
         DATA_AREA                   0
         DATA_FILL                   100
         DATA_KEY_COMPRESSION        yes
         DATA_RECORD_COMPRESSION     yes
         DUPLICATES                  no
         INDEX_AREA                  1
         INDEX_COMPRESSION           yes
         INDEX_FILL                  100
         LEVEL1_INDEX_AREA           1
         NAME                        "Account number"
         PROLOG                      3
         SEG0_LENGTH                 4
         SEG0_POSITION               9
         TYPE                        string
```

Figure 9.7   An FDL file.

9.10.1.2   CREATE/FDL

The file described in the above FDL file can be created by the command:

```
$ CREATE/FDL=customer.fdl
```

The file created is customer.dat as specified in the fdl file. The file name can be overridden by giving it on the command line as:

```
$ CREATE/FDL=customer.fdl  test.dat
```

The file specifications for the created file can be seen as

```
$ DIR/FULL customer.dat

Directory SYS$SYSDEVICE:[TECH4]

CUSTOMER.DAT;1                 File ID:  (5836,18,0)
Size:            52/52        Owner:    [1,1]
Created:  16-FEB-1989 17:28   Revised:  16-FEB-1989 17:28 (1)
Expires:  <None specified>    Backup:   <No backup recorded>
File organization:  Indexed, Prolog: 3, Using 1 key
                              In 2 areas
File attributes:    Allocation: 52, Extend: 12, Maximum bucket size: 3
                    Global buffer count: 0, No version limit
                    Contiguous best try
Record format:      Fixed length 180 byte records
Record attributes:  Carriage return carriage control
Journaling enabled: None
File protection:    System:RWED, Owner:RWED, Group:RE, World:
Access Cntrl List:  None

Total of 1 file, 52/52 blocks.
```

9.10.1.3   ANALYZE/RMS/FDL

This command is used to extract the FDL specification of an existing file. The FDL file can then be modified to create a new data file which has the same RMS parameters as the original file except for the modifications performed on it. The command syntax is

```
$ ANALYZE/RMS/FDL  file-spec
```

File-spec is the data file. The FDL file created has the same file-spec except for the file name extension which is .fdl. For example,

```
$ ANALYZE/RMS/FDL  account.dat
```

creates the file account.fdl.

9.10.2   DUMP

This command has the following qualifiers:

/ascii |
/decimal |Specifies display data representation.
/hex |By default hex and ascii values are displayed.
/octal |

/byte |
/longword |Specifies grouping for the displayed data.
/word |

/record   Specifies logical record display.

/block   Specifies display of blocks of the file. Optionally the starting
              record or block number and the ending or count of the number
              of records or blocks can be specified. For example:
              DUMP/RECORD=(START:3,END:5)   customer.dat
              DUMP/RECORD=(START:3,COUNT:3)   customer.dat

Figure 9.8 shows an example usage of the command.

9.10.3 CONVERT

The command is used to convert (or restructure) a file of one organization to another. The syntax of the command is :

```
$ CONVERT/qualifiers  input-file-spec  output-file-spec
```

Some of the qualifiers are:

/exceptions_file   Creates a file of records which are could not be copied to
                    the output file because of format errors. It is recom-
                    mended that this qualifier be always used.

```
$ DUMP/RECORD=(START:2,COUNT=3) customer.fdl

Dump of file SYS$SYSDEVICE:[TESTING.DATA]CUSTOMER.FDL;2
on 17-FEB-1989 17:47:10.26
File ID (6510,3,0)   End of file block 2 / Allocated 2

Record number 2 (00000002), 48 (0030) bytes

 39312D42 45462D36 31220954 4E454449 IDENT."16-FEB-19 000000
 41562020 2037333A 36323A37 31203938 89 17:26:37   VA 000010
 22726F74 69644520 4C444620 31312D58 X-11 FDL Editor" 000020

Record number 3 (00000003), 6 (0006) bytes

                    4D45 54535953 SYSTEM.......... 000000

Record number 4 (00000004), 17 (0011) bytes

 4D562F58 41560909 09454352 554F5309 .SOURCE...VAX/VM 000000
                             53 S.............. 000010
```

Figure 9.8 DUMP command output.

/fdl = file-spec	Creates the output file using the FDL specifications from the file specified.
/merge	Specifies that records are to be inserted in an existing index file.
/pad = x /pad = %by	If the output file has fixed length record format and the input record has a smaller record size the records are padded with character specified. x is any ascii character. y is a number in the base given by b. b can be "d" for decimal, "h" for hex or "o" for octal. For example /pad = %h45 specifies the pad character to be hex 45 (or ascii "E").
/statistics	Outputs summary information like number of records converted after the conversion is complete.
/truncate	If the output file has fixed length record format and the input records have a larger record size then the records are truncated to the output record size before writing.

For example, the file INPUT.DAT is sequential and contains four records which are to be loaded in the indexed file CUSTOMER.DAT created by the CREATE/FDL command above. Here is the sequence of commands:

```
$ DIR/FULL input.dat

Directory SYS$SYSDEVICE:[TESTING.DATA]

INPUT.DAT;1                 File ID:  (6497,5,0)
Size:            1/2        Owner:    [1,1]
Created:  21-FEB-1989 11:56  Revised:  21-FEB-1989 11:56 (1)
Expires:  <None specified>   Backup:   <No backup recorded>
File organization:  Sequential
File attributes:    Allocation: 2, Extend: 0, Global buffer count: 0, No version
 limit
Record format:      Variable length, maximum 25 bytes
Record attributes:  Carriage return carriage control
Journaling enabled: None
File protection:    System:RWED, Owner:RWED, Group:RE, World:
Access Cntrl List:  None

Total of 1 file, 1/2 blocks.

$ TYPE input.dat

SMITH A. 2547 TEST DATA 1
BEY J.   7123 TEST DATA 2
BELL A.  8213 TEST DATA 3
HOLMES K.3987 TEST DATA 4

$ CONVERT/MERGE/PAD=0 input.dat  customer.dat

$ TYPE customer.dat

SMITH A. 2547 TEST DATA 1000000000...
HOLMES K.3987 TEST DATA 4000000000...
BEY J.   7123 TEST DATA 2000000000...
BELL A.  8213 TEST DATA 3000000000...
```

Customer.dat is sorted by the key at position 9. The padding character is zero so each record has zeros appended to make the record size 180 bytes. More records can be added to customer.dat by using the same CONVERT command line.

9.11 FURTHER READING

Guide to VMS File Applications, Vol. 6A, VMS Programming Manuals.
Record Management Services, Vol. 6B, VMS Programming Manuals.

10

Advanced Programming Features

Most applications can be designed using basic programming features which are specific to the programming language being used. General programming techniques and a good understanding of file and record locking is all that is required. The topics discussed here are useful when developing complex applications which use features specific to VAX/VMS.

The chapter discusses:

- Interprocess synchronization and communications, including mailboxes, shared logical names, global sections, event flags, locks for shared resources
- Object libraries
- Shared images
- Asynchronous system traps (ASTs)
- Exit handlers
- Task-to-task communications across the DECnet network

10.1 INTERPROCESS COMMUNICATIONS AND SYNCHRONIZATION

Consider this application. A small bank has a VAX with 30 terminals, two disk drives of capacity 1 Gbytes each and 16 Mbytes of main memory. Twenty terminals are used by tellers for account inquiry and update, five terminals are used for running background and batch jobs, and five terminals are used for program development and testing. The tellers use forms displayed on the screen for data entry and access the same database files. Does this application require any special program design?

The answer is no. Each teller can run one program which handles

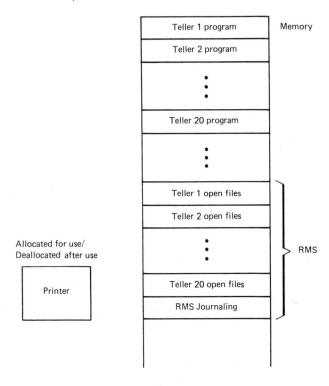

Figure 10.1   A poorly designed application.

database updates by locking critical. records during updates. The screens can be part of the programs or standard forms management systems like DECforms, FMS, or TDMS. Each teller runs the same program, so the system will have 20 processes running the same program. Data can be communicated between processes by creating a common file whose records can be read and updated by all the processes. RMS file journaling can be used to recover the database in case of a power failure (this does not require any special consideration by the programs). See Fig. 10.1.

The application design suffers from some drawbacks:

- Each process (program) accommodates code for the entire application. This can lead to insufficient memory if, say, the number of tellers increase to 130.

- The programs cannot be easily written in a modular fashion with each programmer developing and testing a part of the application.

- Communicating data between the processes requires the data to be written out to disk. Data should be communicated in memory unless it has to be written out to disk.

- The database may consist of, say, 20 files. All these files will be opened by each process causing RMS to run inefficiently.

- A printer or some other resource may be shared by the processes. The resource will have to be allocated and deallocated every time a process needs to use it.

Figure 10.2 shows a more efficient version of the application.

10.2 PROGRAM COMMUNICATIONS

There are three main methods for program communications:

- *Mailboxes:* These are used to send streams of data from one process to another. Normally, one or more processes would send data to a mailbox and one process would process the data.

- *Logical names:* These are used to send small amounts of data like status and counts from one process to another. They can be thought of as common "registers."

- *Global sections:* These are common areas of memory for use by all or some processes.

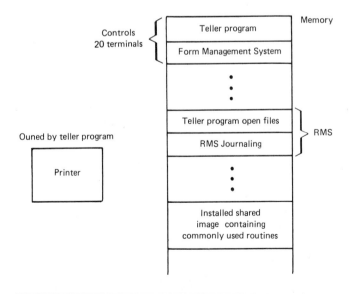

Figure 10.2   A more optimized application.

The words "processes" and "programs" are used interchangeably since a program, when run, is a process. Most of the examples used in this section show communications between two processes, but the techniques can be extended for communications between more processes. Also, processes are assumed to be running from terminals so that output can be displayed, but the techniques apply to processes which do not have attached terminals (like detached or batch processes).

10.2.1 Mailboxes

A typical use of a mailbox is for sending a stream of data from one process to another without using disks. Mailboxes are software devices. The device driver is SYS$SYSTEM:MBDRIVER.EXE and the generic device name is MB:. A sample mailbox device is "MBA12:". One process would normally create a mailbox and other processes would assign channels from their process to the mailbox. Processes can then use QIO functions (system services) to read from or write to the mailbox. Here are two programs, MB_WRITE.C and MB_READ.C, where one program creates the mailbox, and writes data to it, while the other program opens a channel to the mailbox and reads data and displays it on the terminal.

```
/* MB_READ.C
 * This program demonstrates usage of mailboxes for sending streams of
 * data from one process to another.
 *
 * The program opens an existing mailbox, reads it and prints the
 * data read onto the terminal. The mailbox is created by the program
 * MB_WRITE.C which also writes to this mailbox. The mailbox is defined by
 * the logical name MAILBOX_TEST.
 */

#include stdio
#include descrip
#include iodef
#include ssdef
main()
{
int status;
short mbx_chan;               /* i/o channel to mailbox */
$DESCRIPTOR(mbx_logical_name,"MAILBOX_TEST");

/* variables for QIO input from mailbox */
struct {short cond_value; short count; int info;} io_status_block;
char message[256];
int message_len = 255;

/* system service call to assign a channel to the mailbox */
status = sys$assign(    &mbx_logical_name,
                        &mbx_chan,
                        0,              /* access mode. Full access */
                        0               /* associated mailbox name. Not used */
            );
```

```c
    if (status != SS$_NORMAL) lib$stop(status);        /* error? */

    /* read a message from the mailbox */
    status = sys$qiow (      0,                         /* event_flag */
                             mbx_chan,
                             IO$_READVBLK,
                             &io_status_block,
                             0,                         /* ast_address */
                             0,                         /* ast_parameter */
                             message,                   /* parameter P1 */
                             message_len,               /* length, parameter P2 */
                             0,0,0,0                    /* P3, P4, P5, P6 */
                      );
    if (status != SS$_NORMAL) lib$stop(status);        /* error? */

    printf ("%s",message);
}
```

```c
/* MB_WRITE.C
 * The program creates a mailbox, writes a message to it and waits
 * for the message to be read.
 */
#include stdio
#include descrip
#include iodef
#include ssdef

main()
{
int status;
/* variables used for creating mailbox */
char permanent_mbx = 1;             /* temporary mailbox */
short mbx_chan;                     /* i/o channel to mailbox, returned by the
                                       $CREMBX call */

int   max_message_size = 0;         /* use VMS default */
int   max_buf_size = 0;             /* system dynamic memory for buffering
                                       messages to mailbox. Use default */
int   protection_mask = 0;          /* access for all users */
int   access_mode = 0;              /* most privileged access mode */
$DESCRIPTOR(mbx_logical_name,"MAILBOX_TEST");
char tmp[100];

/* variables for QIO output to mailbox */
struct {short cond_value; short count; int info;} io_status_block;
char *message = "Test message to mailbox";
int tmp1;
/* system service call to create mailbox and assign it a logical name */
status= sys$crembx(      permanent_mbx,
                         &mbx_chan,
                         max_message_size,
                         max_buf_size,
                         protection_mask,
                         access_mode,
                         &mbx_logical_name
                  );
if (status != SS$_NORMAL) lib$stop(status);        /* error creating mailbox? */

/* send a message to the mailbox, wait until it is read */
tmp1 = strlen(message);
status = sys$qiow (      0,                         /* event_flag */
                         mbx_chan,
                         IO$_WRITEVBLK | IO$M_NOW,
                         &io_status_block,
                         0,                         /* ast_address */
                         0,                         /* ast_parameter */
                         message,                   /* parameter P1 */
                         (int) strlen(message),     /* length, parameter P2 */
                         0,0,0,0                    /* P3, P4, P5, P6 */
                  );
if (status != SS$_NORMAL) lib$stop(status);        /* error? */
gets(tmp);
}
```

Following are some notes on mailboxes:

- Mailboxes are temporary or permanent. A temporary mailbox is deleted by VMS if no processes are accessing it. A permanent mailbox will remain in the system until a reboot or if the mailbox is explicitly deleted by the $DELMBX system service.
- Mailboxes can be written to and read from by multiple processes.
- Mailboxes are VMS devices, so device operations like setting access protections can be performed on them. To see mailboxes in the system, use:

```
$ SHOW DEVICE  MB
```

or

```
$ SHOW DEVICE/FULL  MB
```

10.2.2 Logical names

Logical names have already been described. Logical names created at the group or system level can be shared by other users. Group logical names can be read by members of the same group while system logical names can be accessed by all processes. Here is a program, LOGNAM, which modifies or displays a group logical name called WRITE_COUNT. The program can be run by two users in the same UIC group from different terminals. Any modification made to the logical name by one user can be displayed by the other user. The users will require the GRPNAM privilege to modify group logical names.

```
Identification Division.
   Program-id.   Logical-names.
   Author.       Jay Shah.
   Installation. VAX/VMS V5.2.

* This program demonstrates how small amounts of data can be transferred from
* one process to another; effectively performing task to task communications.
* The program creates a group level logical name, WRITE_COUNT, if it does not
* exist. This requires the privilege GRPNAM. The program then loops infinitely
* to allow the user to display the equivalent name or enter a new equivalent
* name for the logical name. The program can be run by different users in the
* group. Modifications made to the logical name by one user will be "seen" by
* the other users. To run the program use:
* $cobol lognam
* $link lognam
* $run lognam

Environment Division.
Configuration Section.
Special-names.
         symbolic user-mode is 4.

Data Division.
Working-storage Section.
```

```
      01  lognam-attributes         pic 9(9)  comp value 0.
      01  lognam-table              pic x(9)  value is "LNM$GROUP".
      01  lognam                    pic x(11) value is "WRITE_COUNT".
     * access mode is user (not super, exec or kernel).
      01  access-mode               pic x     value user-mode.
      01  itemlist.
          03  eqv-len               pic 9(4)  comp value 10.
     *       lnm$ string has a value of 2. This is used for equivalent name.
          03  item-code             pic 9(4)  comp value 2.
          03  eqv-addr              usage is  pointer value is reference eqv-nam.
          03  ret-len-addr          usage is  pointer value is reference ret-len.
          03  terminator            pic 9(9)  comp value 0.
      01  eqv-nam                   pic x(10).
      01  ret-len                   pic 9(4)  comp.
      01  call-status               pic s9(9) comp.
     * A value SS$_NOLOGNAM is returned when attempting to use a logical name
     * which is not defined.
     * SS$_NOLOGNAM is declared in the system object library file, STARLET.OLB.
     * It's value is 444 in VMS version 5.2. Since it's value can change when the
     * operating system is upgraded, the value is 'picked' up by the linker from
     * the object library, STARLET.OLB, when the "value external" clause is used
     * as shown here.
      01  no-lognam                 pic s9(9) comp value external SS$_NOLOGNAM.
      01  response                  pic x.

     Procedure Division.
     10-start.
     * Check if the logical name is created; if not then create it.
           call "sys$trnlnm" using

                                 by reference  lognam-attributes,
                                 by descriptor lognam-table,
                                 by descriptor lognam,
                                 by reference  access-mode,
                                 by reference  itemlist,
                                 giving        call-status.
           if call-status = no-lognam
                   move "            " to eqv-nam
                   call "sys$crelnm" using
                                 by reference  lognam-attributes,
                                 by descriptor lognam-table,
                                 by descriptor lognam,
                                 by reference  access-mode,
                                 by reference  itemlist,
                                 giving        call-status
           end-if.
           if call-status is failure then call "sys$exit" using
                                 by value call-status.
     20-menu.
     * loop to display the logical name or change the value of the logical name.
           display " ".
           display "Group logical name WRITE_COUNT has a value of: ", eqv-nam.
           display " ".
           display "Enter 1 to modify the value, 2 to see current value: "
                                 with no advancing.
           accept response.
           if response = "1" then
                   display "Enter new value for WRITE_COUNT: " with no advancing
                   accept eqv-nam
                   call "sys$crelnm" using
                                 by reference  lognam-attributes,
                                 by descriptor lognam-table,
                                 by descriptor lognam,
                                 by reference  access-mode,
                                 by reference  itemlist,
                                 giving        call-status
                       if call-status is failure then call "sys$exit" using
                                 by value call-status end-if
           end-if.
```

```
call "sys$trnlnm" using
                by reference  lognam-attributes,
                by descriptor lognam-table,
                by descriptor lognam,
                by reference  access-mode,
                by reference  itemlist,
                giving        call-status.
if call-status is failure then call "sys$exit" using
                by value call-status.
go to 20-menu.
```

Logical names can be manipulated using system calls or DCL commands, as shown in the following table:

Operation	How to perform the operation	
	From a program	From DCL
Create a name	System call $CRELNM	DEFINE command
Translate a name	System call $TRNLNM	F$TRNLNM lexical function
Delete a name	System call $DELLNM	DEASSIGN command

The logical name value can also be displayed by users in the same group at other terminals by using:

```
$ SHOW  LOGICAL/GROUP  *
```

or

```
$ SHOW  LOGICAL/GROUP  WRITE_COUNT
```

The logical name can be created in the SYSTEM table in which case all processes on the system will be able to read it. The privilege SYSNAM or SETPRV is required for this. If all the processes sharing the logical name are from the same job (created by using the SPAWN or a similar command) then the logical name can be placed in the job table. In this case no special privileges are required to share the logical name.

Data exchange is limited by the size of logical names, which is 255 characters. Multiple logical names can be used, but global sections may be more appropriate for large amounts of data. Multiple DCL command procedures can also communicate using common logical names.

10.2.3 Global sections

The global section is one of the most efficient methods for sharing large amounts of data between processes. A logically contiguous piece of memory can be allocated to a global section for shared use by one or more processes. Some form of synchronization between the processes will be required to avoid multiple processes writing to the same shared area simultaneously. See the next section on interprocess synchronization.

Here are two programs—GBLWR and GBLRD. GBLWR creates a global section of 2048 bytes. The program then reads input from the terminal, and writes it to the global section, repeating the terminal input until the 2048-byte limit of the global section has been reached. The program GBLRD reads the global section from bytes 20 to 40 every 5 seconds and writes the output to its terminal. The programs should be run from two different terminals.

```
/* gblwr.c
 * This program creates a global section, GBL_SECTION_TEST, of 2048 bytes,
 * reads a string entered at the terminal and writes the string to the global
 * section. The string is repeated to fill-up the 2048 bytes of the global
 * section.
 */
#include stdio
#include descrip
#include secdef
#include ssdef

main()
{

char global_memory[2048];
$DESCRIPTOR( gbl_secnam, "GBL_SECTION_TEST" );
struct memrange { char *startaddress; char *endaddress; };
struct memrange inaddress = { global_memory, global_memory + 2047 };
struct memrange retaddress;
char ident[8] = { '\000','\000','\000','\000','\000','\000','\000','\000' };
char *tmpaddress, resp_len;

char response[80];
int status;

/* create the global section */
status = sys$crmpsc(    &inaddress,      /* range of memory to be mapped */
                        &retaddress,     /* actual memory mapped */
                        0,               /* access mode.Full access by others */
                        SEC$M_GBL        /* Global, not private, section */
                      | SEC$M_WRT        /* Read/Write allowed */
                      | SEC$M_EXPREG     /* Map into available space */
                      | SEC$M_PAGFIL,    /* Page file not a disk file section */
                        &gbl_secnam,
                        &ident,          /* version number 0 */
                        0,               /* first page of section to be mapped */
                        (short) 0,       /* channel for file sections */
                        4,               /* number of pages. all */
                        0,               /* first virtual block number of file*/
                        0,               /* protection. none */
                        0                /* page fault cluster size */
                    );
if (status == 1561) printf ("section created\n");
else if (status != SS$_NORMAL) lib$stop(status); /* error? */
```

```
while (TRUE)
        {
        puts("Input a string to be inserted in global section:");
        gets(response);

        /* insert in global memory, repeat input string until global
           memory is filled up */
        tmpaddress = retaddress.startaddress;  /* start of global memory */
        resp_len = strlen(response);

        while (tmpaddress < (retaddress.endaddress - resp_len))
                {
                strcpy( tmpaddress, response);
                tmpaddress = tmpaddress + resp_len;
                };
        };
```

```
/* gblrd.c
 * This program reads a part of the global section created above and writes the
 * contents on the terminal. The two programs should run from two separate
 * terminals.
 */
#include stdio
#include descrip
#include secdef
#include signal
#include ssdef
main()
{
char global_memory[2048];
$DESCRIPTOR ( gbl_secnam, "GBL_SECTION_TEST" );
struct memrange { char *startaddress; char *endaddress; };
struct memrange inaddress  = { global_memory, global_memory + 2047 };
struct memrange retaddress;
char ident[8] = { '\000','\000','\000','\000','\000','\000','\000','\000' };
char *tmpaddress, resp_len;

char response[80];
int status;

/* map the process to the global section created by the execution of the
program, GBLWR.C */
status = sys$mgblsc(     &inaddress,     /* range of memory to be mapped */
                        &retaddress,    /* actual memory mapped */
                        0,              /* access mode.Full access by others */
                        SEC$M_GBL       /* Global, not private, section */
                        | SEC$M_WRT     /* Read/Write allowed */
                        | SEC$M_EXPREG  /* Map into available space */
                        | SEC$M_PAGFIL, /* Page file not a disk file section */
                        &gbl_secnam,
                        &ident,         /* version number 0 */
                        0               /* first page of section to be mapped */
                );
if (status != SS$_NORMAL) lib$stop(status);      /* error? */

printf ("Global section size 2048 bytes.\n");
while (TRUE)
        {
        printf ("bytes 20 to 40 are: %.20s\n",retaddress.startaddress+19);
        printf ("waiting for 5 seconds...\n");
        sleep (5);
        };
}
```

The global section can be seen by:

```
$ INSTALL/LIST/GLOBAL      !List all global sections on system
```

Global sections are allocated pages of memory. Since a page is 512 bytes, the section sizes will be multiples of 512 bytes. Disk file sections allow files to be mapped into memory. This way, a large file's contents can actually be manipulated as if it were memory locations in the program. Also, the section can be written out to disk automatically for use later.

Global sections can be created at the group or system level. *Group global sections* are accessible to processes within the group while *system global sections* are accessible to all processes on the system. The SYSGBL privilege is required to be able to create system global sections.

Global sections can be permanent or temporary. *Temporary global sections* are deleted by the system when no process is mapping to them. *Permanent global sections* can be deleted by the SYS$DGBLSC system call. The PRMGBL privilege is required to create permanent global sections. Note that if multiple processes are mapping to the same global section and one of them deletes the section, the section is actually marked for delete. In this case, the section is deleted only after all the processes release the mapping.

10.3 SYNCHRONIZATION

Synchronization between processes is required when they share common resources and there is a possibility of other processes accessing the resource when one process needs it for exclusive use. Many resources like disks and printer queues do not create contention among processes because the operating system handles synchronization issues for these resources. But resources defined or created by cooperating processes may need to be shared amicably. An example of such a resource could be a common area in memory which is used by one or more processes.

There are two main program synchronization techniques:

1. *Event flags:* These are bit flags managed by the operating system. Processes can decide to wait until an event flag is set (or reset) by another process before continuing execution. When a process waits on an event flag, the operating system puts it in a wait state until the flag is modified.

2. *Locks:* Locks are a few bytes of memory locations. These can be created by cooperating processes and then processes can queue up to use the lock. Once a process has a lock, other processes waiting for the lock will be put in a wait state by the operating system until

the lock is released by the process which has acquired it. ASTs can be used to wait on a lock and continue program execution. ASTs are described later in this chapter.

10.3.1 Event flags

Event flags are bit data structures within the operating system which can be set by one process and tested by the same or another process. They can be used to signal the completion of an event by one process so that another process waiting for the event to be completed can continue execution.

Consider an example. Process 1 handles input from a terminal and stores it in a global section for processing by a "terminal command interpreter" process (Process 2). Every time process 1 receives a terminal input and stores it in the global section, it must inform process 2 that there is a string in the global section for processing. Of course, process 2 could continuously loop to check if a new string has arrived in the global section but this would be a waste of CPU time. Instead, process 2 sets a flag and waits for process 1 to zero it when there is a terminal string ready for processing. Here are programs EVFLAG_WRITER and EVFLAG_READER which use event flags for synchronization.

```
/* EVFLAG_WRITER.C
 * This program demonstrates use of event flags for synchronization between
 * two tasks. The program maps to a global section created by another program,
 * EVFLAG_READER.C and then reads input from the terminal. It waits for a
 * common event flag to be set by the other program, puts the terminal input
 * in the global section and resets the event flag so that the other program
 * can read the global section. The program then reads more terminal input and
 * the operation is repeated.
 *
 * See the Run-time library manual for a description on how to acquire an event
 * flag using the library function LIB$GET_EF.
 */
#include stdio
#include descrip
#include secdef
#include signal
#include ssdef

#define ev_flag1 65
#define ev_flag2 66

main()
{

char global_memory[2048];
$DESCRIPTOR ( gbl_secnam, "GBL_SECTION_TEST" );
struct memrange { char *startaddress; char *endaddress; };
struct memrange inaddress = { global_memory, global_memory + 2047 };
struct memrange retaddress;
char ident[8] = { '\000','\000','\000','\000','\000','\000','\000','\000' };
```

```
char response[80],resp_len;
int status;

$DESCRIPTOR( evflag_cluster_name, "EVFLAG_CLUSTER");

status = sys$mgblsc(    &inaddress,      /* range of memory to be mapped */
                        &retaddress,     /* actual memory mapped */
                        0,               /* access mode.Full access by others */
                        SEC$M_GBL        /* Global, not private, section */
                      | SEC$M_WRT        /* Read/Write allowed */
                      | SEC$M_EXPREG     /* Map into available space */
                      | SEC$M_PAGFIL,    /* Page file not a disk file section */
                        &gbl_secnam,
                        &ident,          /* version number 0 */
                        0                /* first page of section to be mapped */
                    );
if (status != SS$_NORMAL) lib$stop(status);      /* error? */


/* Associate this process with common event flag cluster EVFLAG_CLUSTER */

status = sys$ascefc(    ev_flag1,
                        &evflag_cluster_name,



                        (char) 0,        /* protection: group access  */
                        (char) 0         /* temporary, not permanent cluster */
                    );
if (status != SS$_NORMAL) lib$stop(status);      /* error? */

while (TRUE)
        {
        /* wait for event flag 2 to be set */
        status = sys$waitfr (ev_flag2);
        if (status != SS$_NORMAL) lib$stop(status);       /* error? */
        /* zero event flag 2 */
        status = sys$clref (ev_flag2);
        if ((status && 1) != 1) lib$stop(status);        /* error? */

        /* read terminal input */
        printf("Input a string to be inserted in global section:");
        gets(response);

        /* put terminal input in global section GBL_SECTION_TEST */
        resp_len = strlen(response);
        strcpy( retaddress.startaddress, response);

        /* set event flag 1 */
        status = sys$setef (ev_flag1);
        if ((status && 1) != 1) lib$stop(status);        /* error? */

        };
```

```
/* This is EVFLAG_READER.C
 * This program demonstrates use of event flags for synchronization between
 * two tasks. The program creates a global section and sets a common event
 * flag. Another program, EVFLAG_WRITER.C, puts data in the global section and
 * resets the event flag. This program then processes the global section (in
 * this case it simply prints it's contents out at the terminal) and then sets
 * the event flag to repeat the operation.
 */
#include stdio
#include descrip
#include secdef
#include signal
#include ssdef

#define ev_flag1 65
#define ev_flag2 66

main( )
{

char global_memory[2048];
$DESCRIPTOR( gbl_secnam, "GBL_SECTION_TEST" );
struct memrange { char *startaddress; char *endaddress; };
struct memrange inaddress  = { global_memory, global_memory + 2047 };
struct memrange retaddress;
char ident[8] = { '\000','\000','\000','\000','\000','\000','\000','\000' };

char response[80],resp_len;
int status;

$DESCRIPTOR( evflag_cluster_name, "EVFLAG_CLUSTER");

/* create the global section */
status = sys$crmpsc(    &inaddress,     /* range of memory to be mapped */
                        &retaddress,    /* actual memory mapped */
                        0,              /* access mode.Full access by others */
                        SEC$M_GBL       /* Global, not private, section */
                        | SEC$M_WRT     /* Read/Write allowed */
                        | SEC$M_EXPREG  /* Map into available space */
                        | SEC$M_PAGFIL, /* Page file not a disk file section */
                        &gbl_secnam,
                        &ident,         /* version number 0 */
                        0,              /* first page of section to be mapped */
                        (short) 0,      /* channel for file sections */
                        4,              /* number of pages. all */
                        0,              /* first virtual block number of file*/
                        0,              /* protection. none */
                        0               /* page fault cluster size */
                    );
if (status == 1561) printf ("section created\n");
else if (status != 1) lib$stop(status); /* error? */

/* create a common event flag cluster called EVFLAG_CLUSTER */


status = sys$ascefc(    ev_flag1,
                        &evflag_cluster_name,
                        (char) 0,       /* protection: group access */
                        (char) 0        /* temporary, not permanent cluster */
                    );
if (status != SS$_NORMAL) lib$stop(status);       /* error? */

while (TRUE)
    {
        /* let other process know that it can write to the global section */
        status = sys$clref (ev_flag1);
        if ((status && 1) != 1) lib$stop(status);        /* error? */
        status = sys$setef (ev_flag2);
        if ((status && 1) != 1) lib$stop(status);        /* error? */
```

```
/* wait for the event flag 1 to be set by EVFLAG_WRITER.C
   When the flag is set, EVFLAG_WRITER.C has placed data in
   the global section for this process to read */

status = sys$waitfr(ev_flag1);
if (status != SS$_NORMAL) lib$stop(status);       /* error? */

/* read and display contents of global section */
printf("New data in global section: %s \n ",retaddress.startaddress);

}

}
```

Each process has four sets of 32 event flags. Each set is called a *cluster*. Clusters 0 and 1 (event flags 0 thru 63) are local to the process while clusters 2 and 3 (event flags 64 to 127) are common to processes in the same UIC group. Clusters 2 and 3 have to be given a name by the process that creates them. Cluster 0 and 1 event flags are automatically available to processes while common event flags are available only by "associating" the process with the cluster name (by the $ASCEFC system service).

10.3.2 Locks

Locks can be used in place of event flags. Locks are more general than event flags; they can be used to synchronize usage of resources by multiple processes. In fact, locks are "known" across a cluster so they can be used to synchronize processes across a cluster. Event flags can be used when there are two processes with one process waiting for another to complete a task. Locks can be used when the input is from multiple processes (say a number of processes are writing terminal input to the global section) or multiple output processes (say a number of processes are reading the global section and parsing the terminal input string). Here is a program that reads and writes to a global section. The program can be run from multiple terminals, all the processes will then read and write to the same global section. The lock, GBLSEC_LOCK, will be used for synchronization. The process acquiring the lock can access the global section.

The lock facility is provided by the system but locks are not controlled by the system. A cooperating set of processes define and use locks in an appropriate way. A process can acquire a lock and use the corresponding resource but this does not stop another process from using the resource. The second process should wait for the lock to be released, acquire the lock and then use the resource.

Locks are clusterwide on a cluster.

```
/* LOCK.C
 * This program illustrates use of the lock management facility on VAX/VMS.
 * The program creates a global section and a lock, GBLSEC_LOCK. The program
 * then acquires the lock which allows it to gain exclusive access to the
 * global section. The program prints the contents of the global section,
 * writes new data in the global section and then releases the lock. The
 * The program then waits a random amount of time before reading and
 * writing the global section again.
 *
 * The program can be run from multiple terminals to see varying output at
 * each terminal depending on the order in which processes acquire the lock.
 */
#include stdio
#include descrip
#include secdef
#include lckdef
#include ssdef

/* variables for global section */
char global_memory[2048];
$DESCRIPTOR ( gbl_secnam, "GBL_SECTION_TEST" );
struct memrange { char *startaddress; char *endaddress; };
struct memrange inaddress  = { global_memory, global_memory + 2047 };
struct memrange retaddress;
char ident[8] = { '\000','\000','\000','\000','\000','\000','\000','\000' };

int status;

main()
{
struct {
        short vms_cond;
        short reserve;
        int   lock_id;
        char  lock_val[16];
        } lock_status_block;
$DESCRIPTOR (resource_name,"GBLSEC_LOCK");
char response[80],resp_len;
char this_process_id[80];

create_or_mapto_globalsection();

/* create a string to be put in the global section */
sprintf ( this_process_id,"process id = %d", getpid() );


/* loop forever: acquire lock, read global section, write global section,
                 release lock */
while (TRUE)
        {
        sleep ( rand() & 3);    /* random wait between 0 and 3 seconds */
        status = sys$enqw       /* acquire exclusive access to GBLSEC_LOCK */
                (
                         35,            /* event flag */



        LCK$K_EXMODE,   /* lock mode: exclusive */
        &lock_status_block,
        0,              /* flags: none */
        &resource_name,
        0,              /* parent lock: none */
        0,              /* AST address */
        0,              /* AST parameter */
        0,              /* blocking AST routine: none */
        0,              /* access mode: default */
        0               /* nullarg: reserved */
        );
```

```
              printf ("Global section contains: %s \n",retaddress.startaddress);
              strcpy (retaddress.startaddress, this_process_id);
              status = sys$deq                   /* release lock */
                       (
                                   lock_status_block.lock_id,       /* lock id */
                                   &lock_status_block.lock_val,     /* value block */
                                   0,                               /* access mode */
                                   0                                /* flags */
                       );
              };

};
create_or_mapto_globalsection()
{
/* create the global section (if it does not exist) */
status = sys$crmpsc(     &inaddress,      /* range of memory to be mapped */
                         &retaddress,     /* actual memory mapped */
                         0,               /* access mode.Full access by others */
                         SEC$M_GBL        /* Global, not private, section */
                         | SEC$M_WRT      /* Read/Write allowed */
                         | SEC$M_EXPREG   /* Map into available space */
                         | SEC$M_PAGFIL,  /* Page file not a disk file section */
                         &gbl_secnam,
                         &ident,          /* version number 0 */
                         0,               /* first page of section to be mapped */
                         (short) 0,       /* channel for file sections */
                         4,               /* number of pages. all */
                         0,               /* first virtual block number of file*/
                         0,               /* protection. none */
                         0                /* page fault cluster size */
                   );
if (status == 1561)      {
                         printf ("section created\n");
                         strcpy(retaddress.startaddress,"starting process");
                         }
else if (status != SS$_NORMAL) lib$stop(status); /* error? */
       else

       {
       /* map to existing global section */

       status = sys$mgblsc(
                         &inaddress,      /* range of memory to be mapped */
                         &retaddress,     /* actual memory mapped */
                         0,               /* access mode.Full access by others */
                         SEC$M_GBL        /* Global, not private, section */
                         | SEC$M_WRT      /* Read/Write allowed */
                         | SEC$M_EXPREG   /* Map into available space */
                         | SEC$M_PAGFIL,  /* Page file not a disk file section */
                         &gbl_secnam,
                         &ident,          /* version number 0 */
                         0                /* first page of section to be mapped */
                   );
       if (status != SS$_NORMAL) lib$stop(status);      /* error? */
       };
};
```

Some comments on locks follow:

- When a number of locks are being used by a set of processes, there is a possibility of a deadlock. For example, suppose process A has lock L1 and process B has lock L2. A deadlock occurs if process A waits for lock L2 and process B waits for lock L1 since the processes will be waiting for ever. VMS monitors the system for such deadlocks; if it finds that there is a deadlock, it returns a status of SS$_DEADLOCK to one of the processes. Since VMS arbitrarily decides which programs should receive this message, programs using locks should be able to process this status appropriately.

- Locks in the system can be displayed using the System Dump Analyzer utility (although the output requires a good understanding of VMS internals):

```
$ ANALYZE/SYSTEM
VAX/VMS system analyzer

SDA> SHOW LOCKS
```

The MONITOR utility can display a summary of locks in the system:

```
$ MONITOR LOCKS
```

10.3.3 The distributed lock manager

The distributed lock manager is a superset of the standard lock manager. It can be used for synchronization among processes running on different nodes on a VAXcluster.

10.4 OBJECT LIBRARIES

An object library is a file containing commonly used routines in compiled form (not linked). The advantage is that programmers do not have to write code to perform the functions of these routines; instead, they just use the library. The routines can be used from a program by issuing calls to the routines. In most other respects, the routines can be treated as subroutines defined within the main program.

The main program must be linked against the object library. The next set of steps show how to create an object library of two routines; one displays the current process id and the other reverses an input string. The LIBRARIAN utility is used to create library files.

Here are the two subprograms (functions) which will be inserted in the library.

```
/* PID.C
   function to print process id
*/

pid()
{
printf("\nProcess identification is: %d\n", getpid() );
}
```

```
/* REV.C
   function to reverse an input string
*/

revstr (instr,outstr)
char instr[], outstr[];
{
int tmp,pos;
outstr[0] = '\000';
tmp = strlen(instr);
for (tmp=strlen(instr)-1, pos = 0;  tmp>=0;  tmp--, pos++ )
        outstr[pos] = instr[tmp];
}
```

To create the library, the commands are:

```
$CC  PID         /* compile the two programs */
$CC  REVSTR
$LIBRARY/CREATE/OBJECT  CLIB.OLB      /* Create library. File is CLIB.OLB */
$LIBRARY/INSERT  CLIB.OLB  PID.OBJ, REVSTR.OBJ
                                     /* Insert the modules in the library */
```

The next program calls the two routines in the object library created above.

```
/* mainpgm.c
*/

main()
{
char response[80],reversedstr[80];

pid();
printf("Input a string: "); gets(response);
revstr(response,reversedstr);
printf ("Input reversed is: %s", reversedstr);

}
```

The next set of commands create and run the main program image. The library is specified in the LINK command line.

```
$CC MAINPGM
$LINK  MAINPGM, CLIB.OLB/LIB, SYS$INPUT:/OPTION /* Create object module */
SYS$SHARE:VAXCRTL/SHARE
(Enter CTRL/Z)
$RUN MAINPGM
```

10.5 SHARED IMAGES

When, say, 12 users run the same program, the program is loaded 12 times in memory. This may cause memory to be depleted. The program can be redesigned (if required) so that only one image (of the program) is in memory while any number of other programs can use the image. In most cases the programs do not have to be rewritten, only the LINKER options change. Care must be taken to ensure that the data area is separate for each user using the shared image (and that the shared image is reentrant).

An image on disk which can be installed as a shared image is called a sharable image.

Consider the next file containing two C functions. The first function reverses a specified input string. The second function displays the process-id of the current process (which can also be displayed from DCL by "$SHOW PROCESS".

```
/* File: revpid.c
   The file contains two functions which will be used to crete a sharable
   image.
*/

revstr (instr,outstr)
char instr[], outstr[];
/* the function reverses an input string */
{
int tmp,pos;
outstr[0] = '\000';
tmp = strlen(instr);
for (tmp=strlen(instr)-1, pos = 0;  tmp>=0;  tmp--, pos++ )
      outstr[pos] = instr[tmp];
};

pid()
/* display current process identification */
{
printf("\nProcess identification is: %X\n", getpid() );
};
```

These routines are used by a number of other programs. The routines can be put in an object library but code from object libraries is linked in with the calling program so there is no saving in memory when a number of programs use the routines; the routines will be duplicated in each programs's executable image. If the routines are put in a sharable image, other programs can still link to them; but the routines will be in memory only once. Here is how to create a sharable image of the routines.

```
$ cc revpid                    !compile the function file
$ link/notrace/share revpid,sys$input:/option
sys$share:vaxcrtl/share
universal = pid
universal = revstr

$ copy revpid.exe sys$share:  !move to the sharable image directory
$ install sys$share:revpid.exe /share
```

The LINK command has the "shared" qualifier so the image file is a shared image file. The options file (sys$input: in this case) contains the UNIVERSAL clause which specifies that the function names are available to any other image linking against this image. Consider the C program , mainpgm.c:

```
/* mainpgm.c
*/
#include stdio

main( )
{
char response[80],reversedstr[80];

pid( );
printf("\nInput a string:"); gets(response);
revstr(response,reversedstr);
printf ("Input reversed is: %s", reversedstr);

};
```

This program can be compiled and linked against the shared image by:

```
$link mainpgm,sys$input:/option
sys$share:vaxcrtl/share
sys$share:revpid/share
```

Here is a sample execution of the main program:

```
$ run mainpgm
Process identification is: 1057
Input a string: This is a Test
Input reversed is: tseT a si sihT
```

Note that sharable images can contain a set of commonly used routines. They are similar to object libraries, the main difference is that programs link to one shared image of the common routines in memory while routines from object libraries are included with the program.

Sharable images have another advantage; they can be installed with privileges so they can be designed to perform functions which require privileges which are not assigned to the programs (processes) linking with these privileged shared images.

To see shared images installed in memory use:

```
$ install  list
```

10.6   ASYNCHRONOUS SYSTEM TRAPS (ASTs)

Consider a program which loops indefinitely to accept a line of input from the terminal and display the line. The program should also display "Timer interrupt" every 5 seconds on the terminal. The next program uses ASTs to achieve this.

```
/* AST.C
 * This program demonstrates use of ASTs. The program loops to accept input
 * from the terminal and then display it. A timer will generate an AST
 * every 5 seconds and the AST routine will display a message.
 */
#include stdio
#include descrip
#include ssdef

int status;
char delta_time[8];
$DESCRIPTOR(timbuf,"0 00:00:05.00");    /* 5 seconds */
int ast_routine();                      /* routine declared later */

main()
{
char response[80];

status = sys$bintim              /* convert ascii time to internal form */
            (
            &timbuf,
            delta_time
            );
if (status != SS$_NORMAL) lib$stop(status);

/* set timer to interrupt normal program after specified time */
status = sys$setimr
            (
            35,                        /* event flag */
            delta_time,                /* time before AST interrupt */
            &ast_routine,              /* ast addresss */
            0,                         /* timer id, ignore */
            0                          /* elapsed time, not CPU time */
            );
if (status != SS$_NORMAL) lib$stop(status);

while(TRUE)        /* This loop will be regularly interrupted by the timer */
        {
        printf("Enter any input: "); gets(response);
        printf("You entered %s\n",response);
        };

};
ast_routine()    /* This routine is invoked by timer interrupt AST */
{
printf("\nTimer interrupt\n\n");

/* re-arm the timer */
status = sys$setimr
            (
            35,                        /* event flag */
            delta_time,                /* time before AST interrupt */
            &ast_routine,              /* ast routine addresss */
            0,                         /* timer id, ignore */


            0                          /* elapsed time, not CPU time */
            );
if (status != SS$_NORMAL) lib$stop(status);

};
```

To use ASTs in programs:

- Let the operating system know about the type of AST you wish to enable and the subroutine to be executed when the AST condition is satisfied.

- Continue program execution.

- When the AST condition is satisfied, the operating system will deliver the AST to your program. Effectively, execution control will transfer to the address of the subroutine. When the subroutine completes executing, normal program execution will continue. Note that once an AST has been delivered, the AST is disabled until it is "rearmed" by the subroutine or the program.

- Since the timing of AST delivery is not known to the program (that's why it is called asynchronous), the program and the AST routine should not make assumptions about the state of execution of each other. Specifically, common data access should be synchronized by some means like, say, the AST routine setting a flag when it has data ready for the main program to process.

ASTs can be used to invoke a routine on completion of some system services like $QIO and $ENQ and $SETTIMR. In these calls, the address of the AST routine is given as a parameter. An AST routine can be explicitly invoked by the $DCLAST system service.

10.7 EXIT HANDLERS

A program can be interrupted during normal execution by, say, the user entering CTRL-Y at the terminal. When a program image is stopped, the operating system performs cleanup operations like closing files opened by the image. The operation is called winding down of the image. It may also be crucial for the image to perform its own cleanup before exiting. For example, the image may want to send a warning message to the operator terminal if it is aborted for any reason. Exit handlers are subroutines within programs which are executed if the program image is aborted. The subroutine is "registered" with the operating system at the start of the program so that when the program aborts, the operating system calls it before deleting the image.

Here is a program with an exit handler. To see the exit handler function, abort the program by a CTRL-Y on the terminal (followed by, say, a DIR command so that the image run down starts).

```
/* EXH.C
 * This program demonstrates use of exit handlers. When the program is
 * run, it continuously displays a string on the terminal. If the
 * program is terminated by a control-Y entered at the terminal or by
 * a SYS$FORCEX system call from another process, the program
 * executes the exit handler routine.
 */

#include stdio
int exit_handler(); /* exit handler routine is at end */
int status;
/* data structure required to declare an exit handler */
int cond_val;
struct {
        int vms_reserved;
        char *ex_handler_address; /* address of exit handler      */
        int argument_count;       /* optional arguments           */
        int cond_val_addr;        /* condition value returned by vms */
        } descriptor_block
        = { 0, exit_handler, 0, &cond_val };
main()
{
status = sys$dclexh (&descriptor_block); /* declare the exit handler */
while(TRUE)        /* loop forever until program image is aborted   */
    {
    printf ("Waiting for a control-Y ... ");
    sleep(2);
    };
};

exit_handler()
{
    printf ("This line printed by exit handler routine\n");
};
```

10.8 DISTRIBUTED PROGRAMMING ACROSS VAXes

VAXes can be connected to each other by a DECnet network over Ethernet (multidrop lines), direct DDCMP (point to point) lines, or some other line type. VAXes could also be interconnected by a Computer Interconnect (CI) bus on a VAXcluster. All these VAXes can be used to develop distributed applications like:

- *Distributed databases:* Data are spread on files on disks attached to the various VAXes. Programs on the VAXes communicate to transfer data and perform other data manipulations.

- *Distributed computing:* Applications can be designed so that parts of it run on individual systems for a higher overall throughput. An example could be one VAX handling all terminal I/O including input data validation while another VAX acts as a "database machine" storing and managing data on disk.

- *Resource sharing applications:* One server VAX may have an expensive supercomputer connected to it locally. The server VAX can allow controlled access to the supercomputer by means of appropriate "task-to-task" communications between the VAXes.

This section discusses on how to write programs which interact with other programs over DECnet and VAXclusters.

10.8.1 Programming using DECnet

Chapter 11 shows how to access files over the network and log into other nodes on the network. This section shows how to execute command files over the network and use task-to-task communications programs.

10.8.1.1 Executing command files over the network

A command file can be executed on another machine by simply specifying the node name in the file specification. Here is a command, issued on node SCOOP:: to execute a command file, NETCMD.COM, on node TOPVAX::

```
$ @TOPVAX"SHAH KELTUM":: [TEST] NETCMD.COM
```

The following should be noted:

- The user name and password (SHAH and KELTUM) have to be specified as shown in the above command unless TOPVAX has a proxy account for user SHAH.

- The command effectively performs a log-in on TOPVAX, executes the specified command file there, and then logs off the VAX.

- Output and error messages are displayed on the source node.

10.8.1.2 Task-to-task communications over the network by command files

A command file can initiate the execution of another command file on another node. The command files can then transfer data to each other, effectively allowing communications between the nodes.

Here is an example. TOPVAX is on a DECnet network of VAXes and has a high-speed laser printer attached to it. Users on other VAXes wish to print files on this printer. The command file NETCMD_CLIENT.COM can be on any node in a DECnet network. The command file NETSRV.COM is in the log-in directory of user SHAH on TOPVAX. SHAH must have an account on TOPVAX. When NETCMD_CLIENT is executed, it will execute the command file NETSRV.COM on TOPVAX. The process name would be like SERVER_0012. You will be prompted for the file name of the file to be printed on TOPVAX. The file is copied to TOPVAX by NETCMD_CLIENT.COM and printed by NETSRV.COM. The key command line is

```
$ OPEN/READ/WRITE/ERROR=ERROR_EXIT   NET_IO_CLIENT -
TOPVAX"shah kaltap"::"TASK=NETSRV"
```

Here, the OPEN statement actually performs a network log-in from the current VAX to TOPVAX. The user name and password are specified within double quotes. After the log in, the command file NETSRV.COM is run from the log in directory. To see more information on the connection, use

```
$ NCP:==$NCP
$ NCP show known links
```

The command files then communicate via

- The channel specified in the OPEN statement in the client VAX. In this case the channel is NET_IO_CLIENT.

- The channel created by opening SYSNET: on the server VAX. In this case, the channel is NET_IO.

```
$!File: NETCMD_CLIENT.COM
$!
$! This command file can be used on any node in a network to print a file on
$! that node to a printer attached to the node TOPVAX::. The file NETSRV.COM
$! must be present on TOPVAX:: in your login directory
$!
$! The pair of command files can be modified to write cooperating
$! applications between computers on a network.
$!
$ OPEN/READ/WRITE/ERROR=ERROR_EXIT NET_IO_CLIENT -
                 TOPVAX"SHAH KELTIP"::"TASK=NETSRV"
$ IF P1 .EQS. "" THEN -
           $INQUIRE/NOPUNCTUATION  P1 "File to be printed on TOPVAX: "
$ IF P1 .EQS. "" THEN $EXIT
$ COPY 'P1'  TOPVAX"SHAH KELTIP"::
$ WRITE/ERROR=ERROR_EXIT NET_IO_CLIENT  "''p1'"
$                               !Send file name of command file to be executed
$ DISPLAY:                      ! Display input from the other node
$    READ/END=END_NET/ERROR=ERROR_EXIT NET_IO_CLIENT OUTPUT_LINE
$    WRITE SYS$OUTPUT OUTPUT_LINE
$ GOTO DISPLAY
$ END_NET:
$ CLOSE NET_IO_CLIENT
$ EXIT
$!
$ ERROR_EXIT:
$ WRITE SYS$OUTPUT F$MESSAGE($STATUS)
$ EXIT
```

```
$!File: NETSRV.COM
$!
$! This file acts as a server for network requests from other nodes. The file
$! works in conjunction with NETCMD_CLIENT.COM on oterh VAXes on the network.
$! Presently, it copies and prints a file from the client node onto this node.
$!
$ SET NOON
$ SET VERIFY
$
$ OPEN/READ/WRITE NET_IO SYS$NET:        !Open the channel to the process on
$                                        !the source VAX.
$ READ/END=EXIT NET_IO FIL               !Read filename
$ DEFINE/USER SYS$OUTPUT NET_IO          !Set output for the next command to
$                                        !go over the network to the process
$                                        !which executed this file.
$ PRINT 'FIL
$ CLOSE NET_IO
$ EXIT
```

A file, NETSERVER.LOG, will be created in the log-in directory on TOPVAX. This file will contain the output from the execution of the command file. The output is similar to that produced by executing a file by the SUBMIT command. The file can be used to debug the application.

10.8.1.3 Task-to-task communications over the network by programs

Programs can communicate over the network in a way similar to command file communication described above. Here is an example where two C programs on different nodes communicate with each other. INQ_CLIENT.C can reside on any node on a DECnet network. When its image is run, it executes the command file, INQSER.COM on node TOPVAX. The command file, INQSER.COM, is required on the server node to run the actual C program INQ_SERVER.C. The two C programs can pass data to each other. In this example, the client is asking for a table lookup in the server database.

```
/* This program, inq_client.c, performs a database lookup on a server VAX
 * on the DECNET network. The server VAX runs a command file, INQSER.COM,
 * which in turn runs a program, inq_server.c, which performs the database
 * lookup based on a key passed by this program and returns the looked-up
 * value to this program.
 */

#include stdio
#include file

main ()
{
int net_chan, stat;      /* channel to server VAX */
char *buf;
char inp_buf[80];

/* invoke INQSER.COM on the server VAX */
net_chan = open ("topvax\"shah keltip\"::\"task=inqser.com\"",O_RDWR);
if (net_chan < 0)
    {perror("network command file open error"); exit(SS$_NORMAL);};

buf = "7415";   /* search for this account on server VAX database */
stat = write(net_chan, buf, 4);
if (stat < 0) exit(SS$_NORMAL); /*end of file*/

stat = read(net_chan,inp_buf, 80);               /* read account title sent
                                                    by server VAX */

if (stat < 0) exit(SS$_NORMAL); /*end of file*/
printf ("%s",inp_buf);
if (stat == -1) exit(SS$_NORMAL); /*end of file*/


close (net_chan);
}
```

```
$! File: INQSER.COM
$! Database server for lookup of information on this node by
$! other nodes.
$ SET VERIFY
$ RUN INQ_SERVER.EXE
$ EXIT
```

```c
/* This program, inq_server.c,is run by the command file, INQSER.COM, which
 * is invoked by the program, inq_client.c, on another VAX over the DECNET
 * network. The programs demonstrate a client-server model for distributed
 * applications on a network.
 */

#include stdio
#include file
#include ssdef

main ()
{
int net_chan, chan_stat;        /* channel to client VAX */
char inp_buf[5], *tmp_title;

/* Create a database of account information. In practice, the database would
 * be on disk files.
 */
struct acc_struct
        { char *no;
          char *title;
        };
struct acc_struct acc_info[5] =
                {
                  { "2543", "Mary Smith"       },
                  { "1234", "Peter Kak"        },
                  { "7415", "James Shneider"   },
                  { "8323", "John Bayer"       },
                  { "9231", "Gene Cortess"     },
                };

/* Open the channel to the client VAX */
net_chan = open ("sys$net:",O_RDWR);
if (net_chan == -1) {perror("SYS$NET: open error"); exit(SS$_NORMAL);};

/* Get account number from client VAX */
chan_stat = read(net_chan, inp_buf, 4);
if (chan_stat <= 0 ) {perror("Error on network read");exit(SS$_NORMAL);}

/* Given account number, find account title. In practice, this
   step would be a database lookup on disk. */
tmp_title = "Account does not exist";
if (strcmp(inp_buf,acc_info[0].no) == 0) tmp_title=acc_info[0].title;
else if (strcmp(inp_buf,acc_info[1].no) == 0) tmp_title=acc_info[1].title;
else if (strcmp(inp_buf,acc_info[2].no) == 0) tmp_title=acc_info[2].title;
else if (strcmp(inp_buf,acc_info[3].no) == 0) tmp_title=acc_info[3].title;
else if (strcmp(inp_buf,acc_info[4].no) == 0) tmp_title=acc_info[4].title;

/* Send account title to the client VAX */
chan_stat = write(net_chan, tmp_title, 512);
if (chan_stat <= 0 ) {perror("Error on network write");exit(SS$_NORMAL);}

close (net_chan);
}
```

The sequence of steps are:

- INQ_CLIENT.EXE is run on a VAX.

- The OPEN statement refers to another node, TOPVAX, so DECnet establishes a logical link with TOPVAX.

- The file SYS$SYSTEM:NETSERVER.COM is executed by DECNET on TOPVAX. This file in turn executes SYS$SYSTEM:NETSERVER.EXE. This file, in turn, works in conjunction with the process NETACP and completes the connection. The execution of the command file specified, INQSER.COM, is logged in NETSERVER.LOG in the login directory.

- The device SYS$NET: on the server VAX is used to communicate back with the client VAX. This device is set up when the logical link is established.

Internode communications can be established by creating network objects. This method of communication does not require a command file to be executed on the server node and it can offer more control of the link. For example, a network object can be set up to serve multiple nodes. Creating network objects is not discussed in this book.

10.8.2 Task-to-task communications within a VAXcluster

Normally, communication between tasks on a cluster of different VAXes is performed over DECnet. In this sense, the programs are similar to those described above. While the CI cluster connection can be used for communications, it is not recommended because the CI software and hardware is customized for cluster messages rather than arbitrary user messages. Moreover, the CI is used for disk I/O with HSCs and DECnet over CI may slow down disk I/O.

10.8.3 FURTHER READING

Introduction to System Services, Vol. 4A, VMS Programming Manuals.
Introduction to System Routines, Vol. 3, VMS Programming Manuals.
Guide to Programming Resources, Vol. 1, VMS Programming Manuals.
Networking Manual, Vol. 5A, VMS System Management Manuals.

The DECnet Network

DECnet is DEC's architecture for communications between computers. It attempts to adhere to the OSI standard seven-layer scheme, though it does not comply completely. It also has support for communications with X.25 (packet-switched networks like Tymnet and Telenet) and IBM's System Network Architecture (SNA). This chapter discusses DECnet Phase IV which is currently used at many sites. DECnet Phase V will be OSI-compliant. Many of the services and protocols used currently will be gradually replaced by new ones.

Computers on a network are known as nodes. DECnet interconnects VAX nodes using two main methodologies:

·1. *Ethernet:* Ethernet is usually used when the VAXes are not far from each other, normally within a radius of a few thousand feet. Such a network is called a local area network (LAN). Actually, Ethernet LAN bridges are available which extend the range of Ethernet, even, say, from New York to London. So, the term local area network may be misleading.

2. *DDCMP:* The acronym is for *digital data communications protocol*. This protocol is used when VAXes are using DECnet over communications lines. It is a point-to-point protocol. Two VAXes can be connected to each other by a synchronous or asynchronous line. Line speeds of 9.6 kbits/s or 56 kbits/s are typical. Any two VAXes on a network can communicate with each other provided there is a path between them, either a direct line or via other VAXes.

Note that in this chapter, multipoint and multidrop connections are treated as point-to-point connections. Typical uses of a DECnet network are:

- Copying files.

- Logging into other VAXes.

- Sharing of resources like fast line-printers & software packages.

- Running distributed applications.

Note that terminal servers use Ethernet but they do not use DECnet; they use the LAT protocol. VAXclusters are interconnected VAXes, but the clustering software and hardware are not based on DECnet. Actually, the clustering hardware (the CI bus) can be used by DECnet also, but this is normally not recommended as DECnet is inefficient when used over the CI bus. Local Area VAXclusters use Ethernet for cluster communications but DECnet protocols are not used. See the chapter on VAXclusters for information on clusters.

11.1 BASIC ISSUES

Figure 11.1 shows a hypothetical network. Notes on the network follow:

- Any of the six VAXes can communicate with each other. The communications path between VAXA to VAXF is VAXA to VAXB to VAXE to VAXF. The network databases can be set up to disallow connections between any two VAXes.

- Users need not know the path their data takes from one node to another; only the source and destination node names are required. DECnet uses an adaptive routing algorithm to select intermediate nodes.

- Nodes which do not act as in-between nodes are called *end nodes*. Nodes which can receive messages from one node and send them to

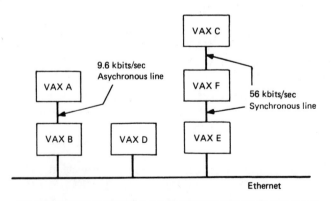

Figure 11.1   A hypothetical DECnet network.

another are called *routers*. Routers also function as end nodes. VAXA, VAXD and VAXC are end nodes (or nonrouters). VAXB, VAXE, and VAXF must be routers.

- Ethernet bandwidth is 10 Mbits/sec so file transfer between, say, VAXB to VAXD is faster than file transfer between VAXA to VAXB.

- Any of the VAXes can be part of VAXclusters.

- Failure of VAXE will partition the network into two subnetworks whose nodes can communicate with other nodes within the subnetwork. Nodes send out messages at regular intervals which effectively say "I am on the network." Other nodes make a note of nodes on the network by listening to these messages. Nodes can also determine if a particular node is on the network by sending out an inquiry message. The network database on each node is automatically updated when nodes enter or leave the network.

11.2 FILE ACCESS ACROSS THE NETWORK

Users on one node can access another node provided they have an account on the node to be accessed. The node to be accessed is called a *host*. Here is the command to copy a file from node VAXE to the current node, which is VAXB:

```
$ COPY  VAXE"username password"::DUA1:TEST.DATA  TEST.DATA
```

Node names are followed by two colons. The user name and password are specified within double quotes. If a proxy account has been created on VAXE for the user then the user name and password need not be specified:

```
$ COPY  VAXE::DUA1:TEST.DATA  *.*
```

Proxy accounts are described in Chapter 14.

Actually, most commands on the system which require a file name can access the file from another node if the node name is mentioned in the file specification. For example, this command displays the files in directory [TEST] on the logical device TEST_DRIVE on node VAXD:

```
$ DIRECTORY  VAXD::TEST_DRIVE:[TEST]*.*;*
```

The logical device name, TEST_DRIVE, is translated into a physical name by the node VAXD (and not the node from which the command is issued).

11.3   LOGIN OVER THE NETWORK

To log into node VAXE:: from the current node VAXB:: the command is

```
$ SET  HOST  VAXE::
```

Node VAXE:: will ask for your username and password. Once logged
into the other node, the terminal works like a terminal on the new
node. The LOGOUT command returns control to the original node.

When logged in across the network, the session can be logged into a
file. All terminal input and output is logged in a file, SETHOST.LOG,
on the original node with the following login command:

```
$ SET  HOST  VAXE::/LOG
```

The log file can be printed out after logging off the host node. In fact,
this method can be used to create a log file of a terminal session on the
current node. The "0" in the next command means the current node:

```
$ SET  HOST 0/LOG
```

Effectively you will be logging into your system again, creating a
second session. The log file can be accessed after logging off from the
second session.

11.4   NETWORKING TERMINOLOGY AND CONCEPTS

11.4.1   Network Control Program (NCP)

NCP is used to configure the network database on each node and to monitor status of connections to other nodes. For example, to know the status
of all nodes configured in the current VAX the commands would be

```
$ NCP :== $NCP
$ NCP SHOW KNOWN NODES

Known Node Volatile Summary as of   9-DEC-1989 17:56:07

Executor node = 1.5 (VAXNV5)

State                 = on
Identification        = DECnet-VAX V5.0,  VMS V5.1-1
Active links          = 1
```

Node	State	Active Links	Delay	Circuit	Next node
1.2 (VAXNE2)	reachable	1	1	BNA-0	1.2 (VAXNE2)
1.3	reachable			BNA-0	1.3
1.4	reachable			BNA-0	1.4
1.6 (VAXNE6)	reachable			BNA-0	1.9
1.9	reachable			BNA-0	1.9
1.421	reachable			BNA-0	1.421

Some notes on the output follow:

- Current node, called the executor node, is VAXNV5. Six other nodes are reachable. Two nodes, VAXNE2 and VAXNE6, were configured when setting up the database, so their node names are displayed. The other four nodes were found to be reachable by messages received from them.

- There is one session between the current node and node VAXNE2 as shown by active links. The session could be for file transfer, a network log in from VAXNE2 to the current node or from the current node to VAXNE2, or some other session.

- All the nodes are adjacent nodes as they are all on Ethernet. Actually, the current node gathers information only on adjacent nodes by listening to other nodes. Information on nonadjacent nodes is displayed only if the network database is configured with nonadjacent node names and DECnet addresses of these nodes.

- The column headed by "next node" displays the node adjacent to the node at the left. Entering the NCP SHOW KNOWN NODES command after logging into that node gives adjacent nodes of that node. This way, it is possible to know all the nodes on the network.

11.4.2 Areas

In DECnet phase IV, the current implementation, a network can be divided into logical areas. Areas are numbered 1 through 63. Area 1 is assumed when not specified. Each area can have up to 1023 nodes. DECnet addresses of nodes are specified as area.node-number like 1.35, 4.32, and 32 (the last address is assumed to be 1.32).

It was mentioned before that routers act as in-between nodes when they receive messages from one node and send them to another. There are two types of routers, intraarea routers (or just routers) and area routers. Area routers can send messages received from a node in one area to a node in another area. Why segment a physically connected network into areas?

- Messages directed within the area are not seen by nodes in other areas except by area routing nodes. This reduces processing overhead by nodes in the network.

- Networks can be logically partitioned for easier management.

- Multiple areas are required if the number of nodes exceed 1023.

Intraarea routers are also known as level 1 routers and interarea routers are also known as level 2 routers.

The next command shows the areas which are accessible to the current node.

```
$ NCP SHOW KNOWN AREA

Known Area Volatile Summary as of 12-DEC-1989 12:35:13

    Area    State         Circuit        Next node to area

    1       reachable                    1.5 (SCOOP5)
    4       reachable     BNA-0          4.129 (TOPVAX)
```

In NCP commands, usually KNOWN NODES, KNOWN LINES, KNOWN CIRCUITS can be replaced by the name of particular entities. For example,

```
$ NCP   SHOW   KNOWN   NODES
$ NCP   SHOW   NODE   VAX5
$ NCP   SHOW   KNOWN   CIRCUITS
$ NCP   SHOW   CIRCUIT   BNA-0
```

11.4.3 Circuits and lines

A circuit is the logical path from a node to another node. A line is the low-level physical data path from a node to the network. For example, a VAX on the Ethernet may have a number of circuits, one for each adjacent node and each called BNA-1. The line could be called BNA-1. There is only one line per physical data path. To see all circuits and lines on the current node the commands are

```
$NCP :== $NCP
$NCP   SHOW KNOWN CIRCUITS

Known Circuit Volatile Summary as of  9-DEC-1989 18:19:38

        Circuit         State              Loopback      Adjacent
                                           Name          Routing Node

    BNA-0           on                                1.3
    BNA-0                                             1.4
    BNA-0                                             1.9
    BNA-0                                             1.2 (VAXNE2)
    BNA-1           on

$NCP   SHOW KNOWN LINES

Known Line Volatile Summary as of  9-DEC-1989 18:19:45

        Line            State

    BNA-0           on
    BNA-1           on
```

Note the multiple circuits to other nodes on line BNA-0. A circuit gets established whenever a new node is accessed. It remains even after the session is terminated. Lines are physical connections, so they will be seen as soon as the system is booted. In this case the VAX is connected to two separate Ethernets so there are two lines BNA-0 and BNA-1.

11.4.4 Logical links

A *logical link* is a session between two nodes. For example, a user copying files from another node sets up a logical link between that node and the current node. Another user may have "set host" to the other node, in which case he or she also has set up a logical link. Both these links may be over the same circuit and line. Logical links can be displayed by

```
$ NCP SHOW KNOWN LINKS


Known Link Volatile Summary as of  9-DEC-1989 18:34:08

   Link        Node          PID     Process     Remote link  Remote user

   8209     1.5 (VAXNV5)   00000112  SHAH4            8210     CTERM
   8195     4.200          00000109  REMACP            114     SYSTEM
```

Here, the first logical link was due to a SET HOST 0 command. The second one is a file transfer between the current node (1.5) and node 4.200. This is determined from the "Process" and "Remote user" columns.

11.4.5 Setting up and maintaining the network database

NCP can be used to set up a node for network operations. Each node will have to be individually set up. As the commands can be cryptic for novice system managers, there is a file, SYS$MANAGER:NETCONFIG.COM, on the system to configure the network database initially. Here is a sample usage of the file:

```
$ SET DEFAULT SYS$MANAGER:
$ @NETCONFIG.COM

    DECnet-VAX network configuration procedure

This procedure will help you define the parameters needed to get DECnet
running on this machine.  You will be shown the changes before they are
executed, in case you wish to perform them manually.

What do you want your DECnet node name to be?              : VAXNV5
What do you want your DECnet address to be?                : 1.5
Do you want to operate as a router?        [NO (nonrouting)]: YES
Do you want a default DECnet account?                  [YES]:

    Here are the commands necessary to setup your system.

------------------------------------------------------------------------
$ RUN SYS$SYSTEM:NCP
    PURGE EXECUTOR ALL
    PURGE KNOWN LINES ALL
    PURGE KNOWN CIRCUITS ALL
    PURGE KNOWN LOGGING ALL
    PURGE KNOWN OBJECTS ALL
    PURGE MODULE CONFIGURATOR KNOWN CIRCUITS ALL
$ DEFINE/USER SYS$OUTPUT NL:
$ DEFINE/USER SYS$ERROR NL:
$ RUN SYS$SYSTEM:NCP       ! Remove existing entry, if any
    PURGE NODE 1.5 ALL
    PURGE NODE VAXNV5 ALL
$ RUN SYS$SYSTEM:NCP
    DEFINE EXECUTOR ADDRESS 1.5 STATE ON
    DEFINE EXECUTOR NAME VAXNV5
    DEFINE EXECUTOR MAXIMUM ADDRESS 1023
    DEFINE EXECUTOR TYPE ROUTING IV
    DEFINE EXECUTOR NONPRIVILEGED USER DECNET
    DEFINE EXECUTOR NONPRIVILEGED PASSWORD DECNET
$ DEFINE/USER_MODE SYSUAF SYS$SYSTEM:SYSUAF.DAT
$ RUN SYS$SYSTEM:AUTHORIZE
    ADD DECNET /OWNER="DECNET DEFAULT" -
        /PASSWORD=DECNET -
        /UIC=[376,376] /ACCOUNT=DECNET -
        /DEVICE=SYS$SPECIFIC: /DIRECTORY=[DECNET] -
        /PRIVILEGE=(TMPMBX,NETMBX) -
        /DEFPRIVILEGE=(TMPMBX,NETMBX) -
        /FLAGS=(CAPTIVE) /LGICMD=NL: -
        /NOBATCH /NOINTERACTIVE
$ CREATE/DIRECTORY SYS$SPECIFIC:[DECNET] /OWNER=[376,376]
$ RUN SYS$SYSTEM:NCP
    DEFINE LINE    BNA-0 STATE ON
    DEFINE CIRCUIT BNA-0 STATE ON COST 4
    DEFINE LINE    BNA-1 STATE ON
    DEFINE CIRCUIT BNA-1 STATE ON COST 4
    DEFINE LOGGING MONITOR STATE ON
    DEFINE LOGGING MONITOR EVENTS 0.0-9



    DEFINE LOGGING MONITOR EVENTS 2.0-1
    DEFINE LOGGING MONITOR EVENTS 4.2-13,15-16,18-19
    DEFINE LOGGING MONITOR EVENTS 5.0-18
    DEFINE LOGGING MONITOR EVENTS 128.0-4
------------------------------------------------------------------------

Do you want these commands to be executed? [YES]:
```

The network database is made up of the following files in SYS$SYSTEM:

NETCIRC.DAT

NETCONF.DAT

NETLINE.DAT

NETLOGING.DAT

NETNODE_LOCAL.DAT

NETNODE_REMOTE.DAT

NETOBJECT.DAT

NETPROXY.DAT

Once configured, the network can be started by

```
$ @SYS$MANAGER:STARTNET
```

DECnet will come up on the node. Three processes will be running on the system:

1. NETACP—handles sessions with other nodes.
2. EVL—event logger (described later).
3. REMACP—handles file operations for files opened on this node by other nodes.

To see adjacent nodes, use

```
$ SHOW  NETWORK
```

or

```
$ NCP  := $NCP
$ NCP  SHOW  KNOWN  NODES
```

The second form requires special privileges and displays more extensive information. DECnet listens to the network and finds out the node addresses of adjacent nodes. DECnet does not find the node names of these nodes. Also nonadjacent nodes are not known automatically. These nodes can be added to the database by

```
$ NCP  DEFINE  NODE  VAXNE4  ADDRESS 4.22
$ NCP  SET  NODE  VAXNE4  ALL
```

11.4.6   NCP commands for maintaining the network database

Each node on the network maintains a database on disk. This database is in a set of files which were mentioned in the section above. When the network is enabled on the node, by executing

```
$ @SYS$MANAGER:STARTNET.COM
```

the database gets loaded in memory. The database on disk is called the permanent database, while the database in memory is the volatile database. The volatile database gets loaded from the permanent database every time the network is enabled. The Network Control Program (NCP) is used to maintain these databases. For example, the next command removes information on node VAX5:: from the permanent database.

```
$ NCP:= = $NCP              !This allows you to use the NCP command
$ NCP PURGE NODE VAX5 ALL !Delete permanent information on the node.
```

Information on node VAX5 is still in the volatile database so the node is still known until the network is disabled and enabled again. The information in the volatile database can be deleted, without disabling the network, by the command

```
$ NCP CLEAR NODE VAX5 ALL
```

The NCP PURGE and NCP CLEAR commands have a similar syntax. PURGEs remove entries from the permanent database, while CLEARs remove entries in the volatile database. Note that DECnet is able to get the node addresses of adjacent nodes on the network, so these nodes need not be created in the volatile database. DECnet does not find node names, so these will have to be entered.

NCP also has two sets of commands to create entries in the permanent and volatile databases: DEFINE and SET. For example,

```
$ NCP DEFINE LINE BNA-0 STATE ON
```

sets the Ethernet line BNA-0 in the ON state in the permanent database. When the network is enabled the next time, the line will be automatically set to the ON state. To set the line ON right now, the volatile database can be changed with:

```
$ NCP SET LINE BNA-0 STATE ON
```

The NCP commands DEFINE, SET, PURGE and CLEAR take the same set of parameters in most cases. They are used to create or remove entries and change parameters in the permanent or volatile database. The NCP HELP command can be used to see what these sub-commands can be used for. Here are some examples of usage of these commands:

```
$ NCP  DEFINE  NODE  VAXNE4  ADDRESS  4.22         !Enter new node
$ NCP  SET     NODE  VAXNE4  ADDRESS  4.22         !Enter new node
                                                   !(temporary)
$ NCP  PURGE   NODE  VAXNE4  ADDRESS  4.22         !Delete node
$ NCP  CLEAR   NODE  NAME VAXNE4 ADDRESS  4.22     !Delete node
                                                   !entry in memory
$ NCP  DEFINE  EXECUTOR  TYPE  ROUTING  IV         !Change parameter
                                                   for !current node
```

The SHOW and LIST commands can be used to see parameters in the permanent and volatile databases; SHOW for the volatile database and LIST for the permanent database. Examples are:

```
$ NCP  SHOW  KNOWN  NODES  !display information in volatile database
$ NCP  LIST  KNOWN  NODES  !display information in permanent database
```

The output of the SHOW command is shown in the next section.

11.4.6.1 Network parameters, counters and events

The sections above describe how to create and delete entries for node names, lines, and circuits. Each one of these has associate parameters which assume default values if not specified. Here is a list of parameters for the current node:

```
NCP SHOW EXECUTOR CHARACTERISTICS


Node Volatile Characteristics as of 12-DEC-1989 11:33:26

Executor node = 1.5 (SCOOP5)

Identification            = DECnet-VAX V4.7,  VMS V4.7
Management version        = V4.0.0
Incoming timer            = 45
Outgoing timer            = 60
NSP version               = V4.0.0
Maximum links             = 32
Delay factor              = 80
Delay weight              = 5
Inactivity timer          = 60
Retransmit factor         = 10
Routing version           = V2.0.0
Type                      = area
Routing timer             = 600
Broadcast routing timer   = 180
Maximum address           = 1023
Maximum circuits          = 16
Maximum cost              = 1022
Maximum hops              = 30
Maximum visits            = 63
Maximum area              = 63
Max broadcast nonrouters  = 64
Max broadcast routers     = 32
Area maximum cost         = 1022
Area maximum hops         = 30
Maximum buffers           = 100
Buffer size               = 576
Nonprivileged user id     = DECNET
Default access            = incoming and outgoing
Pipeline quota            = 3000
Default proxy access      = incoming and outgoing
Alias maximum links       = 32
```

Some of the parameters are described here:

- *Maximum links.* These are the maximum number of sessions which can be established between this node and all other nodes on the network. The parameter can be changed by:

```
$ NCP SET EXECUTOR MAXIMUM LINKS 58
```

- The node is an area router as shown by the TYPE parameter.
- It can have 16 circuits. Since usually one circuit is established for connection with one other node, up to 16 nodes can be communicating with this VAX simultaneously.
- Timer parameters are specified in seconds and they mainly specify timeouts.
- *Maximum buffers* specifies number of transmit buffers.
- *Maximum cost* specifies the upper limit on the cost of a packet going out from the node. The cost is determined by adding the costs of all lines on the way to the destination from the source node to the current node when a packet is routed through multiple nodes. If the cost exceeds this parameter value then the packet is dropped.
- *Maximum hops* specifies the upper limit on the number of lines a packet going out of this node can travel. If the destination is not reached within the limit, the packet is discarded.

While most of these parameters can be changed, the default values are adequate for most applications. The parameters should be changed, keeping other nodes in mind as reckless changes to parameters can create a detuned network.

Here is another example of node characteristics. The node is an SNA gateway used for communicating with IBM mainframes:

```
$ NCP SHOW NODE SNAGWY CHARACTERISTICS

Node Volatile Characteristics as of 12-DEC-1989 11:34:03

Remote node =   1.221 (SNAGWY)

Service circuit        = BNA-0
Hardware address       = 08-00-2B-0D-26-3D
Load file              = SYS$COMMON:[SNA$CSV]SNACST010.SYS
Dump file              = SYS$COMMON:[SNA$CSV]SNAGWY.DMP
Access                 = incoming and outgoing
```

Counts of various operations are maintained for

1. The current node

2. Lines on the current node

3. Circuits on the current node.

These are useful for performance evaluation and network tuning. Here are some examples; the parameters are fairly obvious.

```
$ NCP SHOW EXECUTOR COUNTERS

Node Counters as of 12-DEC-1989 12:41:22

Executor node = 1.5 (SCOOP5)

    11214  Seconds since last zeroed
    27685  Bytes received
    27754  Bytes sent
      604  Messages received
      607  Messages sent
        3  Connects received
        3  Connects sent
        1  Response timeouts
        0  Received connect resource errors
        2  Maximum logical links active
        0  Aged packet loss
        0  Node unreachable packet loss
        0  Node out-of-range packet loss
        0  Oversized packet loss
        0  Packet format error
        0  Partial routing update loss
        0  Verification reject


$ NCP SHOW KNOWN LINE COUNTERS


Known Line Counters as of 12-DEC-1989 12:42:41

Line = BNA-0

   >65534  Seconds since last zeroed
   525927  Data blocks received
   432947  Multicast blocks received
        0  Receive failure
 48772033  Bytes received
 42512836  Multicast bytes received
        0  Data overrun
        0  Local buffer errors
   133841  Data blocks sent
    39153  Multicast blocks sent
        5  Blocks sent, multiple collision
        5  Blocks sent, single collision
       58  Blocks sent, initially deferred
  8494976  Bytes sent
  3621016  Multicast bytes sent
        0  Send failure
        0  Collision detect check failure
        0  Unrecognized frame destination
        0  System buffer unavailable
        0  User buffer unavailable
```

```
$ NCP SHOW CIRCUIT BNA-0  COUNTERS

Known Circuit Counters as of 12-DEC-1989 12:43:40

Circuit = BNA-0

       >65534  Seconds since last zeroed
         1291  Terminating packets received
         1446  Originating packets sent
            0  Terminating congestion loss
        24769  Transit packets received
        24769  Transit packets sent
            0  Transit congestion loss
            0  Circuit down
            0  Initialization failure
        61484  Data blocks sent
      4672648  Bytes sent
       459227  Data blocks received
     44243711  Bytes received
            0  Unrecognized frame destination
            0  User buffer unavailable
```

Counter values can be zeroed by commands such as

```
$ NCP  ZERO  LINE  BNA-0  COUNTERS
$ NCP  ZERO  KNOWN  LINES  COUNTERS
$ NCP  ZERO  CIRCUIT  BNA-1  COUNTERS
```

Events are changes in the state of the network. Examples of events are a new node entering the network or a line state changed from on to off. Different events will be seen on different nodes on a network. The process EVL is an network event logger. It sends event messages to the OPCOM process, which logs them in the operator log file and displays them on operator consoles. A terminal can receive console messages on network events by:

```
$ REPLY/ENABLE=NET   !Send network messages to this terminal.
```

Here are some network messages seen on the console or in the operator log file.

```
%%%%%%%%%% OPCOM   9-DEC-1989 08:45:45.71  %%%%%%%%%%
Message from user DECNET
DECnet starting
%%%%%%%%%% OPCOM   9-DEC-1989 08:45:52.47  %%%%%%%%%%
Message from user DECNET
DECnet event 4.10, circuit up
From node 1.5 (SCOOP5),  9-DEC-1989 08:45:51.20
Circuit BNA-0
%%%%%%%%%% OPCOM   9-DEC-1989 08:45:52.50  %%%%%%%%%%
Message from user DECNET
DECnet event 4.15, adjacency up
From node 1.5 (SCOOP5),  9-DEC-1989 08:45:52.26
Circuit BNA-0, Adjacent node = 1.4
%%%%%%%%%% OPCOM   9-DEC-1989 08:49:18.39  %%%%%%%%%%
Message from user DECNET
DECnet event 4.7, circuit down, circuit fault
From node 1.5 (SCOOP5),  9-DEC-1989 08:49:18.37
Circuit BNA-1, Line synchronization lost
%%%%%%%%%% OPCOM   9-DEC-1989 15:04:59.95  %%%%%%%%%%
Message from user DECNET
DECnet event 4.18, adjacency down
From node 1.5 (SCOOP5),  9-DEC-1989 15:04:59.94
Circuit BNA-0, Dropped by adjacent node, Adjacent node = 1.2 (SCOOP2)
```

Note that each message is identified by an event number. An event number consists of two parts: an event class (followed by a dot), followed by an event type. An example is 4.18. The event classes and types are described in the NCP section of *VMS System Management Manual*.

It is possible to log only certain types of event messages and avoid logging of events which generate a lot of message output and are of no concern on the particular node. The @SYS$MANAGER:- NETCONFIG.COM command generates the network database and sets events to be logged. See the NETCONFIG session above for the list of events which are logged. To log only certain events, use

```
$ NCP  SET  LOGGING  MONITOR  STATE  ON
$ NCP  SET  LOGGING  MONITOR  EVENTS  0.3-5   !Events  0.3,0.4,0,5
$ NCP  SET  LOGGING  MONITOR  EVENTS  3.*     !All events of class 3
```

Note that SET is for the volatile database in memory while DEFINE is for the permanent database on disk.

Event monitoring for specific events can be disabled by a command such as

```
$ MCR  NCP  CLEAR  LOGGING  MONITOR  EVENT 0.7 !Disable load request
                                               !messages
```

Normally, events are logged on each node. The installation may have a network operator who monitors events on a number of nodes. He or she can set up the nodes so that all network messages are sent to a particular node. Then the operator has to monitor only the network console on that node. To send all event messages on the current node to the node VAXN5 also, use:

```
$ NCP  SET  LOGGING  MONITOR  STATE  ON
$ NCP  SET  LOGGING  MONITOR  SINK  VAXN5 !Log events to node VAXN5
$ NCP  SET  LOGGING  CONSOLE  STATE  ON   !Log events on this system
                                          !also.
$ NCP  SET  LOGGING  CONSOLE  KNOWN  EVENTS
```

11.5 ETHERNET

Figure 11.2 shows a sample Ethernet-based network. Logically, each node has a Ethernet controller card which is connected to the Ethernet cable by a transceiver cable. The H4005 allows a transceiver cable to be tapped into the Ethernet cable. The DELNI allows eight transceiver cables to be plugged into it and the corresponding nodes to communicate with each other.

Various pieces of hardware are available to support thin-wire Ethernet, Ethernet repeaters, LAN-bridges, and so on. In fact, a DELNI can be used to interconnect the transciever cables from vari-

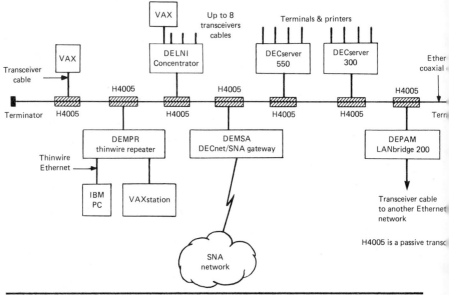

Figure 11.2   A network showing Ethernet components.

ous nodes without using any Ethernet backbone cable. The logical network is not changed by these products.

Logically, Ethernet can be considered a bus; each node on the network can communicate directly with any other node. The bus usage is
quite straightforward. A node wishing to send out data, sends the data
to the Ethernet controller card. The connection between the node CPU
and the card is referred to as a LINE in NCP commands. The card "listens" to note if the Ethernet is in use. If no node is using the network,
the card sends the data on the Ethernet. It listens again to note if another node also sent data on the Ethernet simultaneously. If there is
such a collision, the data has to be retransmitted. This technique of
usage is known as *Carrier Sense, Multiple Access with Collision Detect
(CSMA/CD)*. Each Ethernet controller continuously monitors the
Ethernet to determine if there is any traffic for itself. If there is, the
data received is sent to the lower layers of DECnet software on that
node and ultimately to the application. Ethernet bandwidth is 10
Mbits/sec, though collisions and other factors reduce the actual
throughput to a much lesser value.

DEC has exploited Ethernet technology fully for DECnet and other
uses like LAT (which is described later). An Ethernet node is identified by a 48-bit (12 hex digit) *hardware address*. This address is hard-
wired in the Ethernet controller card. This address is not used for
DECnet communications. DECnet writes a new address in the controller card when DECnet is brought up on the node. This address, called
the *physical address*, is calculated as a function of the DECnet area

and node number of the node on which the card resides. The physical address is used when a node addresses another node on the network. The reason for doing this is that the transmitting node can determine the physical address of the Ethernet card on the other node by looking up the DECnet address of the destination node from its NCP database. This way, nodes do not have to maintain (in their databases) a list of Ethernet addresses of other nodes on the network.

There is another reason why hardware addresses are converted to physical addresses. Many companies make Ethernet cards. Since a limited set of addresses is allocated to DEC, the hardware addresses are converted to physical addresses for use by the controller cards. The physical address is determined from the DECnet node address, so it is unique on any particular network.

The network setup commands mentioned in previous sections are valid for Ethernet connections. All nodes on an Ethernet should be in the same area as otherwise communications between nodes in different areas will be via area routers although they can directly communicate over the Ethernet. If lanbridges or other devices are used to divide an Ethernet network into segments, then the lanbridges may restrict traffic from one segment to another.

Multiple controllers can be used for redundancy to connect a VAX to Ethernet but only one NCP LINE should be enabled as otherwise both controllers will attempt to send data on the Ethernet causing collisions. If the first controller does not function then it's line should be disabled before enabling the second controller's line:

```
$ NCP  SET  LINE  BNA-1  STATE  OFF
$ NCP  SET  LINE  BNA-0  STATE  ON
```

Two separate Ethernets can be used for redundancy. Each VAX will have two controllers, one connected to each Ethernet. Again, only one Ethernet should be enabled at any one time. This can be achieved by setting the controller line states to off for all controllers connected to one Ethernet.

The Ethernet card is controlled by software drivers like any other driver on the VAX. The cards are different depending on the bus used on the particular VAX. For example, a Ethernet controller on VAXBI buses is called DEBNA while the card for Q-bus VAXes is DESQA. The software drivers are different for the different cards. A typical driver is SYS$SYSTEM:ETDRIVER.EXE and the corresponding device name is ETAnn:. These drivers are used by DECnet, but programmers can write software to bypass DECnet and send output for other nodes directly to Ethernet by using "ET" devices.

TCP/IP is a commonly used protocol on Ethernet, but VAX/VMS uses the DECnet protocol so TCP/IP is not discussed here. TCP/IP can run with DECnet on the same Ethernet hardware if required.

11.6   DDCMP

DDCMP (digital data communications protocol) is used for point-to-point connections between nodes. Example connections are 1200-baud asynchronous (RS232C based) and 56-Kbaud synchronous (using DMV11 cards). Modems can be installed at the two ends but that is of no concern to DECnet.

To use a permanently connected asynchronous terminal line between the two systems for DECnet, the system managers on the systems at both ends must install the driver NODRIVER and set the terminal line as:

```
$ SYSGEN  : = =  $SYSGEN              !Enable SYSGEN as a command
$ SYSGEN  CONNECT  NOA0:/NOADAPTER    !Load driver NODRIVER
$ SET  TERMINAL/PROTOCOL=DDCMP  TXA2:
```

The necessary line and circuit NCP commands must be issued on both systems:

```
$ SET  LINE  TX-0-2  STATE  ON  RECEIVE  BUFFERS  4
$ SET  CIRCUIT  TX-0-2  STATE  ON
```

The lines are then ready for communications.

For synchronous lines only the line and circuit NCP commands are required. The line name is determined by the card used. For the DMV-11 card the line name is DMP. Here is how to initialize the lines

```
$ SET  LINE  DMP-0  PROTOCOL  DDCMP  POINT  STATE  ON
$ SET  CIRCUIT  DMP-0  STATE  ON
```

The DEFINE commands can be used instead of SET to make the changes permanent in the network database on disk.

11.7   SNA CONNECTIVITY

DEC has a set of hardware and software products for accessing SNA networks (which allows access to IBM mainframes). What can such a cross-network connection be used for?

1. *Terminal emulator:* DEC terminals can be used as IBM 3270 equivalents. CICS, TSO and similar applications can be accessed.

2. *Remote job entry:* Accesses IBM RJE facilities.

3. *Application programming interface (API):* Emulates IBM Logical Unit 0.

4. *Data transfer facility:* Allows file transfer and sharing between VAXes and IBM MVS systems. Also allows programs to access files on the mainframes.

5. *Disoss interface:*   Disoss is an office automation system on the mainframe.

6. *Distributed host command facility (DHCF):*   Allows IBM 3270 terminals to act as line-oriented terminals on VAX systems.

7. *Printer emulator:*   Allows IBM print output to be routed to a VAX.

8. LU 6.2 program to program communications (APPC).

To the IBM systems, the connection from the VAX is through a 37×5 communications controller as either a physical unit type 2 or directly as a channel device.

There are two types of gateways:

1. *VMS/SNA gateway:*   This is a DPV-11 (or similar) synchronous card in the VAX backplane connected to a 37×5 controller on the IBM network.

2. *DECnet/SNA gateway:*   This is a small box (with a microVAX in it) which connects to Ethernet on the VAX side. There are two forms of this gateway; the ST, which connects to the 37×5 controller, or the CT, which connects as a channel to an IBM mainframe. These gateways have the advantage of direct connection by any VAX on the Ethernet. For small applications the VMS/SNA gateways may be more cost-effective.

Figure 11.3 shows the three types of inter-connections.

The basic software is different for each type of gateway, but the functionality is similar. Typically, 128 terminal (3270) sessions can be used on each gateway through the VAXes.

SNATRACE is a utility which logs every packet sent between the gateway and the IBM 37×5 or the channel hardware. It is useful for link-level debugging of applications. SNAP is a utility which shows which LU sessions are currently being used on the gateway. SNAP also displays CPU and memory usage within the gateway.

The Ethernet gateways show up as nodes on the DECnet network. These gateways have to be loaded with software every time they reboot. The VAXes on the Ethernet which can load the gateways are called load hosts. Loads can also be initiated by the NCP commands LOAD or TRIGGER issued from one of the VAXes. The LOAD command loads the gateway from the software on the VAX issuing the command:

```
$ NCP LOAD NODE SNAGWY   !Load the gateway from this node.
```

The gateway parameters, like passwords for each logical session, are loaded from the current node. The current node must be configured for loading the gateway software. The TRIGGER command sends

1. Direct connection from a VAX

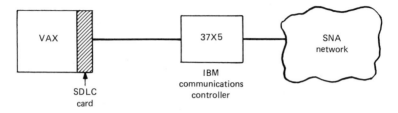

2. Ethernet connection shared by VAXES, type 1

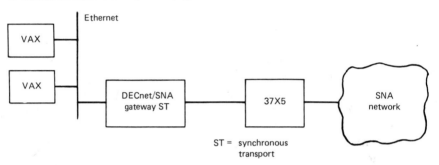

3. Ethernet connection shared by VAXES, type 2

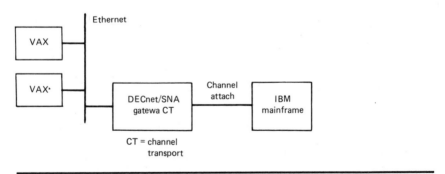

Figure 11.3   SNA network connectivity.

a message to the gateway telling it to ask for a load from the network. Nodes which have the gateway set up in their NCP databases will respond by a message effectively saying "I can load you". The gateway then tells the first node responding to load it. This technique is also used by the gateway when it is first powered up.

```
$ NCP  TRIGGER  NODE  SNAGWY  !Tells gateway to ask for a load.
                              !This node may or may not load the
                              !software.
```

If there are a number of VAXes on the Ethernet which can load the gateways and some of them are powered down, the TRIGGER command issued from any VAX will cause the gateways to be reloaded from any VAX which is up and has the load software.

11.8 FURTHER READING

Networking, Vol. 5A, System Management Manuals
DECnet/SNA VMS Gateway Management Manual.
Digital Technical Journal, Issue 3: "Networking Products." Digital Press, Maynard, Mass., 1986.
Digital Technical Journal, Issue 9: "Distributed Systems." Digital Press, Maynard, Mass., 1989.
Malamud, Carl, *DEC Networks and Architectures*, McGraw-Hill, New York 1989.

Chapter

12

VAXclusters

A VAXcluster is two or more VAXes sharing resources like disk drives and print queues. The words VAXcluster and cluster are used synonymously in this book. Figure 12.1 shows a small cluster. What is the advantage of such a configuration over three VAXes with their own disk and tape drives connected together by an Ethernet based DECnet network?

1. The disk and tape drives on the cluster can be used as local devices by the three VAXes. On Ethernet, a user would have to log in to the other VAX (either directly or indirectly when using say a COPY command) to use its devices.

2. Disk files can be shared on the cluster. Three applications, one on each VAX on the cluster, can access the same database files on a common disk. Record locking is implemented by the cluster software. Data sharing is possible over Ethernet (via DECnet), but programs are more complicated and may contain esoteric code.

3. When a VAX on the cluster accesses disk data, the VAX does not require assistance of another VAX. Effectively, system throughput is nearly three times that of an individual VAX on the cluster. On Ethernet, when one VAX accesses files on a disk attached to the other VAX, CPU time is consumed on both the VAXes.

4. The cluster has high availability. In a well-planned cluster, a single hardware failure will have minimal impact on operations. Also managing a cluster is easier than managing a set of VAXes connected via Ethernet.

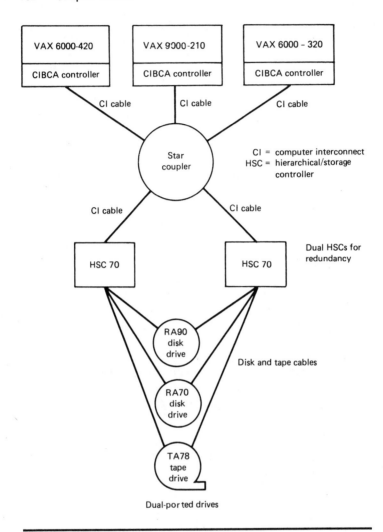

Figure 12.1   A CI-based three-VAX cluster.

12.1   CLUSTER BASICS

Computer interconnect (CI) is a bus. Ethernet is also a bus. But the protocols used on the the buses are different. CI has a bandwidth of 70 Mbits/sec. In contrast, Ethernet has a theoretical bandwidth of 10 Mbits/sec while practical throughput may be about 3 Mbits/sec because of message collisions. Each VAX on a CI based cluster has a CI device controller in its cabinet. The controller is connected to a passive junction box called the star coupler (currently, the product name is SC008). VAXes and HSC controllers are considered as nodes. The

HSC (Heirarchical Storage Controller) is an intelligent disk and tape drive controller which allows VAXes on the cluster to share these devices. The devices are 'seen' as local devices on the VAXes. Disk files can be shared by the VAXes effectively allowing cluster-applications with a throughput approaching the sum of CPU speed of the individual VAXes.

A cluster can also be configured over Ethernet, although it would have a much lower throughput than a CI-based cluster. An Ethernet-based cluster is called a Local Area VAXcluster (LAVc). A CI-based cluster and a LAVc can join to form a mixed-interconnect cluster. On a LAVc, the Ethernet is used for DECnet and cluster communications though each use a different protocol.

12.2 CLUSTER TERMINOLOGY

VAXport drivers are the software device drivers, similar to other device drivers on the nodes. There are two VAXport drivers: PADRIVER.EXE and PEDRIVER.EXE. PADRIVER.EXE is used by CI-based VAXes to communicate on the cluster hardware. PEDRIVER.EXE is used by Ethernet based LAVcs.

System communications services (SCS) is the software on each cluster node which implements communications in a cluster. It makes use of the VAXport drivers.

Connection manager is the software on each node that manages cluster connectivity. It is a layer above SCS.

Distributed file services is the cluster software on each node which manages disk and file sharing. It also controls record locking by users on the cluster. It is a form of distributed RMS for file access.

Distributed lock manager is used to synchronize operations between nodes. It is used by other cluster software like the distributed file service and distributed job controller. Users can synchronize clustered applications by using $ENQ and $DEQ system calls.

Distributed job controller is used to manage cluster-wide batch and print queues. For example, a printer attached to one VAX can be used by all the VAXes in the cluster with the DCL PRINT command. Batch queues can be set up to distribute jobs to VAXes which are least busy. The jobs can be submitted from any VAX.

A *star coupler* is a junction box where the CI cables from all the nodes on the cluster are interconnected. Each CI connection from the node to the star coupler is dual-pathed for redundancy. Currently, the cable length cannot exceed 45 meters, effectively, all the nodes have to be within a 90 meters diameter circle. The star coupler is not used by Ethernet based clusters.

Heirarchical storage controller is an intelligent node on the CI cluster which controls disk and tape drives. Currently, it is does not have a VAX CPU. The HSC70 can control more devices than the HSC50, but otherwise they serve a similar function. The HSC connects to the star coupler with CI cables. It optimizes response time when a number of I/O requests are received from VAXes on the cluster.

12.3   SETTING UP A CLUSTER

System files, including the operating system, drivers, and layered software products, can be on a common disk for all nodes on the cluster. If the same files are used by all the VAXes, the configuration is a common environment (*homogeneous*) cluster. If the files are different for different VAXes, whether they are on one disk or on different disks, the configuration is a multiple environment (*heterogeneous*) cluster. The advantage of a common environment cluster is that operating system upgrades and installation of layered products has to be done only once for all the VAXes. Also, systems management is simplified since common command procedures can be placed in a common directory. If a product is licensed for a particular VAX in the cluster then it should be installed in that VAXes system directories only.

12.3.1   The common system disk

Most system files, the operating system, drivers, compilers, and utilities, can be common for all the VAXes in a cluster. Any system disk will contain the directory [VMS$COMMON] which contains subdirectories for common system files shared by all nodes. Each node on the cluster will also have its own system directory: [SYS0], [SYS1], [SYS2], and so on. All references to system directories are via the logical name SYS$SYSROOT. SYS$SYSROOT is defined as a search list consisting of two logical names, SYS$SPECIFIC and SYS$COMMON. SYS$SPECIFIC points to the node's private system directory. SYS$COMMON is an alias for the shared system directory [VMS$COMMON]. An alias is a different name for the same file. So, for example, [SYS0]SYS$COMMON.DIR is an alias for [000000]VMS$COMMON.DIR. (Aliases can be created by the "$ SET FILE/ENTER" command.)

Here are the logical name translations for SYS$SYSROOT on two nodes on a VAXcluster:

```
Translation of SYS$SYSROOT
---------------------------

(on node VAXTOP in a cluster)

$ SHOW LOGICAL SYS$SYSROOT
   "SYS$SYSROOT" = "SYS$SPECIFIC" (LNM$PROCESS_TABLE)
        = "SYS$COMMON"
 1 "SYS$SPECIFIC" = "DUB6:[SYS0.]" (LNM$SYSTEM_TABLE)
 1 "SYS$COMMON" = "DUB6:[SYS0.SYSCOMMON.]" (LNM$SYSTEM_TABLE)

(on node SCOOP in the same cluster)

$ SHOW LOGICAL SYS$SYSROOT
   "SYS$SYSROOT" = "SYS$SPECIFIC" (LNM$PROCESS_TABLE)
        = "SYS$COMMON"
 1 "SYS$SPECIFIC" = "DUB6:[SYS1.]" (LNM$SYSTEM_TABLE)
 1 "SYS$COMMON" = "DUB6:[SYS1.SYSCOMMON.]" (LNM$SYSTEM_TABLE)
```

When DCL commands are entered or any system files are accessed, the operating system first searches for files in the node-specific system directories (under SYS$SPECIFIC) . If the files are not in there, the operating system scans the common system directories (under SYS$COMMON, effectively under [VMS$COMMON]). So if a product is to be installed for clusterwide use, it should be installed under [VMS$COMMON]; if the product is for a specific VAX, it should be installed under SYS$SPECIFIC of that VAX. Some files like page and swap files cannot be common to all nodes so they are found under SYS$SPECIFIC of each node. Figure 12.2 shows the directory layout of the system disk on a common-disk cluster.

12.4   ALLOCATION CLASS

Two HSCs can be connected to one disk drive. This way, if one HSC fails, the VAXes on the cluster can access the disk drive via the other HSC. If the HSCs were independent, the drive might have two names depending on which HSC is being used to access the drive. For example, if the HSCs are NODEH1 and NODEH2, the drive names could be NODEH1$DUA1: and NODEH2$DUA1:. If these names were used then every time there is an HSC failure, the applications would have to check for the failure and use the other path. To circumvent this, the HSCs are given the same *allocation class*. This command has to be issued from each HSC console:

```
HSC> SET ALLOCATION DISK 5
```

The disk drive is now known as 5DUA1:. The cluster will use one of the two HSCs to access the disk. in case an HSC fails, the cluster will automatically use the other HSC.

Allocation classes can be used when there are dual paths to devices. This way if one path fails, the other is automatically used.

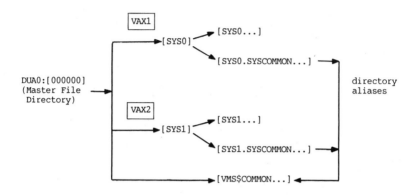

Figure 12.2   Directory structure of the common disk on a two-VAX cluster.

12.5   VOTES AND QUORUM

The design of the clustering architecture is such that if adequate care is not taken, the cluster can be partitioned into two smaller independent clusters which can lead to erratic behavior and disk corruption. To ensure that there is only one logical cluster on the CI hardware or Ethernet, each VAX is assigned a VOTE and it will join a cluster (or form a cluster) only if the sum of votes of the VAXes in the cluster exceeds a specified value called a QUORUM. VOTES is a SYSGEN parameter and QUORUM is calculated by the clustering software.

Here is how the scheme works. Suppose there are 5 VAXes in a cluster and each VAX has a vote of 1. HSCs do not have a vote. Suppose the quorum is set to 3. Total votes are 5, which is greater than the quorum value, so the cluster functions normally. Suppose a VAX fails. The total votes are 4, still greater than the quorum so the cluster functions normally. In fact, one more hardware failure will not matter. But if 3 VAXes fail, there will be only two VAXes up which would contribute a total of 2 votes which is less than the quorum value. In this case the cluster cannot continue. The main reason is, if the 3 failed VAXes come up, they can possibly form their own separate cluster which would cause two clusters to co-exist.

Typical value for a vote for each VAX is 4. The quorum is set by

$$QUORUM = (\text{Sum of all votes} + 2) / 2$$

Five VAXes in a cluster, each with a vote of 4 will have a quorum of 11.

The part of the VAX clustering software handling votes and quorum is called the Connection Manager. It reads a SYSGEN parameter, EXPECTED_VOTES, from the first VAX on the cluster and uses this to calculate a quorum value. The quorum value is then updated dynamically as VAXes join the cluster.

VOTES is a SYSGEN parameter on each node. It specifies the votes contributed to the cluster by the node. The EXPECTED_VOTES parameter is specified on each node. It is an estimate of the sum of all votes of all the cluster VAXes. It is used by the Connection Manager to calculate an initial QUORUM value. As VAXes join the cluster, the QUORUM value is adjusted by using the calculation shown above.

12.5.1 Quorum Disk

On a two-VAX cluster, the vote-and-quorum algorithm mentioned above cannot work, because if one VAX breaks down, the quorum algorithm shown above causes the remaining machine to be without a quorum. Hence, the cluster must fail. If the cluster does not fail, the system can have a one-VAX cluster which may cause a situation where each of the two VAXes function as an independent cluster. The way around this is to assign any disk shared by the VAXes as a quorum disk. The disk contributes votes to the cluster. This way, if one VAX fails, the other VAX with the quorum disk remains clustered. The failed VAX cannot come up and form a cluster unless it also uses the quorum disk or the other VAX, effectively ensuring that there is only one cluster.

If a quorum disk is used, each VAX has a SYSGEN parameter DISK_QUORUM which specifies the name of the disk. The votes contributed by the quorum disk are given by the SYSGEN parameter QDSKVOTES.

12.6 FURTHER READING

VAXcluster Systems Handbook.
VAXcluster Manual, Vol. 1B, System Management Manual.
Guide to Setting up a System, Vol. 1A, System Management Manual.
Digital Technical Journal, Issue 5: "VAXcluster Systems." Digital Press, Maynard, Mass., 1987.
"VAXclusters: A Closely-Coupled Distributed System." *ACM Transactions on Computer Systems*, May 1986, pp.130–146.

Chapter

13

Systems Management and Operator Functions

Systems managers and operators have the common function of ensuring smooth daily operation, operations planning, and user support. In a small organization, the system manager may be the operator (and even a programmer), while in a very large organization, system management functions may be handled by network managers, system performance reviewers, capacity planners, and operations managers. Typical system management tasks are

- Booting (bringing up) and shutting down the system.
- Creating and modifying user profiles: accounts, privileges and quotas.
- Monitoring system activity. Monitoring users, CPU, memory, disk usage, network operations and processes.
- Enforcing security for the system, individual applications, and users.
- Enforcing resource quotas for users.
- Generating accounting reports on resource usage by users.
- Scheduling and monitoring batch and print jobs.
- Installing and upgrading software products.
- Monitoring system reliability; monitoring and auditing hardware errors.
- Monitoring system performance and behavior.
- Auditing system performance and user requirements for capacity planning.
- Customizing system command files and SYSGEN parameters.
- LAT terminals and terminal server management.

- Mounting and dismounting devices.
- Performing disk backups.
- Checking disks for file corruptions.
- Disk management.

All of these tasks are discussed in this chapter unles they have been covered elsewhere in this book.

13.1 BOOTING THE SYSTEM

Each system has one terminal called the *console terminal*. This is the only terminal which can interact with the system even when the system is "halted." On the 8000 series VAXes, the console actually consists of a microcomputer with its own hard disk and floppy drives. The console is used to start the system and can also be used as a regular terminal after the system is booted. Obviously, the console should be placed where it is secure from access by unauthorized personnel.

To start the system, the operating system must be residing on a disk connected to the system. In a new installation, the operating system is loaded on disk from tape by the standalone BACKUP program which can be loaded from tape. The distribution operating system is also available on media like CDROM.

The information in this paragraph applies to most VAXes, though not all. The console prompt is > > >. If this prompt is not seen, then a CTRL/P should be entered. The system can be booted by first halting the system and then issuing the BOOT command with the disk name of the disk containing the operating system:

```
> > >  HALT
> > >  BOOT DUA4
```

On a cluster, each VAX (node) will have to be booted individually. The operating system is loaded in memory. Initialization of operating system data structures and memory are then performed by the operating system. The core of the operating system is contained in the disk directory SYS$LOADABLE_IMAGES:. Other files accessed are RMS.EXE, DCL.EXE, SYS$LIBRARY:DCLTABLES.EXE, F11AACP.EXE, F11BXQP.EXE, SYS$MESSAGE:SYSMSG.EXE, STARTUP.COM, LOGINOUT.EXE. The loading process takes a few minutes (up to 15 minutes on some VAXes).

Just after the load, the operating system executes the command file SYS$MANAGER:SYSTARTUP_V5.COM. (If the operating system version is below V5.0 then the file is SYS$MANAGER:SYSTARTUP.COM). The system manager usually puts system startup commands in this file.

Here is a simplified start up file:

```
$ SET NOON
$ WRITE SYS$OUTPUT "The VAX/VMS system is now executing SYSTARTUP_V5.COM"
$!
$ DEFINE /SYSTEM /EXEC SYS$SYLOGIN SYS$MANAGER:SYLOGIN
$ DEFINE /SYSTEM SYS$ANNOUNCE "@SYS$MANAGER:ANNOUNCE.TXT"
$ DEFINE /SYSTEM SYS$WELCOME "@SYS$MANAGER:WELCOME.TXT"
$!
$ @SYS$MANAGER:STARTNET          !Start DECNET
$!
 $@SYS$MANAGER:LTLOADTERM          !Start LAT and customize terminals
$!
$ MOUNT/NOASSIST/SYSTEM DUA5: USERDISK
$ MOUNT/NOASSIST/SYSTEM DJB1: DEVELOP
$!
$!Startup files for layered products
$ @SYS$MANAGER:FMSTARTUP          !Forms Management System
$ @SYS$MANAGER:CDDSTRTUP.COM      !Common Data Dictionary
$ @SYS$MANAGER:SDD$STARTUP        !VAXsim
$ @SYS$SYSTEM:STARTUP SMISERVER   !Required by SYSMAN
$!Start the queue manager and queues
$ @SYS$MANAGER:STARTQUE
$ EXIT
```

Once the file is executed, the system is ready for use. Terminals on DECservers can access the system only if the file @SYS$MANAGER:LTLOAD.COM is executed to enable LAT terminals.

The file SYS$MANAGER:SYLOGIN.COM executes every time a user logs into the system. The file can be customized to perform initializations for every user. It may contain, say, definition of a DCL symbol which will be used by everyone.

13.2   SHUTTING DOWN THE SYSTEM

To bring down the system, the command to be entered is

```
$ @SYS$SYSTEM:SHUTDOWN.COM
```

The system should be checked for activity before this command is used. Useful commands to check the system are:

```
$ SHOW SYSTEM              !Any processes which are not supposed to
                           !be executing?
$ SHOW BATCH               !Any jobs in background?
$ MONITOR  :==  $MONITOR   !Declare MONITOR to be a foreign DCL
                           !command.
$ MONITOR SYSTEM           !What is the CPU and memory utilization?
```

Any user having the OPER privilege can shut down the system. The command can be issued from any terminal—not necessarily the console. The command file issues warning messages to all users before proceeding further. The command file then executes another command file SYS$MANAGER:SYSHUTDWN.COM. This file can be customized to include commands for bringing down applications and perform cleanups required for the installation. Note that the file SYS$SYSTEM:SHUTDOWN.COM must not be modified. The system can be rebooted automatically if specified when answering the shutdown questions. If automatic reboot is not specified, the system can be rebooted later from the system console.

Here is a sample shutdown process (slightly modified).

```
$ @SYS$SYSTEM:SHUTDOWN

       SHUTDOWN -- Perform an Orderly System Shutdown

How many minutes until final shutdown [0]: 5
Reason for shutdown [Standalone]: Testing reboot
Do you want to spin down the disk volumes [NO]?
Do you want to invoke the site-specific shutdown procedure [YES]?
Should an automatic system reboot be performed [NO]? YES
When will the system be rebooted [shortly via automatic reboot]:
Shutdown options (enter as a comma-separated list):
  REBOOT_CHECK        Check existence of basic system files
  SAVE_FEEDBACK       Save AUTOGEN feedback information from this boot

Shutdown options [NONE]: reboot_check
%%%%%%%%%%  OPCOM    8-JUN-1989 16:23:00.91  %%%%%%%%%%
Operator _RTA3: has been enabled, username TECH4

%SHUTDOWN-I-OPERATOR, This terminal is now an operator's console.
%%%%%%%%%%  OPCOM    8-JUN-1989 16:23:00.92  %%%%%%%%%%
Operator status for operator _RTA3:
CENTRAL, PRINTER, TAPES, DISKS, DEVICES, CARDS, NETWORK, CLUSTER, SECURITY,
LICENSE, OPER1, OPER2, OPER3, OPER4, OPER5, OPER6, OPER7, OPER8, OPER9, OPER10,
OPER11, OPER12

%SHUTDOWN-I-DISLOGINS, Interactive logins will now be disabled.
%SET-I-INTSET, login interactive limit = 0, current interactive value = 5
%SHUTDOWN-I-SHUTNET, The DECnet network will now be shut down.
%SHUTDOWN-I-STOPQUEMAN, The queue manager will now be stopped.
%JBC-E-JOBQUEDIS, system job queue manager is not running

SHUTDOWN message from user TECH4 at _RTA3:   16:23:03
SCOOP will shut down in 0 minutes; back up shortly via automatic reboot.
Please log off node SCOOP.
Testing reboot
7 terminals have been notified.

%SHUTDOWN-I-SITESHUT, The site-specific shutdown procedure will now be invoked.
%SHUTDOWN-I-STOPUSER, All user processes will now be stopped.
%SHUTDOWN-I-REMOVE, All installed images will now be removed.
%SHUTDOWN-I-DISMOUNT, All volumes will now be dismounted.
%SHUTDOWN-I-DISMOUNTDEV, Dismounting device _DUA0:.
%SHUTDOWN-I-DISMOUNTDEV, Dismounting device _DJC3:.

%%%%%%%%%%  OPCOM    8-JUN-1989 16:23:08.78  %%%%%%%%%%
Message from user TECH4
_RTA3:, SCOOP shutdown was requested by the operator.

%%%%%%%%%%  OPCOM    8-JUN-1989 16:23:09.00  %%%%%%%%%%
Logfile was closed by operator _RTA3:
Logfile was SYS$SYSROOT:[SYSMGR]OPERATOR.LOG;13

%%%%%%%%%%  OPCOM    8-JUN-1989 16:23:09.10  %%%%%%%%%%
Operator _RTA3: has been disabled, username TECH4
```

13.3   SYSTEM CRASH

The system can be stopped abruptly by entering a CTRL/P followed by the HALT command at the console terminal. This is not recommended but may be required in an emergency. The system will also shut down abnormally in case of a power failure or operating system failure. When the system is later rebooted, the disks will not be corrupted, although files open for write may be. Incomplete batch and print jobs can be restarted from the beginning. The effect on applications would depend on how the applications are designed. DECnet and the cluster will resynchronize with the other nodes, but network operations which were in progress during the crash will have to be redone.

13.4   USER ACCOUNTS

Account information is stored in the indexed file SYS$SYSTEM:-SYSUAF.DAT. Here the word account means profile. The file is accessed by the AUTHORIZE utility:

```
$ SET  DEFAULT  SYS$SYSTEM:    !Change current directory
$ RUN  AUTHORIZE
UAF>
```

The UAF> prompt is issued by the AUTHORIZE utility. UAF is an acronym for User Authorization File. Although, normally the system manager will maintain accounts, any user on the system with the necessary privileges can manipulate accounts. An example of creation of a new account is:

```
UAF>  ADD SHAH /DIR=[SHAH]/DEV=DUA3:/UIC=[122,33] -
/PASSWORD=JALQUL/FLAG=NODISUSER
```

Here a user, SHAH, is added to the system. His default directory at log-in will be [SHAH] on the disk DUA3:. His user identification code (UIC) will be [122,33] and his log-in password will be JALQUL. All other parameters will have default values. A new record will be inserted in the file SYSUAF.DAT. Once the account is created, SHAH can log into the system with username SHAH and password JALQUL.

The MODIFY command is similar to the ADD command except that it changes account information of an existing user:

```
UAF>  MODIFY SHAH/PASS=TIMPAL
```

The SHOW command displays information on one or more users.

```
UAF> SHOW SHAH

Username: SHAH                          Owner:
Account:                               UIC:    [122,33] ([SHAH])
CLI:    DCL                            Tables: DCLTABLES
Default:  DUA3:[SHAH]
LGICMD:   LOGIN
Login Flags:
Primary days:   Mon Tue Wed Thu Fri
Secondary days:                     Sat Sun
Primary   0000000000011111111112222  Secondary 0000000000011111111112222
Day Hours 012345678901234567890123  Day Hours 012345678901234567890123
Network:  ##### Full access ######             ##### Full access ######
Batch:    ##### Full access ######             ##### Full access ######
Local:    ##### Full access ######             ##### Full access ######
Dialup:   ----- No access ------             ----- No access ------
Remote:   ##### Full access ######             ##### Full access ######
Expiration:           (none)   Pwdminimum:  6   Login Fails:     0
Pwdlifetime:        30 00:00   Pwdchange:       (pre-expired)
Last Login:           (none)  (interactive),          (none) (non-interactive)
Maxjobs:         0  Fillm:       20  Bytlm:      10000
Maxacctjobs:     0  Shrfillm:     0  Pbytlm:         0
Maxdetach:       0  BIOlm:       18  JTquota:     1024
Prclm:           2  DIOlm:       18  WSdef:        200
Prio:            4  ASTlm:       24  WSquo:        500
Queprio:         0  TQElm:       10  WSextent:    1000
CPU:        (none)  Enqlm:       30  Pgflquo:    10000
Authorized Privileges:
  TMPMBX NETMBX
Default Privileges:
  TMPMBX NETMBX
```

The fields are described in Table 13.1. Most of the fields can be modified by specifying them as a qualifer with a value. For example, to modify the owner field the command would be

```
UAF> MODIFY  SHAH/OWNER="Jay Shah"
```

13.4.1 Proxy accounts

To copy a file over the network from system TOPPER to the current system, the user can enter a command like:

```
$ COPY  TOPPER"SMITH JAYKAP"::TEST.DATA  *.*
```

The file TEST.DATA will be copied from system TOPPER to the current system. The user has to enter his or her user name and password (SMITH and JAYKAP) after the node name for his account on system TOPPER. The string

```
"SMITH JAYKAP"
```

is called the access control string. It will normally be required for every command accessing other nodes over the network. The problem is that people standing nearby or someone eavesdropping the network can note your password for the system TOPPER. To avoid entering the username and password, a network proxy account for you can be created by the system manager on system TOPPER.

TABLE 13.1   Account information

Field	Description
Username	User name for log-in.
Owner	Can be used to store user's full name.
Account	Used by the account report generator. Users on the same project can be given a common account name so that a common resource usage report is generated.
UIC	User identification code.
CLI	Default command interpreter. Do not change this.
Tables	Default table which contains command definitions. Do not change this.
Default	Specifies user's default device and directory. To specify this use the qualifiers /DEVICE and /DIRECTORY.
LGICMD	This command file is executed by the system just after a successful login. The file should be in the default device and directory. Normally, this file is LOGIN.COM. Users can put in commands which will be automatically executed on login.
Login flags	These flags are set by the system manager. An example is DISUSER. This flag does not allow the user to log in, although the account file has a valid user name and password.
Primary and Secondary days and day hours	These are used to specify the days and hours of access to the system. Note that the hours are read off with first digit on one line and the second digit on the next line. In this case, the hours are from 00 through 23. For example,
	UAF> MODIFY SHAH/ACCESS = (PRIMARY,9-17)
	UAF> MODIFY SHAH/NOACCESS = SECONDARY
	allows access Monday through Friday 9 am to 5 pm and no access on Saturday and Sunday.
Network, Batch, Local, Dialup, Remote	These five fields can be used to restrict the type of access by primary and secondary days and hours.
Expiration	Specifies when the account expires.
Pwdminimum	Specifies the minimum length of the password which will be accepted when changed.
Login Fails	Number of log-in failures due to invalid passwords. Possible intrusion attempt.
Pwdlifetime	After a password change, the user of the account must change the password again within Pwdlifetime time. Otherwise the account will be disabled.
Pwdchange	Specifies when the password was last changed. Preexpired is for new accounts. It means that the current password is valid for one log-in only; the user will have to change the password after logging in.
Last Logon	Last time of log-in both interactive and noninteractive (noninteractive could be network or batch log-in).
Maxjobs	maximum number of processes allowed.
Maxacctjobs	maximum number of processes allowed excluding network logins.

TABLE 13.1   Account information (*Continued*)

Field	Description
Maxdetach	maximum detached jobs allowed. Detached processes may be created by the $RUN/DETACH command.
Prclm	Maximum sub-processes allowed.
Prio	Priority of processes. A value above 8 for normal processes is not recommended.
Queprio	Priority of batch and queue jobs. 0 means use default.
CPU	Specifies maximum CPU time allowed per process.
Fillm	maximum number of open files allowed.
Shrfillm	maximum number of open shared files allowed.
BIOlm	Buffered i/o limit. This is the maximum number of buffered i/o operations like terminal i/o which can be outstanding at any time.
DIOlm	Direct i/o limit. This is the maximum number of direct i/o operations like disk i/o which can be outstanding at any time.
ASTlm	Specifies maximum number of ASTs which can be outstanding at any time. ASTs are queued for scheduled wakeups like running of print and batch jobs at a preset time.
TQElm	Timer queue limit. Specifies maximum timer queue entries and event flag clusters which can be outstanding.
Enqlm	Enqueue limit. Specifies maximum number of lock queue entries which can be outstanding.
Bytlm	Maximum number of bytes of nonpaged dynamic memory which can be used at any time. This memory may be used for I/O buffering.
Pbytlm	?
JTquota	Size in bytes for jobwide logical name table.
WSdef	Initial working set size in pages for the process. A page is 512 bytes.
WSquo	Working set size the process can expand to if it needs extra memory.
WSextent	The process can expand more than the number of pages specified by WSquo if the system has additional free pages. WSextent is the limit for this expansion.
Pgflquo	Maximum number of pages the process can use in the system paging file.

The command would be:

```
UAF> ADD/PROXY SCOOP::SMITH SMITH
```

Here, user SMITH on node SCOOP is given access to the current node TOPPER with the account on the current node to be used being SMITH. Now when SMITH performs network operations from node SCOOP to node TOPPER, the username and password need not be specified:

```
$ COPY TOPPER::TEST.DATA *.*
```

Note that if SMITH is logged on system TOPPER and he wishes to access system SCOOP using a proxy account, then the proxy account has to be created on SCOOP. This way, the passwords are not entered on terminals or command files.

To see all the network proxys, the command is

```
UAF > SHOW/PROXY  *
```

The database for proxy accounts is in the file SYS$SYSTEM:-NETPROXY.DAT and the AUTHORIZE program maintains this database.

13.4.2 Rights identifiers

Objects (files, devices, logical name tables, queues, and global sections) can be protected by using UIC-based protection. But suppose a file is to be set up so that it can be accessed by Mary and Joe only. Mary is in UIC [200,5] and Joe is in UIC [122,32]. UIC-based protection cannot be used since Mary and Joe are in separate UIC groups. Also, other users may share UIC groups with Mary and Joe, but they should not be allowed to access the file. The solution is to assign a *rights identifier*, say, SECURE_DATA to Mary and Joe. The file can then be protected (by ACLs as explained later) so that only users holding the SECURE_DATA rights identifier can access the file. In future, another user can be given access to the file by granting the user the rights identifier SECURE_DATA.

Rights identifier information is stored in the file SYS$SYSTEM:RIGHTSLIST.DAT. The AUTHORIZE program is used to maintain the rights database. Normally, when a new account is created, one right is granted to the user. The name of the right is the user's username. New identifiers can be created as

```
UAF > ADD/IDENTIFIER  SECURE_DATA
```

To grant the SECURE_DATA identifier to MARY and JOE the commands are

```
UAF > GRANT/IDENTIFER  SECURE_DATA  MARY
UAF > GRANT/IDENTIFER  SECURE_DATA  JOE
```

Now when the SHOW MARY command is issued, the account information for MARY along with the rights identifiers held by MARY is displayed. Rights identifiers can be granted to other rights identifiers which allows a tree structure of rights to be built. The next section describes how to use these rights identifiers for protection of objects.

13.5   ACCESS CONTROL LISTS (ACLs)

Continuing the example above, the file EMPLOYEE.DATABASE can be protected so that only Mary and Joe can access it.

```
$ SET  ACL  EMPLOYEE.DATABASE
              /ACL=(IDENTIFIER=[*,*],ACCESS=NONE)
$ SET  ACL  EMPLOYEE.DATABASE
              /ACL=(IDENTIFIER=SECURE_DATA,ACCESS=READ+WRITE)
```

Here two ACEs are created on the file. The second ACE effectively says that the ACL protection is based on rights list identifiers and the holder of the identifier SECURE_DATA can perform READ and WRITE operations on the file (but no DELETE, EXECUTE, or CONTROL operations). The first ACE effectively says that the protection is based on UIC and that users having any UIC group and member have no access to the file. The ACEs are inserted at the top of the list so note that the second ACL will be checked before the first one when a user attempts to access the file.

The command DIRECTORY/ACL EMPLOYEE.DATABASE will list the two access control entries (ACEs) for the file. The set of ACEs for an object is called an access control list (ACL). As many ACEs as required can be created for an object. Identifiers can be specified as UICs or rights identifiers.

Note that when a user attempts to access an object, the ACL is checked first; the UIC protection is checked only if no ACL entry matches. For simplicity, it is better to set access by UIC such that no one is allowed access to the object if no ACL entry matches the user's identifiers.

In summary,

- Rights identifiers are useful to protect an object so that only a specified set of users and no one else can access the object. Decide on the name of an identifier for the object to be protected.

- Declare the name in the rights identifier database by the command

```
UAF> ADD/IDENTIFER  id-name
```

- Set ACLs on the object so that only owners of the identifier can access then object. Use the command

```
$ SET  ACL  object-name /ACL=(Access Control Entry)
```

- Grant the identifier to authorized users by the command

```
UAF> GRANT/IDENTIFIER  id-name  user-name
```

13.6 DISK BACKUPS

The BACKUP command can be used to back up complete disks or selected files onto tapes or other disks. The same command is used for restore operations. The files being backed up should not be open for write when the backup is in progress. This ensures integrity of the backup contents.

13.6.1 Complete disk backups

Here is a set of commands to back up the complete disk DUB5: to tapes on MUA1:,

```
$ DISMOUNT/NOUNLOAD  DUB5:    !In case there was a previously mounted
                             !tape.
$ MOUNT  DUB5:  DISK5        !DISK5 is the volume label for DUB5:
$ INITIALIZE  MUA1:  D5BCK   !Label the tape D5BCK.
$ MOUNT/FOREIGN  MUA1:       !Mount the tape for the backup.
$ BACKUP/IMAGE  DUB5:  MUA1: !Perform the disk to tape backup.
```

/IMAGE records volume initialization information like disk label and cluster size. When /IMAGE is used, only complete volumes can be backed up; selected files cannot be backed up. More than one tape may be required in which case the system will prompt for a new tape to be mounted when the previous one is used up. These commands are convenient to back up all disks regularly. The tape is mounted with the /FOREIGN qualifier for most BACKUP commands.

In case the disk is subsequently corrupted, the backed up data can be restored by

```
$ MOUNT/FOREIGN  MUA1:
$ BACKUP/IMAGE  MUA1:D5BCK/SAVE_SET  DUB5:
```

The disk is mounted as a normal Files-11 device. The complete disk backup and restore operation is also useful to make all files contiguous on highly fragmented disks. Selected files can also be restored from the image backup by (DUB5 is mounted normally):

```
$ BACKUP  MUA1:D5BCK/SAVE_SET/SELECT=(*.COB;*, *.DATA;*)
   DUB5:[TOPLEVEL...]
```

13.6.2 Backup of selected files and directories

Here is a set of commands to back up the files in directory [TOPLEVEL] and all its subdirectories to tape

```
$ MOUNT/FOREIGN  MUA1:
$ BACKUP  DUB5:[TOPLEVEL...]*.*;*  MUA1:TOP.BCK/SAVE_SET
```

The files will be backed up on tape in a backup file called TOP.BCK. This file is called a save set. Save sets are container files which contain other files and they can be processed by the BACKUP command only. Note that the /SAVE_SET qualifier must follow the name of the save set. The files can be restored by

```
$ BACKUP  MUA1:TOP.BCK/SAVE_SET  DUB5:[TOPLEVEL...]
```

If the files are already present on disk then they will not be restored unless the /OVERLAY, /NEW_VERSION, or /REPLACE qualifier is specified on the command line.

All the files under [TOPLEVEL] in the tape save set can be restored to another directory tree under the directory [NEWTOP.TOPLEVEL] by the command:

```
$ BACKUP  MUA1:TOP.BCK/SAVE_SET  DUB5:[NEWTOP...]
```

It is possible to create multiple save sets on one tape. For example, if the backup of [TOPLEVEL] was followed by the command:

```
$ BACKUP  DUB5:[APPL...]  MUA1:APPL.BCK/SAVE_SET
```

then directory [APPL] and all its subdirectories are backed up to a second save set on the tape.

13.6.3 Directory of backups

The save sets on a tape with the files they contain can be listed by

```
$ BACKUP/REWIND/LIST  MUA1:*
```

The files in a particular save-set, say, APPL.BCK, can be listed by

```
$ BACKUP/REWIND/LIST MUA1:APPL.BCK/SAVE_SET

Listing of save set(s)

Save set:            APPL.BCK
Written by:          SHAH4
UIC:                 [000001,000032]
Date:                1-DEC-1989 15:23:45.68
Command:             BACKUP DUB5:[APPL...] MUA0:APPL.BCK/SAVE
Operating system:    VAX/VMS version V4.7
BACKUP version:      V4.7
CPU ID register:     01200123
Node name:           _SCOOP::
Written on:          _MUA0:
Block size:          8192
Group size:          10
Buffer count:        3

[APPL.TMP]CPU.COM;1                    1    9-NOV-1988 13:41
[APPL.TMP]DIRSEARCH.COM;2              1   27-OCT-1988 16:09
[APPL.TMP]EBC1.DAT;1                   1   25-MAY-1989 14:59
[APPL.TMP]REPRINT_REPORT.COM;46        8   11-APR-1989 11:53

Total of 4 files, 11 blocks
End of save set
```

13.6.4   Network backups

Files and directories can be backed up to a save set on another VAX/VMS system on the network:

```
$ BACKUP  DUB5:[TOPLEVEL...]*.*;*  BACVAX::DJC1:TOP.BCK/SAVE_SET
```

Here the directory [TOPLEVEL] and its subdirectories are backed up from the current system to the system BACVAX::.

Note that it is not possible at the current time to restore a save set over the network (the save set being on one system and the restore to be performed on another).

13.6.5   Other qualifiers

The /LOG qualifier displays the list of files as they are being backed up or restored.

The /VERIFY qualifier causes backup to compare the original files and the files backed up after the files are backed up. It increases confidence in the integrity of the backup.

The /REWIND qualifier can be used to create the save set at the beginning of the tape. If this qualifier is not specified, the save set is created after any save sets existing on the tape.

The /NOASSIST qualifier causes messages to be sent to the terminal issuing the command. Normally, messages are sent to the operator console.

13.6.6   Standalone backup

Standalone backup is used to load VMS. It can also be used to perform backups just like the normal VMS BACKUP utility.

Although not required, when backing up the complete system disk, standalone backup can be used if there are files open for write, like the system operator log file.

Standalone backup has similar commands to normal backup except that it can be used to back up and restore complete devices (files cannot be selected for backup). To boot standalone backup, normal VMS has to be shutdown and the following command can be issued from the console:

```
>>>BOOT/R5=E0000000  DUA0:
```

or

```
>>>BOOT  MUA0:
```

where DUA0: and MUA0: are devices containing the standalone backup. Standalone backup can be created on any disk or tape by running

@SYS$UPDATE:STABACKIT.COM. The command file will prompt for the device on which standalone backup is to be created. The device could be the disk on which the operating system is resident.

Standalone backup on tape is useful to restore the system disk when the system does not boot due to corruption of the system disk. Many sites do not use standalone backup as this involves shutting the system down which may not be acceptable. In this case, they should ensure that disk activity on the disk being backed up will not affect the backup operation.

13.7 SECURITY ISSUES

Broadly, there are two classes of protections that can be enforced:

1. Protection of access to objects like files, disks and global sections.

2. Protection against unauthorized access to the system.

13.7.1 Protection of objects

Objects are files, devices, logical name tables, queues and global sections. UIC-based protection was discussed in the chapter on files and directories. It can be used to protect objects based on user type (system, owner, group, and world) and protection type (read access, write access, delete privilege, and execute access).

Objects can also be protected by ACLs as discussed above. ACL access types are also read access, write access, delete privilege, execute access. Each user can be assigned a subset of these access types against each object.

To see the UIC- and ACL-based protections set on a file, the command is

```
$ DIRECTORY/SECURITY  *.COB
```

One problem with UIC- and ACL-based protection is that the protections can be modified by users having the SETPRV (or some other) process privileges. Effectively, system administrators and similar "superusers" have access to all files on the system. One solution for the owner of the file is to encrypt files so that the contents cannot be determined. Encryption algorithms are widely available. DEC also has a software product called VMS Encryption. This product is a software implementation of the *National Bureau of Standards Data Encryption Standard* (DES).

13.7.2 Log-ins and passwords

Since passwords are stored in disks using one-way encryption algorithms, anyone reading the password file SYS$SYSTEM:SYSUAF.DAT will be able to see other log-in parameters for users but not the password. In fact, if users forget passwords, system managers usually give them a new password since even he or she cannot find out user passwords from the system.

A user name and password are normally required to log into the system. Since user names are not secret, a potential intruder can use someone else's user name and try guessing passwords. What can be done to protect the system against such a possibility?

On most VMS systems, three log-in attempts are allowed before the log-in process terminates. Usually, this is not considered a break-in attempt (no action is taken) and users can continue attempting log-ins. (They will have to redial into the system if using DIALUP lines.) System managers can set up security alarms (described later) so that a message prints out at the console terminals giving information about the user name and terminal from which the log-in failed. Actually, three log-in attempts are allowed in 20 seconds. These two parameters are SYSGEN parameters which can be changed even when the system is running:

SYSGEN parameter LGI_RETRY_LIM, default value 3 attempts

SYSGEN parameter LGI_RETRY_TMO, default value 20 seconds

To change these parameters until the system is rebooted use

```
$ RUN SYS$SYSTEM:SYSGEN
SYSGEN> SET LGI_RETRY_LIM 6
SYSGEN> SET LGI_RETRY_TMO 30
SYSGEN> WRITE ACTIVE
SYSGEN> EXIT
```

Constant monitoring of the console terminal is required to note log-in failures. This may not be convenient.

Better solutions are to disable the user account permanently until further action is taken or disable the user from logging in again for a period of time. These can be done automatically if the system detects a break-in attempt.

What is a *break-in attempt*? Two SYSGEN parameters control when failed log-ins are considered as break-in attempts:

SYSGEN parameter LGI_BRK_TMO, default value 300 seconds

SYSGEN parameter LGI_BRK_LIM, default value 5 attempts

These parameters imply that, on the average, one login failure will be tolerated every 300 seconds or 5 minutes. If more than five consecutive failures occur within 25 minutes then the login is considered a break-in attempt. These parameters can be changed by using the SYSGEN utility.

Two actions will be taken by the system on attempted break-ins:

1. Disable further log-ins for some time from that terminal or user name. By default, log-ins are disabled from the particular terminal by the username. This method is useless if the terminal is on a terminal server since terminal names change from one session to another. (For example, the terminal name could be LTA21: on the first log-in attempt and LTA33: on another log-in attempt from the same terminal). In this case, the solution is to set the SYSGEN parameter LGI_BRK_TERM to 0 so that a user name is disabled regardless of the terminal used. The duration the user will have to wait before the system will validate log-ins is a random number (to fox the potential intruder) based on the system parameter LGI_HID_TIM.

2. Automatically disable the user account by setting the log-in flag /DISUSER in the authorization file, SYS$SYSTEM:SYSUAF.DAT. This action is drastic and will be taken only if the SYSGEN parameter LGI_BRK_DISUSER is set to 1 (normally it is 0).

To see a list of intruders use

```
$ SHOW INTRUSION
```

Intrusion	Type	Count	Expiration	Source
NETWORK	INTRUDER	5	14:48:21.29	SCOOP::SHAH4
TERMINAL	SUSPECT	3	14:38:21.29	_LTA23:
TERMINAL	SUSPECT	3	14:38:29.18	_LTA24:
TERMINAL	SUSPECT	3	14:38:21.29	_LTA23:SHAH4

Intrusion type is SUSPECT when the user cannot log in in the default three attempts; it is INTRUDER when a log-in is a break-in attempt.

Intrusion entries can be deleted by

```
$ DELETE/INTRUSION_RECORD "SCOOP::SHAH4"    !Delete one intrusion
                                             entry.
```

13.7.3   Security audits (Since VMS V5.2)

Security-related information is processed by the process AUDIT_SERVER on the system. Previously, the events were logged in the operator log file SYS$MANAGER:OPERATOR.LOG, but since the release of VMS V5.2, the events are logged in SYS$MANAGER:SECURITY_AUDIT.AUDIT$JOURNAL and optionally logged in the operator log file. The SECAUDIT.COM file used (previous to V5.2) to display security events is replaced by ANALYZE/AUDIT command.

The command to enable logging of security messages is:

```
$ SET  AUDIT √ALARM/ENABLE=alarm-types
```

where alarm-types are

ACL	Display objects which are accessed and has an ACL alarm set.
ALL	All types of alarms should be reported.
AUDIT	Display any SET AUDIT command executed.
AUTHORIZATION	Display fields modified in the system authorization files. (SYS$SYSTEM:SYSUAF.DAT, RIGHTSLIST.DAT, NETPROXY.DAT).
BREAKIN = ALL	Log-in break-ins.
FILE_ACCESS = ALL	File access by use of special privileges and unsuccessful file access attempts.
INSTALL	Installation of images.
LOGFAILURE = ALL	
LOGIN = ALL	
LOGOUT = ALL	
MOUNT	Use of any MOUNT or DISMOUNT command for volumes.

Keywords other than =ALL are also possible; the HELP command or the manuals should be used to see all the options.

When the system boots, a default set of alarms are set by the system effectively using the command:

```
$ SET  AUDIT /ALARM/ENABLE=(AUDIT,AUTHORIZATION,BREAKIN=ALL)
```

To display a summary of logging status including what events are being logged the command is

```
$ SHOW AUDIT/ALL

List of audit journals:
    Journal name:          SECURITY
    Journal owner:         (system audit journal)
    Destination:           SYS$COMMON:[SYSMGR]SECURITY_AUDIT.AUDIT$JOURNAL
    Monitoring:            free disk space
    Warning threshold:     1000 blocks
    Action threshold:      250 blocks
    Resume threshold:      750 blocks

Security auditing server characteristics:
    Final resource action:  crash system

Security archiving information:
    Archiving events:      none
    Archive destination:

Security alarm failure mode is set to:
    WAIT         Processes will wait for resource

Security alarms currently enabled for:
    AUTHORIZATION
    BREAKIN:     (DIALUP,LOCAL,REMOTE,NETWORK,DETACHED)
```

The messages are stored in an internal binary format. The ANALYZE/AUDIT command can be used to display these messages in various forms. Here are some examples (the output is edited for brevity):

```
$ ANALYZE/AUDIT/SUMMARY
```

Total records read:	1272		Records selected:	1272
Record buffer size:	512		Format buffer size:	256
Server messages:	0		Customer messages:	0
Digital CSS messages:	0		Layered prod messages:	0
Audit changes:	14		Installed db changes:	145
Login failures:	99		Breakin attempts:	12
Successful logins:	368		Successful logouts:	229
System UAF changes:	249		Network UAF changes:	0
Rights db changes:	70		Object accesses:	0
Volume (dis)mounts:	86			

```
$ ANALYZE/AUDIT/BRIEF
```

Date / Time	Type	Subtype	Node	Username	ID	Term
17-FEB-1990 18:29:55.95	LOGIN	REMOTE	TOPVAX	SHAH4	21A00A55	_RTA1:
17-FEB-1990 18:29:58.06	LOGOUT	REMOTE	TOPVAX	SHAH4	21A00A55	⁻RTA1:
17-FEB-1990 18:31:15.31	BREAKIN	REMOTE	SCOOP1	SHAH4	217BB8BE	⁻RTA2:
17-FEB-1990 18:31:30.98	SYSUAF	SYSUAF_MODIFY	TOPVAX	SHAH4	21A00A43	⁻
17-FEB-1990 18:33:21.92	LOGOUT	LOCAL	TOPVAX	SHAH4	21A008C8	_LTA429
					(SRVR4⁷PORT_5	
17-FEB-1990 18:59:36.25	LOGOUT	BATCH	TOPVAX	MIXERFUN1	21A00A58	
17-FEB-1990 18:59:47.51	LOGIN	LOCAL	TOPVAX	0207	21A00A59	_OPA0:
17-FEB-1990 18:59:54.72	LOGOUT	LOCAL	TOPVAX	MIXERFUN1	21A00A56	_LTA471
					(LAT_08002B10E7997PORT_7	⁻
17-FEB-1990 19:00:27.86	MOUNT	VOL_MOUNT	TOPVAX	0207	21A00A59	
17-FEB-1990 19:56:33.38	LOGOUT	DETACHED	TOPVAX	TEST1	21A00A5E	
17-FEB-1990 20:03:15.60	LOGIN	SUBPROCESS	TOPVAX	TEST1	21A00A5F	

```
$ ANALYZE/AUDIT/FULL/SINCE:TODAY
```

```
%AUDSRV-I-NEW_FILE, now analyzing file SYS$COMMON:[SYSMGR]SECURITY_AUDIT.AUDIT$JOURNAL;3
Security alarm (SECURITY) and security audit (SECURITY) on TOPVAX, system id: 1035
Auditable event:        Remote interactive login
Event time:             17-FEB-1990 18:29:55.95
PID:                    21A00A55
Username:               SHAH4
Terminal name:          _RTA1:
Remote nodename:        TOPVAX          Remote node id:         1035
Remote username:        SHAH4
```

```
Security alarm (SECURITY) and security audit (SECURITY) on TOPVAX, system id: 1035
Auditable event:        Remote interactive logout
Event time:             17-FEB-1990 18:29:58.06
PID:                    21A00A55
Username:               SHAH4
Terminal name:          _RTA1:
Remote nodename:        TOPVAX          Remote node id:         1035
Remote username:        SHAH4
```

```
Security alarm (SECURITY) and security audit (SECURITY) on SCOOP1, system id: 1036
Auditable event:        Remote interactive breakin detection
Event time:             17-FEB-1990 18:31:15.31
PID:                    217BB8BE
Username:               SHAH4
Password:               SDF
Terminal name:          _RTA2:
Remote nodename:        TOPVAX          Remote node id:         1035
Remote username:        SHAH4
```

```
Security alarm (SECURITY) and security audit (SECURITY) on TOPVAX, system id: 1035
Auditable event:          System UAF record modification
Event time:               17-FEB-1990 18:31:30.98


PID:                      21A00A43
Username:                 SHAH4
Image name:               $1$DUSO:[SYSO.SYSCOMMON.][SYSEXE]AUTHORIZE.EXE
Object name:              SYS$COMMON:[SYSEXE]SYSUAF.DAT;1
Object type:              file
User record modified:     SHAH4
Fields modified:          FLAGS

Security alarm (SECURITY) and security audit (SECURITY) on TOPVAX, system id: 1035
Auditable event:          Local interactive logout
Event time:               17-FEB-1990 18:33:21.92
PID:                      21A008C8
Username:                 SHAH4
Terminal name:            _LTA429: (SRVR4/PORT_5)

Security alarm (SECURITY) and security audit (SECURITY) on TOPVAX, system id: 1035
Auditable event:          Batch process login
Event time:               17-FEB-1990 18:59:23.06
PID:                      21A00A58
Username:                 MIXERFUN1

Security alarm (SECURITY) and security audit (SECURITY) on TOPVAX, system id: 1035
Auditable event:          Volume mount
Event time:               17-FEB-1990 19:00:41.96
PID:                      21A00A59
Username:                 0207
Image name:               $1$DUSO:[SYSO.SYSCOMMON.][SYSEXE]BACKUP.EXE;2
Object name:              _$1$MUAO:
Object type:              device
Object owner:             [OPER,0207]
Object protection:        SYSTEM:RWEDC, OWNER:RWEDC, GROUP:C, WORLD:C
Logical name:             TAPE$PAGESW
Volume name:              PAGESW
Mount flags:              /FOREIGN/NOASSIST/MESSAGE/NOCACHE/NOJOURNAL


$ ANALYZE/AUDIT/FULL/EVENT_TYPE=LOGFAIL

%AUDSRV-I-NEW_FILE, now analyzing file SYS$COMMON:[SYSMGR]SECURITY_AUDIT.AUDIT$JOURNAL;3
Security alarm (SECURITY) and security audit (SECURITY) on TOPVAX, system id: 1035
Auditable event:          Local interactive login failure
Event time:               17-FEB-1990 18:43:50.70
PID:                      21A00A57
Username:                 <login>
Terminal name:            _OPAO:
Status:                   %LOGIN-F-CMDINPUT, error reading command input

Security alarm (SECURITY) and security audit (SECURITY) on TOPVAX, system id: 1035
Auditable event:          Local interactive login failure
Event time:               17-FEB-1990 19:16:19.94
PID:                      21A00A5A
Username:                 MIXERCAT1
Terminal name:            _LTA472: (LAT_08002B10E799/PORT_7)
Status:                   %LOGIN-F-INVPWD, invalid password
```

13.7.4   Security audits (before VMS V5.2)

When the command

```
$ SET  AUDIT /ALARM/ENABLE=ALL
```

is issued, the system records security related information in the oper-

ator log file, SYS$MANAGER:OPERATOR.LOG, and displays mes-
sages on operator terminals which have security logs enabled by the
command

```
$ REPLY/ENABLE=ALL    !Display all console messages here.
```

or

```
$ REPLY/ENABLE=SECURITY   !Display security messages.
```

Actually, a subset of the messages can be logged by using

```
$ SET  AUDIT /ALARM/ENABLE=alarm-types
```

where alarm-types are:

ACL	Display objects which are accessed and have an ACL alarm set.
ALL	All types of alarms should be reported.
AUDIT	Display any SET AUDIT command executed.
AUTHORIZATION	Display fields modified in the system authorization files. (SYS$SYSTEM:SYSUAF.DAT, RIGHTSLIST.DAT, NETPROXY.DAT).
BREAKIN	Log-in break-ins.
FILE_ACCESS	File access by use of special privileges and unsuccessful file access attempts.
INSTALL	Installation of images.
LOGFAILURE	
LOGIN	
LOGOUT	
MOUNT	Use of any MOUNT or DISMOUNT command.

For example,

```
$ SET  AUDIT /ALARM/ENABLE=(AUTHORIZATION,BREAKIN,LOGIN)
```

There is a command file on the system, SYS$MANAGER:-
SECAUDIT.COM, which can be used to extract security messages
from the operator log file for regular audits. Here is a sample usage of
the file

```
$ @SYS$MANAGER:SECAUDIT /OUTPUT=SECURITY.LOG

$ TYPE SECURITY.LOG

%%%%%%%%%% OPCOM   1-JUN-1989 19:17:02.49  %%%%%%%%%%
Security alarm / Security audit alarms enabled
        Time:           01-JUN-1989 19:17:01.95
        PID:            00000103
        User Name:      SYSTEM
        Audits Modified:
            ACL
            MOUNT
            AUTHORIZATION
            AUDIT
            BREAKIN:    (DIALUP,LOCAL,REMOTE,NETWORK,DETACHED)
            LOGIN:      (DIALUP,LOCAL,NETWORK)
            LOGFAILURE: (BATCH,DIALUP,LOCAL,REMOTE,NETWORK,SUBPROCESS,DETACHED)

%%%%%%%%%% OPCOM   1-JUN-1989 21:58:09.29  %%%%%%%%%%
Security alarm / Local interactive login failure
        Time:           01-JUN-1989 21:58:09.22
        PID:            00000114
        User Name:      JAY2
        Status:         %LOGIN-F-INVPWD, invalid password
        Dev Name:       _LTA1:

%%%%%%%%%% OPCOM   2-JUN-1989 09:13:22.40  %%%%%%%%%%
Security alarm / Network login
        Time:           02-JUN-1989 09:13:22.39
        PID:            00000117
        User Name:      JIM2
        Source:         1.2  SCOOP2::SUPERPRINT

%%%%%%%%%% OPCOM   2-JUN-1989 10:03:16.23  %%%%%%%%%%
Security alarm / Successful file access
        Time:           02-JUN-1989 10:03:16.23
        PID:            0000011E
        User Name:      SHAH3
        Image:          DUA4:[SYS0.][SYSEXE]CMS.EXE;1
        File:           _DUA4:[000000]SHAH1.DIR;1
        Mode:           READ WRITE
        Privs Used:     BYPASS
```

13.7.5 Ethernet protection

Ethernet traffic can be monitored by any VAX on the Ethernet. This can seriously jeopardize security if a programmer on the network analyzes the traffic for passwords and other supposedly secure information. The DESNC hardware product allows encryption of packets transmitted by a node in a way that only a preprogrammed DESNC at a receiving node can decrypt. The product required extensive maintenance of software keys and programming of the DESNCs on the Ethernet.

13.8 BATCH AND PRINT JOBS

Batch programs and file printing have very little in common but they are discussed together because they use queues on the system. Queues here refer to those managed by the job controller; not to be confused with queues which are operating system data structures.

Users can run batch jobs by using a command like:

```
$ SUBMIT MYPROG.COM
```

MYPROG.COM is a command file containing DCL commands. The effect is somewhat similar if the file was run from the user's terminal by using:

```
$ @MYPROG.COM
```

The major difference is that the output goes to a file, MYPROG.LOG rather than the terminal. The queue manager runs the job as a detached process. LOGIN.COM will be executed for the user before the file is executed. LOGIN.COM will run with SET VERIFY so that the commands executed in LOGIN.COM and the file submitted MYPROG.COM will be echoed in the log file MYPROG.LOG. These echoes can be disabled by a SET NOVERIFY in the LOGIN or MYPROG command files.

Execution can be scheduled for a later time (or date) by

```
$ SUBMIT MYPROG.COM/AFTER=19:00    !Run after 7.00 pm.
```

Files to be printed are specified with the PRINT command:

```
$ PRINT MYPROG.LOG,OUTPUT.REPORT
```

The output goes to the queue SYS$PRINT by default. Other queue can be specified as in

```
$ PRINT/QUEUE=LN03$PRINT   MYPROG.LOG,OUTPUT.REPORT
```

If the system fails while a long job is being printed. The PRINT command can be used to print only certain page of a file:

```
$ PRINT MYPROG.LOG/PAGES=(12:234)    !Print pages 12 thru 234.
```

The system manager has to set up queues on a new system. The steps in setting up a print queue are:

1. Start the queue manager.
2. Initialize one queue per device.
3. Spool the device to the queue.
4. Start the queue.

A batch queue can be created by initializing and starting a queue for batch. Here is a sample initialization:

```
$!Commands to initialize queues.
$!Required once when the system is newly created.
$!The procedure initializes
$!      a queue for line printer (LPA0:),
$!      a queue for a LN03 laser printer on a terminal server LAT port,
$!      a batch queue.
$!
$!The "FLAG" is a banner page before the actual job or file.
$!
$ START/QUEUE/MANAGER/BUFFER_COUNT=10/EXTEND_QUANTITY=25
$!
$!LN03 printer
$ INITIALIZE /QUEUE LN03$PRINT/ON=LTA34: /PROCESSOR=LATSYM
$ SET DEVICE /SPOOLED=(LN03$PRINT, SYS$SYSDEVICE:) LTA34:
$!
$!line printer
$ INITIALIZE /QUEUE /ON=LPA0: SYS$PRINT
$ SET DEVICE LPA0: /SPOOLED=(SYS$PRINT, SYS$SYSDEVICE:)
$!
$!batch queue
$ INITIALIZE/QUEUE SYS$BATCH /BATCH /JOB_LIMIT:4    !up to 4 jobs running
$                                                   !concurrently as 4 processes.
```

When the system is booted, the queues can be started by

```
$!Start queues every time the system is booted. Put in SYSTARTUP_V5.COM.
$ START/QUEUE/MANAGER
$ START/QUEUE  SYS$PRINT
$ START/QUEUE  SYS$BATCH
$ SET TERMINAL  LTA34:/PERMANENT/FORMFEED/PAGE=66/NOWRAP
$ START/QUEUE  LN03$PRINT
```

Batch and print jobs are controlled by the process JOB_CONTROL
which runs when the START/QUEUE/MANAGER command is run.
The list of queues can be seen by

```
$ SHOW QUEUE/FULL

Printer queue LN03$PRINT, on LTA310:, mounted form LN03 (stock=DEFAULT)
        /BASE_PRIORITY=4 /DEFAULT=(FEED,FORM=DEFAULT) /OWNER=[1,4]
        /PROTECTION=(S:E,O:D,G:R,W:W)

Batch queue SYS$BATCH
        /BASE_PRIORITY=4 /DISABLE_SWAPPING /JOB_LIMIT=1 /OWNER=[1,4]
        /PROTECTION=(S:E,O:D,G:R,W:W) /WSDEFAULT=1024 /WSQUOTA=1024

Printer queue SYS$PRINT, stalled, on LPA0:, mounted form DEFAULT
        /BASE_PRIORITY=4 /DEFAULT=(FEED,FLAG,FORM=DEFAULT) /OWNER=[1,4]
        /PROTECTION=(S:E,O:D,G:R,W:W) /RETAIN
```

The jobs awaiting execution in each queue can be seen by

```
$ SHOW QUEUE/FULL

Printer queue LN03$PRINT, on LTA310:, mounted form LN03 (stock=DEFAULT)

Batch queue SYS$BATCH

    Jobname      Username     Entry  Status
    --------     --------     -----  ------
    MYPROG       SHAH4        1824   Executing


Printer queue SYS$PRINT, on LPA0:, mounted form DEFAULT

    Jobname      Username     Entry  Blocks  Status
    --------     --------     -----  ------  ------
    MYPROG       SHAH         1739      1    Printing
    EMPLOY       CARR         1694      9    Pending
```

Jobs can be stopped by:

```
$ STOP/ENTRY=1824   SYS$BATCH      !Abort a running job
$ DELETE/ENTRY=1694 SYS$PRINT      !Remove a queued job awaiting
                                    execution.
```

13.9   INSTALLING SOFTWARE LICENSES

Since VMS V5.0 was released in 1987, most software layered products can be used only if a license is entered in the system. (Products can be installed without a license.) Licensing information is supplied on a piece of paper which is called a *product authorization key* (PAK). The license must be entered into the system. The LICENCE LIST (or SHOW LICENSE) command displays a list of products whose licenses are installed on the system. Obviously, the scheme discourages software piracy.

Most license information is stored in the file SYS$COMMON:[SYSEXE]LMF$LICENSE.LDB. The commands LICENSE REGISTER and LICENSE LOAD commands can be used to enter a license into the license database and to activate the license. The interactive command procedure SYS$UPDATE:VMSLICENSE.COM can also be used

```
$ @SYS$UPDATE:VMSLICENSE.COM

    VMS License Management Utility Options:

        1.  Register a Product Authorization Key
        2.  Amend an existing Product Authorization Key
        3.  Exit this procedure

Select option: 1
* Do you have your Product Authorization Key? Y

    When prompted for input, enter data from corresponding fields on
    your Product Authorization Key (PAK) or Product Authorization
    Amendment (PAAM).
```

Some prompts display a default reply (shown in brackets). To use
the default, press the RETURN key. To replace default data, enter
the new data to be used. To cancel the use of default data without
entering new data, enter the backslash (\) character.

You will have the opportunity to review and correct your responses
before actually registering this license. If you wish to exit from
giving responses, do so by typing CTRL/Z.

```
  PAK ID:
* Issuer [DEC]:
* Authorization Number: ALS-WM-21212-12
  PRODUCT ID:
* Product Name: DTR
* Producer [DEC]:
  NUMBER OF UNITS:
* Number of Units: 400
  KEY LEVEL:
* Version (v.u):
* Product Release Date (dd-mmm-yyyy):
  KEY TERMINATION DATE:
* Key Termination Date (dd-mmm-yyyy):
  RATING:
* Availability Table Code: F
* Activity Table Code:
  MISCELLANEOUS:
* Key Options: MOD_UNITS
* Product Token:
* Hardware ID:
* Checksum: 1-PQPQ-PQPQ-PQPQ-PQPQ


              LMF Database:  SYS$COMMON:[SYSEXE]LMF$LICENSE.LDB
                    Issuer:  DEC
      Authorization Number:  ALS-WM-21212-12
              Product Name:  DTR
                  Producer:  DEC
           Number of Units:  400
                   Version:
      Product Release Date:

        Key Termination Date:
     Availability Table Code:  F
         Activity Table Code:
                 Key Options:  MOD_UNITS
               Product Token:
                 Hardware ID:
                    Checksum:  1-PQPQ-PQPQ-PQPQ-PQPQ

* Is this information correct? Y
     DEC DTR has been registered.
* Do you want to LOAD this license on this system [YES]?
%LICENSE-I-LOADED, DEC DTR was successfully loaded with 400 units

* Do you want to register another PAK? N
  Cleaning up ...

  VMS License Management Utility Options:

     1.  Register a Product Authorization Key
     2.  Amend an existing Product Authorization Key
     3.  Exit this procedure

Select option: 3
$
```

13.10   INSTALLING NEW SOFTWARE PRODUCTS

The operating system is usually loaded on a new system by the standalone backup utility. Once the operating system is copied on disk, the disk can be booted. All further products, including operating system updates, are installed with the utility SYS$UPDATE:VMSINSTAL.COM.

The installation process will depend on the product being installed. Normally, the network should be shut down and all users should be logged off when installing products. Each product comes with a small installation guide which should be read before installation. Installations should normally be performed form the SYSTEM account. As an example, here is the installation of the Datatrieve language product.

```
$ @SYS$UPDATE:VMSINSTAL

        VAX/VMS Software Product Installation Procedure V5.1-1

It is 25-MAY-1989 at 12:21.
Enter a question mark (?) at any time for help.

%VMSINSTAL-W-DECNET, Your DECnet network is up and running.
* Do you want to continue anyway [NO]? y
* Are you satisfied with the backup of your system disk [YES]?
* Where will the distribution volumes be mounted: MUA1:

Enter the products to be processed from the first distribution volume set.
* Products: dtr
* Options:
The following products will be processed:
  DTR V4.2
        Beginning installation of DTR V4.2 at 12:21

%VMSINSTAL-I-RESTORE, Restoring product saveset A ...
%VMSINSTAL-I-RELMOVED , The product's release notes have been
                                successfully moved to SYS$HELP.
        Product:      DTR or DTR-USER
        Producer:     DEC
        Version:      4.2
        Release Date: 1-MAY-1988

* Does this product have an authorization key registered and loaded? y
* Do you want to use default answers for all questions [NO]? y

    **************************************************************

    The Language-Sensitive Editor is not installed on your
    system.  To have the Language-Sensitive Editor support,
    you must:

        1.  Install the Language-Sensitive Editor
        2.  Install or reinstall this product

    **************************************************************

* Do you want to continue the installation [NO]? y

        The installation of VAX DATATRIEVE will now continue for
        10 minutes to 30 minutes.
```

```
%VMSINSTAL-I-RESTORE, Restoring product saveset B ...
%VMSINSTAL-I-SYSDIR, This product creates system
                            disk directory  VMI$ROOT:[DTR].
%VMSINSTAL-I-SYSDIR, This product creates system
                            disk directory VMI$ROOT:[SYSTEST.DTR].

    During the installation, a file called
    DTRSTUP.COM has been added to SYS$MANAGER:


The site-dependent start-up file, SYS$MANAGER:SYSTARTUP.COM
(if you are running under VMS V4.x) or SYS$MANAGER:SYSTARTUP_V5.COM
(if you are running under VMS V5.0) should have the following line added:

    $     @SYS$MANAGER:DTRSTUP.COM


**************************************************************

VAX DATATRIEVE User Environment Test Packages (UETPs)
have been provided and can be run after the installation is
complete. They are invoked from VAX DATATRIEVE as follows:

DTR> @sys$common:[systest.dtr]dtr     ! The general test
DTR> @sys$common:[systest.dtr]plots   ! The plots test
DTR> @sys$common:[systest.dtr]rdb     ! The Rdb test

**************************************************************

%VMSINSTAL-I-MOVEFILES, Files will now be moved to their target directories...

Executing IVP for:  VAX DATATRIEVE V4.2-1

Running the general IVP test ...
    Test completed successfully

*************************************

VAX DATATRIEVE V4.2-1

IVP COMPLETED SUCCESSFULLY

*************************************

IVP completed for:  VAX DATATRIEVE V4.2-1

Restoring VAX DATATRIEVE demonstration RDB/VMS database

Exported by Rdb/VMS V2.1-5 Backup/Restore utility
A component of Rdb/VMS V2.1-5
Previous name was DTR$LIBRARY:PERSONNEL.RDB
It was logically exported on  4-MAR-1987 11:24
IMPORTing relation COLLEGES
IMPORTing relation DEGREES
IMPORTing relation DEPARTMENTS
IMPORTing relation EMPLOYEES
IMPORTing relation JOBS
IMPORTing relation JOB_HISTORY
IMPORTing relation SALARY_HISTORY
IMPORTing relation WORK_STATUS
        Installation of DTR V4.2 completed at 12:30

Enter the products to be processed from the next distribution volume set.


* Products: <CTRL/Z>

        VMSINSTAL procedure done at 11:08
```

In a typical product install, the following operations are performed:

- Release notes containing latest information are moved to SYS$HELP:.

- Executable images are moved to SYS$SYSTEM:.

- Error message files are moved to SYS$MESSAGE:.

- Library files are moved to SYS$LIBRARY:.

- The file SYS$LIBRARY:DCLTABLES.EXE is modified to incorporate one or more DCL commands.

- The file SYS$HELP:HELPLIB.HLB is modified to incorporate help on the product (see the HELP command).

- Sample examples on using the product are stored in SYS$EXAMPLES:.

- A startup command file is moved to SYS$STARTUP:.

- Directories and accounts may be created for the product's use.

- An installation verification procedure is run to confirm that the product is properly installed.

13.10.1 Disk installation

Normally, products are installed from tape. When you have to install the product on a number of machines or the product has to be reinstalled at a later time, it is convenient to copy the product tape to a disk and install the product from the disk files. To copy a product to disk, use

```
$ MOUNT  MUA0: /OVERRIDE=IDENTIFICATION
$ COPY  MUA0:  DUB2:[PRODUCTS] /LOG
```

The product consists of files in BACKUP save sets format. To install the product from disk, specify the disk name and directory when prompted for the source during installation.

13.11   LAT TERMINALS AND TERMINAL SERVER MANAGEMENT

Terminal servers on Ethernet communicate with VAXes using the LAT protocol. Terminal servers allow terminals (and other asynchronous devices like the LN03 printer) to create virtual connections to VAXes. Currently there are four types of terminal servers: DECserver 100 (8 lines), DECserver 200 (8 lines), DECserver 300 (16 lines), and DECserver 550 (128 lines). Figure 13.1 shows a possible configuration.

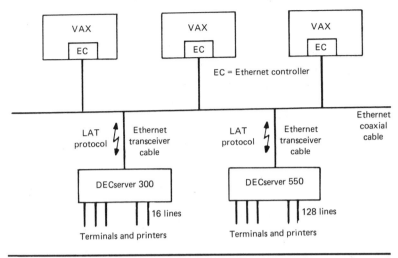

Figure 13.1   Terminal servers on Ethernet.

The server normally displays a prompt to attached terminals which look like this:

```
Local>
```

Users can connect to VAXes on the Ethernet by the command:

```
Local>CONNECT service-name
```

Normally, a VAX on the Ethernet will offer a LAT service whose name is the same as the VAX node name.

LAT commands can be given on a VAX by using the LATCP utility which is run by

```
$ LCP   :== $LATCP    !Define it as a DCL command
$ LCP
LCP>                  !LAT commands can be given here
```

VAXes which support log-ins from terminal server terminals must have LAT started. This is achieved by executing:

```
$ @SYS$MANAGER:LTLOAD.COM
```

The execution performs the following operations:

- Enables the LAT terminal driver

```
$ RUN  SYS$SYSTEM:SYSGEN
CONNECT  LTA0/NOADAPTER
```

- Creates a service with the node name as the service name

```
$LCP : = $LATCP
$LCP  CREATE  SERVICE /ID
```

- Enables the service

```
LCP  START  NODE
```

The VAX is now set to accept connections from terminals on terminal servers. The advantage of terminal servers is that users can directly log into any VAX on the Ethernet. If terminals are directly connected to VAXes and then to log into another VAX, the user would have to use the $ SET HOST command which consumes CPU time for terminal I/O on two machines. See the chapter on the hardware environment for more information on terminal servers.

LAT terminals are named like LTA2: and LTA33: on the host VAXes. The number is allocated dynamically by the VAX as users log in. So, logging in at two different times from the same terminal server port will generate two different terminal names. The SET TERMINAL command can be used to change terminal characteristics information like device type and speed. For example, the next command disables broadcast messages to LTA526: from other users

```
$ SET  TERMINAL  LTA26:/NOBROADCAST/PERMANENT
```

Other users will not be able to use REPLY and PHONE to "contact" that terminal.

13.12 HARDWARE MALFUNCTIONS

The SHOW DEVICES command displays error counts of hardware errors logged by the system on each device.

```
$ SHOW DEVICES
```

Device Name	Device Status	Error Count	Volume Label	Free Blocks	Trans Count	Mnt Cnt
DUA4:	Mounted	0	PRIMDISK	176890	3	1
DUA5:	Mounted	21	TESTDISK	219396	1	1

Device Name	Device Status	Error Count
LTA0:	Offline	0
TXA0:	Online	0
TXA1:	Online	0
VTA0:	Offline	0

Device Name	Device Status	Error Count
LIA0:	Online	0

Device Name	Device Status	Error Count
ETA0:	Online	0
PUA0:	Online	2

Further information on these errors is recorded in binary form in the file SYS$ERRORLOG:ERRLOG.SYS by the process ERRFMT. To see a detailed description of these errors use the command

```
$ ANALYZE/ERROR_LOG
```

The output is mainly of interest to the hardware engineer, but system managers should be aware of device problems. The /SINCE qualifier reports errors after a particular date (or time) and the /INCLUDE qualifier reports errors for selected devices

```
$ ANALYZE/ERROR_LOG /SINCE:22-DEC-1989/INCLUDE=(DUA5:,PUA0:)
```

Here is a typical errorlog report entry.

```
V A X / V M S       SYSTEM ERROR REPORT       COMPILED  6-OCT-1989 13:35
                                                                   PAGE  1.
*************************** ENTRY   6325. ***************************
ERROR SEQUENCE 3.                        LOGGED ON:        SID 06800C32
DATE/TIME  6-OCT-1989 05:23:03.08                    SYS_TYPE 070009F9

DEVICE ATTENTION   KA85    REV# 0.
                   CPU # 1.

"DSA" PORT SUB-SYSTEM, UNIT _PTA0:, INIT SEQUENCE COMPLETED

       SA             4051
                               CONTROLLER MICRO-CODE #1.
                               PORT IS TU81P
                               STEP 4

INIT SEQUENCE

       UCB$W_PORTSTEP1    0980
                               PORT ALLOWS HOST ODD ADDRESSES
                               ENHANCED DIAGNOSTICS IMPLEMENTED
                               STEP 1
       UCB$W_HOSTSTEP1    A4C6
                               INTERRUPT VECTOR 430 (OCTAL)
                               INTERRUPT ENABLE
                               16. RING RESPONSE SLOTS
                               16. COMMAND RING SLOTS
       UCB$W_PORTSTEP2    10A4
                               16. RING RESPONSE SLOTS
                               16. COMMAND RING SLOTS
                               STEP 2
       UCB$W_HOSTSTEP2    CDC8
       UCB$W_PORTSTEP3    20C6
                               INTERRUPT VECTOR 000430 (OCTAL)
                               INTERRUPT ENABLE
                               STEP 3
       UCB$W_HOSTSTEP3    0003
                               MAPPING REGISTER #486 SELECTED
       UCB$W_PORTSTEP4    4051
                               CONTROLLER MICRO-CODE #1.
                               PORT IS TU81P
                               STEP 4
       UCB$W_HOSTSTEP4    0003
                               GO
                               HOST REQUESTS "LAST FAIL"
                               "BURST", 2. 16-BIT TRANSFER(S)
```

```
MAPPING ALLOCATION INFORMATION

    VEC$L_MAPREG     000A81E6
                                   "MPR" #486. STARTING MAP REGISTER
                                   "MPR"(S) PERMANENTLY ALLOCATED
                                   10. MAP REGISTER(S) ALLOCATED
                                   DIRECT DATAPATH


 ORB$L_OWNER      00000000
                                   OWNER UIC [000,000]
 UCB$L_CHAR       0C450000
                                   SHARABLE
                                   AVAILABLE
                                   ERROR LOGGING
                                   CAPABLE OF INPUT
                                   CAPABLE OF OUTPUT
 UCB$W_STS             0000
 UCB$L_OPCNT       00000000
                                   0. QIO'S THIS UNIT
 UCB$W_ERRCNT          0001
                                   1. ERRORS THIS UNIT
 UCB$W_NUMBINITS       0001
                                   1. INIT SEQUENCE(S)
```

13.13 CHECKING DISKS FOR FILE CORRUPTIONS

When a disk is in use and there is a system failure due to ,say, power failure or a fatal bug, file (and directory) pointers on the disk may be corrupted. For example, if the DELETE command deletes all the headers for a file. It is possible that power fails when only some headers are deleted. In this case, the file space may be only partially deallocated. The ANALYZE/DISK_STRUCTURE command can be used to check or repair the damage:

```
$ ANALYZE/DISK_STRUCTURE DUB6:        !Report corruptions
$ ANALYZE/DISK_STRUCTURE/REPAIR DUB6:
                                      !Report and repair corruptions
                                      !Repaired files are stored in
                                      !the directory [SYSLOST].
$ ANALYZE/DISK_STRUCTURE/REPAIR/CONFIRM DUB6:
                                      !Report corruptions. Repair each
                                      !corruption if confirmed by the
                                      user.
```

The operation should be performed on privately mounted disk volumes. Here is an example.

```
$ ANALYZE/DISK_STRUCTURE DJA5:

%VERIFY-I-OPENQUOTA, error opening QUOTA.SYS
-SYSTEM-W-NOSUCHFILE, no such file
%VERIFY-W-DELHEADER, file (3196,19,1)
        marked for delete
%VERIFY-W-DIRNAME, directory file [SHAH.PGM]CALC.DIR;2 is not named '.DIR;1'
%VERIFY-W-LOSTHEADER, file (26,3,1) SETHOST30MAR89.LOG;1
        not found in a directory
```

13.14   OPERATOR MESSAGES

Any terminal on the system can be enabled to receive operator messages like the security messages shown above. To enable a terminal as an operator console,the command is:

```
$ REPLY /ENABLE
```

Operator   messages   are   also   logged   in   the   file SYS$MANAGER:OPERATOR.LOG. The file can be printed, say, every night for recordkeeping. A new log file can be created by using

```
$ REPLY /LOG
```

13.15   THE SYSMAN UTILITY

This utility allows the system manager to issue commands on any node on a DECnet network or VAXcluster. It is convenient for managing a number of systems without explicitly logging into them. SYSMAN is also used to set up startup commands for products during system startup.

To run SYSMAN, the commands are

```
$ SYSMAN  : = =  $SYSMAN
$ SYSMAN
SYSMAN>
```

SYSMAN communicates with the process SMISERVER on other VAXes when executing DCL commands.

DCL commands can be specified preceded by the word DO:

```
SYSMAN> DO DIR [SHAH]
```

To execute commands on another node, say, TOPVAX, use

```
SYSMAN> SET ENVIRONMENT/NODE=TOPVAX
Remote Password:

%SYSMAN-I-ENV, current command environment:
        Individual nodes: TOPVAX
        At least one node is not in local cluster
        Username SHAH       will be used on nonlocal nodes

SYSMAN> DO SHOW SYSTEM

%SYSMAN-I-OUTPUT, command execution on node TOPVAX
VAX/VMS V5.1-1  on node TOPVAX 29-DEC-1989 18:53:12.46    Uptime   1 03:47:59
   Pid   Process Name    State  Pri    I/O         CPU        Page flts Ph.Mem
00000081 SWAPPER         HIB     16      0    0 00:00:05.82         0        0
00000084 ERRFMT          HIB      8   1191    0 00:00:18.36        76      101
00000085 OPCOM           HIB      9   3867    0 00:02:12.02       647      166
00000086 JOB_CONTROL     HIB      9    207    0 00:00:03.03       132      357
00000087 NETACP          HIB     10   6447    0 00:02:40.34       189      367
00000088 EVL             HIB      6     90    0 00:00:19.92     26577       51  N
00000089 REMACP          HIB      8      8    0 00:00:00.29        68       36
000000A5 SMISERVER       LEF      8    231    0 00:00:03.88       377      514

SYSMAN>
```

The system contains a startup database, SYS$START-UP:VMS$LAYERED.DAT, which contains commands which are executed when the system boots. The database is maintained by SYSMAN STARTUP commands.

13.16 FURTHER READING

VMS System Management Manuals.

14

System Utilities

In this chapter we look at some tools available to the system programmer and manager. The discussion is on

- System parameters and the SYSGEN utility.
- Modifying system parameters: the AUTOGEN utility.
- The INSTALL utility.
- System dump analyzer (SDA), which is used for examining system code and data.

14.1 STARTING UP THE SYSTEM

The operating system is loaded in memory from the system disk by a BOOT command on the console. The sequence of steps are

1. The console loads the boot block (block 0) on disk into memory and passes control to it. This process is different for the various types of VAXes. The console may be a separate microcomputer as in the case of the 8000 series VAXes, or it may be a terminal with a CPU built-in with the standard VAX CPU.
2. Usually, the boot block contains a small program which loads the file SYS$SYSTEM:VMB.EXE from the disk. VMB is the primary bootstrap program. All modules executed after it are independent of the VAX CPU type.
3. VMB loads the file SYS$SYSTEM:SYSBOOT.EXE. SYSBOOT is the secondary bootstrap program. It loads the base operating system called the executive. Major files accessed are SYS.EXE, TTDRIVER.EXE, PAGEFILE.SYS, and other driver files. These

files are in the directory accessed by the logical SYS$LOADABLE_IMAGES:.

4. Control passes to module INIT in SYS.EXE. INIT enables memory management, and initializes VMS data structures.

5. Control then passes on to the SYSINIT module in SYS.EXE. This module sets up the page and swap file data structures, sets up RMS and creates the first normal process on the system: STARTUP.

6. The STARTUP process uses DCL to execute SYS$SYSTEM:-STARTUP.COM. The operations performed are

   a. Setting up system logical names like SYS$SYSROOT and SYS$MESSAGE.

   b. Starting of three detached processes: Error log formatter (ERRFMT), Batch and queue job controller (JOB_CONTROL) and the operator communications process (OPCOM).

   c. Install of some commonly used images.

   d. Invoking of SYSGEN to load device drivers.

   e. Execution of the command file SYS$MANAGER:-SYSTARTUP_V5.COM.

At this stage the system is ready for log-ins. SYSTARTUP_V5.COM can be customized to perform system startup functions like setting up queues, installing commonly used images, starting DECnet, running startup procedures for layered products, and starting LAT for terminals on terminal servers.

14.2   USER LOG-INS

Once booted, the system is ready for log-ins. When a user presses the RETURN key on a local teminal or issues the CONNECT command on terminal servers, the system receives a hardware interrupt and VMS creates a process to handle log-in on that terminal. The name of the process is the terminal name like _TXA1: or _LTA23:. The process then executes the image SYS$SYSTEM:LOGINOUT.EXE. This image prompts the user to enter a user name and password, validates the input against the authorization file SYS$SYSTEM:SYSUAF.DAT, sets up DCL in process P1 space, reads in process quotas from SYSUAF.DAT, renames the process as the user name of the user, and passes control to DCL. DCL executes LOGIN.COM if it exists in the user's log-in directory. The user is then set to execute DCL commands.

DCL issues a QIOW call to the operating system, which will return one line of input from the terminal. This will be the command entered by the user at the terminal. The QIOW specifies a local event flag (LEF) which is to be set by the opeating system when the user enters a line of input. The process will wait until the flag is set by the operating system which is when the operating system receives a complete line of terminal input. The $ SHOW SYSTEM command will show the state of processes as LEF when the processes are waiting for a LEF to be set (or reset).

Once the user enters a complete line, the operating system sends the line to DCL in the process, which then parses it and either executes an internal DCL command (like SHOW DEFAULT) or runs an image (like for a COBOL compilation). A CTRL/T entered by the user will show what image is currently executing in the process.

As more users log in, the CPU switches among its own tasks (like getting a line from the terminal) and the user processes.

14.3 CPU USAGE

The CPU is idle just after the system is booted unless processes are created during the startup phase by the execution of SYSTARTUP_V5.COM. Normally, every key received from users generates a hardware interrupt causing the CPU to take action. Once a number of users are logged in, the CPU performs operations (like I/O) on behalf of the users and also executes code in user processes. If all users are logged in but sitting idle, then there will be one process per user in the system but the CPU will be idle. But users are usually performing various operations like compilations, running utilities, and running applications.

Processes are assigned software priorities ranging from 0 through 31. Priorities 16 through 31 are used by high-priority real-time processes. Default priority for each user is specified in SYSUAF.DAT and is usually 4. The $ SHOW SYSTEM command displays process priorities. Priorities can be changed by the $ SET PROCESS/PRIORITY command. When a number of processes need CPU time, the operating system assigns the CPU to the process with the highest priority. If there are a number of processes with the highest priority, the CPU is assigned to each of these process a small time interval at a time. The time interval is called a time slice, and the method of allocating the CPU to each process one by one is called *round robin scheduling*. The time slice is determined by the system parameter QUANTUM. This parameter can be displayed and changed by the SYSGEN utility. A typical value is 20. The value is multiplied by 10 milliseconds to arrive at the time slice which would be 200 milliseconds for a QUANTUM value of 20. The scheduling method implies that low-priority processes may not get CPU time until the high-priority processes run to completion (or do not need the CPU). Actually, processes may issue operating system calls for I/O or other services. In this case, the process waits until the operating system performs the service. The CPU is then allocated to other processes in the mean time. There are a number of wait states for a process. Here is a list of possible process states:

COLPG •   Collided page wait. Occurs when a process tries accessing a shared page which is being brought into memory by another process.

CEF   Common event flag wait.

LEF   Local event flag wait.

PFW   Page fault wait. Occurs when a physical page is referenced by the process and the page is not in memory.

HIB   Hibernate wait. Occurs when a process issues the SYS$HIBER system service call. The HIB state is exited when a $WAKE or $SCHDWK call is issued, an AST is delivered, or the process is deleted.

SUSP   Suspended wait. A process enters this state when the SYS$SUSPND system service call is used to suspend it. The process can be resumed by another process issuing the SYS$RESUME call.

FPG   Free page wait. Occurs when the process's working set is to be expanded but the free page list is depleted.

MWAIT   Miscellaneous wait. Occurs for waits not classified by other states. An example is a wait for memory from a depleted nonpaged pool.

COM   Computable. Waiting for CPU to be assigned to the process.

CUR   Currently executing.

States for processes swapped out to SWAP file.

LEFO   Local event flag wait (swapped out).

HIBO   Hibernate wait (swapped out).

SUSPO   Suspended wait (swapped out).

COMO   Computable (swapped out).

Processes which are waiting for CPU time will be in the COM (computable) state. While the one process which the CPU is executing will be in the CUR (for current) state. Again, the "$SHOW SYSTEM" command displays this information.

14.4   I/O

Processes perform I/O to devices by using a QIO (queued I/O) or QIOW (queued I/O with wait) system service call. High-level languages use statements like READ and WRITE and the compiler converts these to equivalent QIOs. QIOs and QIOWs are similar except that a QIO returns immediately to the program whether the I/O is completed or not, while a QIOW waits in the operating system for the I/O to complete. For example, to determine whether there is any input entered from a user terminal, a QIO can be used while to get input from the user a QIOW can be used; the QIOW will wait until the user enters input and during that time the process will be in a LEF wait state.

The operating system maintains queues for pending I/O operations and so the term QIO. CPU executes code in processes and in the operating system. Normally, the operating system has priority over user processes.

14.4.1 Hardware interrupts

I/O devices generate interrupts when they need the attention of the operating system. Interrupts are normally handled by the appropriate software device drivers. The VAX has 16 hardware *interrupt priority levels* (IPLs): 16 through 31. Interrupts from 25 to 31 are used for urgent and emergency purposes like power failure and system bug checks.

The operating system sets up interrupt vectors in the *system control block* (SCB) which point to routines which will service interrupts. When an interrupt occurs, execution of current code by the CPU is suspended and the interrupt routine specified by the interrrupt vector for the interrupt is executed. The base of the interrupt vectors is given by the CPU register SCBB (*system control block base*).

On an interrupt, the CPU registers PC and PSL are automatically stacked by the hardware. The interrupt handler routine must save contents of registers it uses. On completion of the routine, the REI (*return from interrupt*) must be executed. The PC and PSL are unstacked automatically. The CPU then continues executing its original code.

14.5   PAGING AND SWAPPING

The page files are used by VMS to swap out pages of memory when physical memory is depleted (or a process's quota, WSMAX is exceeded) and more memory is required by processes. There are other uses of the page file. Normally, there is one at least one page file on the system. Another page file can be used by

```
$ SYSGEN   : = =   $SYSGEN
$ SYSGEN   CREATE   SYS$SYSTEM:PAGEFILE1.SYS   /SIZE=20000
$ SYSGEN   INSTALL   SYS$SYSTEM:PAGEFILE1.SYS   /PAGEFILE
```

The swap files are used when a process needs to be swapped out because of depletion of balance slots (more processes being created). All the pages constituting the process are swapped to the swap file. The primary swap file is automatically installed by the system startup command file SYS$SYSTEM:STARTUP.COM. More swap files can be created by commands similar to those used for creating page files as shown above. Effective with VMS V5.0, the operating system uses the swap file for paging when the page file is full. Similarly, the page file may be used for swapping.

To see the page and swap files in use the command is

```
$ SHOW MEMORY/FILES

                System Memory Resources on 26-DEC-1989 14:20:13.33
Paging File Usage (pages):                       Free  Reservable       Total
    DISK$VMSRL5:[SYS0.SYSEXE]SWAPFILE.SYS        17296     17296        17296
    DISK$VMSRL5:[SYS0.SYSEXE]PAGEFILE.SYS        92348     32854        98000
```

Note that the AUTOGEN procedure is used by the system to create initial page and swap file sizes. Unless there is a special requirement, AUTOGEN should be allowed to modify the sizes depending on SYSGEN parameters like GBLPAGFIL.

14.6 VMS MEMORY USAGE

System code resides in static virtual memory in S1 space. Data structures like process control block are defined in the files SYS$SYSTEM:LIB.MLB and SYS$SYSTEM:STARLET.MLB. Most data is maintained in dynamic memory. Dynamic memory is also known as pool. There are two types of pool: paged and nonpaged. Pool usage is described here, first, the nonpage pool:

Variable-size blocks, each a multiple of 16 bytes.	Used for buffered I/O, job information block, process control block.
Small request packets (SRPs)	Used for buffered I/O, file (window) control blocks, device data block, timer queue elements. Size determined by SYSGEN parameter SRPSIZE. Initial count given by SYSGEN parameter IRPCOUNT.
Intermediate request packets (IRPs)	Used by buffered I/O, volume control block. Size of each block is fixed at 160 bytes. Initial count given by SYSGEN parameter IRPCOUNT.
Large request packets (LRPs)	Used mainly for DECnet buffers. (LRPs). Size determined by SYSGEN parameter LRPSIZE. Initial count given by SYSGEN parameter LRPCOUNT.

Features of paged pools are

Variable-size blocks, each a multiple of 16 bytes.	Used for information on INSTALLed images, group and system logical names.
Process allocation region.	Used for process logical names, information on privately mounted volumes.

The size of paged dynamic memory is given by the SYSGEN parameter PAGEDYN. The size of nonpaged dynamic memory is initially given by NPAGEDYN and the memory can grow up to NPAGEVIR.
To see memory utilization the command is

```
$ SHOW MEMORY/POOL
                 System Memory Resources on 26-DEC-1989 16:35:19.33
Fixed-Size Pool Areas (packets):    Total       Free     In Use       Size
  Small Packet (SRP) List            2109       1440        669         96
  I/O Request Packet (IRP) List      1542       1337        205        176
  Large Packet (LRP) List             100         64         36       1648
Dynamic Memory Usage (bytes):       Total       Free     In Use    Largest
  Nonpaged Dynamic Memory          2665984     453488    2212496     389568
  Paged Dynamic Memory             1362944     795968     566976     793888
```

14.7 SYSTEM PARAMETERS AND THE SYSGEN UTILITY

Normally, the SYSGEN utility is used by the system manager. The system has about 226 parameters which can be modified to customize the system for specific requirements. These parameters are stored in the file SYS$SYSTEM:VAXVMSSYS.PAR, which is read when the system is booted. Some of these parameters can be changed after the system is booted so that they are in effect until the next boot. The modified parameters can also be saved by the SYSGEN utility so that they are in effect every time the system boots, but this is not recommended. Refer to the next section to understand how to change system parameters. The parameters are grouped into categories shown in Table 14.1.
To see the list of SYSGEN parameters, their current value, and the range of values they can take, use

```
$SYSGEN  :==  $SYSGEN  !Define SYSGEN as a foreign DCL command.
```

```
$SYSGEN SHOW /ALL        !Show all parameters
(only some parameters shown here)
```

```
Parameters in use: Active
```

Parameter Name	Current	Default	Minimum	Maximum	Unit	Dynamic
GBLSECTIONS	540	250	20	4095	Sections	
GBLPAGES	70700	10000	512	-1	Pages	
GBLPAGFIL	1024	1024	128	-1	Pages	
MAXPROCESSCNT	240	32	12	8192	Processes	
BALSETCNT	187	16	4	1024	Slots	
IRPCOUNT	1542	60	0	32768	Packets	
IRPCOUNTV	6168	250	0	32768	Packets	
WSMAX	16400	1024	60	100000	Pages	
NPAGEDYN	2665984	300032	16384	-1	Bytes	
NPAGEVIR	9997824	1000000	16384	-1	Bytes	
PAGEDYN	1362944	190000	10240	-1	Bytes	
VIRTUALPAGECNT	98536	8192	512	600000	Pages	
QUANTUM	20	20	2	32767	10Ms	D
WSINC	150	150	0	-1	Pages	D
WSDEC	250	250	0	-1	Pages	D
FREELIM	150	32	16	-1	Pages	
FREEGOAL	655	200	16	-1	Pages	
GROWLIM	654	63	0	-1	Pages	D
BORROWLIM	818	300	0	-1	Pages	D
CLISYMTBL	500	250	10	500	Pages	D
LOCKIDTBL	1200	200	40	65535	Entries	
SCSNODE	"	"	"	"	"ZZZZ"	Ascii	
UAFALTERNATE	0	0	0	1	Boolean	
LGI_BRK_TERM	1	1	0	1	Boolean	D
LGI_BRK_DISUSER	0	0	0	1	Boolean	D
TTY_TYPAHDSZ	78	78	0	-1	Bytes	
RMS_DFMBFIDX	0	0	0	127	Buffers	D
RMS_EXTEND_SIZE	0	0	0	65535	Blocks	D
PQL_DFILLM	16	16	-1	-1	Files	D
PQL_DWSDEFAULT	242	100	-1	-1	Pages	
ACP_DINDXCACHE	93	25	2	-1	Pages	D
ACP_EXTCACHE	64	64	0	-1	Extents	D
DEFPRI	4	4	1	31	Priority	D
IJOBLIM	64	64	1	1024	Jobs	D
BJOBLIM	16	16	0	1024	Jobs	D
NJOBLIM	16	16	0	1024	Jobs	D
RJOBLIM	16	16	2	254	Jobs	D
LGI_BRK_LIM	5	5	0	255	Failures	D
LGI_BRK_TMO	300	300	0	-1	Seconds	D
LGI_HID_TIM	300	300	0	-1	Seconds	D
VOTES	1	1	0	127	Votes	

The D (for dynamic) at the end of some lines means the parameter can be changed when the system is running. These parameters can be changed by the SYSGEN SET command. For example,

```
$ SYSGEN  SET  LGI_BRK_LIM  10
$ WRITE  ACTIVE
```

The parameter is effective until the next system boot.

14.7.1 Loading drivers

The SYSGEN utility is also used to load device drivers. Normally, the command

```
$SYSGEN  AUTOCONFIGURE  ALL
```

TABLE 14.1   Sysgen Parameter Groups

ACP	File system parameters. An example is ACP_DIRCACHE, which specifies the number of pages for caching file directory blocks in memory.
CLUSTER	Parameters for a VAXcluster. An example is VOTES, which specifies the number of votes this node contributes on a cluster.
JOB	Parameters for user jobs. A job is all the processes, including the top process and all spawned processes. An example parameter is DEFPRI, which specifies the default priority for processes.
LGI	Parameters for user log-in security. An example is LGI_BRK_DISUSER which specifies if the DISUSER log-in flag in the user authorization file should be set if a break-in is attempted by someone using the user name.
PQL	Process quotas. Process quotas are set in the authorization file, but these parameters are used if the SYS$CREPRC system service or the DCL RUN command is used. An example is PQL_DFILLM, which specifies the default open file limit for a process.
RMS	Parameters for RMS (files). An example is RMS_EXTEND_SIZE, which specifies the number of blocks by which to extend files when they are being written into.
SCS	Parameters for System Communications Services. Mainly used by VAXclusters. An example is SCSNODE which specifies the node name of the VAX in a cluster. Normally this is the same as the DECnet node name.
SYS	System operations parameters. An example is BALSETCNT which specifies the number of balance sets in memory, effectively the number of processes which can remain in memory. If more processes are created some will be swapped out.
TTY	Terminal parameters. An example is TTY_TYPAHDSZ, which specifies the number of characters which can be typed ahead in the terminal. These characters are buffered in the operating system until requested for by the process's DCL or program image.
Others	These are parameters not classified in the above groups. An example is CHANNELCNT which specifies the number of I/O channels available to the system.

will load drivers for all devices properly attached to the system. This command is executed during system boot. But drivers may have to be loaded after the boot. Some products also create drivers for "software" devices. For example, the DEC Test Manager (DTM) software loads a driver PCDRIVER.EXE when the DTM startup file is executed. The LOAD command loads a driver. The RELOAD command loads the latest version of a driver. An example usage is

```
$ IF F$GETDVI("_PTY:","EXISTS") THEN SYSGEN RELOAD
    SYS$SYSTEM:PCDRIVER.EXE
$ SYSGEN CONNECT PC/NOADAPTER/DRIVER=PCDRIVER
```

14.7.2   Other SYSGEN Uses

SYSGEN is used to create and install page and swap files as shown
before in this chapter. It is also used to set up shared memory on some
older multi-CPU systems like the VAX 11/782.

14.8   MODIFYING SYSTEM PARAMETERS: THE AUTOGEN UTILITY

For a new system, system parameters are calculated automatically by
the AUTOGEN utility. These parameters are based on CPU size,
memory, and estimated work load. The parameters may have to be
modified if required by software products and new hardware products.
Although system parameters can be modified by the SYSGEN WRITE
command, this is not recommended since the modifications are not
documented and the parameters may be reset if AUTOGEN is used for
parameter modifications later. Moreover, parameters are interdependent, so if one parameter is modified, AUTOGEN will modify other
parameters whose values depend on the modified parameter.
AUTOGEN has internal algorithms to do this.

14.8.1   An example

The system parameter GBLPAGES specifies the number of global
pages set up in the system for use by global sections. A software product may require 20000 global pages. SYSGEN shows that there are
10000 global pages in the system.

```
$SYSGEN SHOW GBLPAGES

Parameters in use: Active
Parameter Name              Current  Default  Minimum  Maximum Unit  Dynamic
---------------             -------  -------  -------   ------- ---   -------
GBLPAGES                    10000    10000    512       -1 Pages
```

All modifications to SYSGEN parameters should be specified in the
file SYS$SYSTEM:MODPARAMS.DAT. If the file does not exist, the
file can be created using an editor. One of the next two lines can be
entered in the file:

```
$ TYPE  SYS$SYSTEM:MODPARAMS.DAT

ADD_GBLPAGES=10000
GBLPAGES=20000
```

The parameter prefixed by an ADD_ is the preferred form since if
the system recalculates the parameter for it's own requirements, then

10,000 pages will be added to the newly calculated value rather than fixing the size at 20,000.

To make the parameter effective, run AUTOGEN by

```
$ @SYS$UPDATE:AUTOGEN   SAVPARAMS   REBOOT
```

The system parameters will be modified and the system will reboot with the new parameter value for GBLPAGES.

14.8.2 AUTOGEN details

AUTOGEN.COM is a DCL command file in the directory SYS$UPDATE. When the utility is run, it has phases of execution which are given by the parameters on the command line. The starting and ending phases are given by P1 and P2 on the command line. All in-between phases are executed also. In the example above, the phases SAVPARAMS through REBOOT are executed by AUTOGEN. Each phase uses various input and output files. Briefly, the files VMSPARAMS.DAT and MODPARAMS.DAT are used to generate VAXVMSSYS.PAR. The final file used by VMS to determine system parameters during a boot is VAXVMSSYS.PAR. The phases of execution are described in Table 14.2.

AUTOGEN uses feedback information from system operations to tune system parameters. If feedback information is not to be used then specify P3 as NOFEEDBACK:

```
$ @SYS$UPDATE:AUTOGEN   SAVPARAMS   REBOOT   NOFEEDBACK
```

To see a brief HELP on AUTOGEN, use

```
$ @SYS$UPDATE:AUTOGEN   HELP
```

14.9 THE INSTALL UTILITY

Normally, this utility is used by the system manager. Installing an image will set up various data structures in memory so that the image is "known" to the operating system. Executable images can be installed if they are used frequently. This will reduce the overhead of setting up the file header in the operating system when the image is run (by the DCL RUN command). Sharable images normally are installed before they are used (if they are not installed, each process using them has a separate copy of the image). Sharable images are mapped to global sections. Privileges can be assigned to installed images so that nonprivileged users can run the image and effectively use the extra privileges for the duration of the image execution.

An example of installing a shared image is

TABLE 14.2 AUTOGEN phases (All files are in SYS$SYSTEM)

Phase	Input files	Output files	Description
SAVPARAMS	None	AGEN$FEEDBACK.DAT	Collect feedback information from the running system. Output file will be used by GETDATA phase.
GETDATA	VMSPARAMS.DAT MODPARAMS.DAT AGEN$FEEDBACK.DAT	PARAMS.DAT	Use base system parameters (VMSPARAMS.DAT), user specified modifications (MODPARAMS.DAT) and feedback information to create PARAMS.DAT which is used by further phases.
GENPARAMS	PARAMS.DAT AGEN$ADDHISTORY.DAT	SETPARAMS.DAT VMSIMAGES.DAT AGEN$FEEDBACK.REPORT AGEN$ADDHISTORY.TMP	Generate new system parameters and create the installed image list. The history file stores AUTOGEN update logs.
TESTFILES	PARAMS.DAT	SYS$OUTPUT AGEN$FEEDBACK.REPORT	Display the page, swap, and dump file sizes calculated by AUTOGEN.
GENFILES	PARAMS.DAT	PAGEFILE.SYS SWAPFILE.SYS SYSDUMP.DMP Secondary page and swap files AGEN$FEEDBACK.REPORT	Generate new page, swap, and dump files if required.
SETPARAMS	SETPARAMS.DAT AGEN$ADDHISTORY.TMP	VAXVMSSYS.PAR VAXVMSSYS.OLD AUTOGEN.PAR AGEN$ADDHISTORY.DAT	Run SYSGEN to set system parameters specified in SETPARAMS.DAT and to generate a new AUTOGEN.PAR file. Current parameters are retained in VAXVMSSYS.OLD.
SHUTDOWN	None	None	Shutdown system after update of system parameters.
REBOOT	None	None	Shutdown then automatically reboot system with new parameters.

```
$ INSTALL  ADD  DUB6:[SYSCODE]INITDB.EXE
/OPEN/HEADER/PRIVILEGED/SHARED
```

To see a list of installed images the command is

```
$ INSTALL  LIST
```

Here is a sample usage of the command

```
$ INSTALL LIST
(output is edited to reduce size)

DISK$VMSRL5:<TESTB$PROD>.EXE
   TESTB_CALL;2
                  Open Hdr Shar              Lnkbl              Wrt

DISK$VMSRL5:<SYS0.SYSCOMMON.SYSEXE>.EXE
   ANALIMDMP;1                      Prv
   AUTHORIZE;1                      Prv
   CDU;1          Open Hdr          Prv
   CMS;2          Open     Shar
   COPY;2         Open Hdr Shar
   DCL;2          Open Hdr Shar              Lnkbl
   DELETE;1       Open Hdr Shar
   DIRECTORY;2    Open Hdr Shar

DISK$VMSRL5:<SYS0.SYSCOMMON.SYSLIB>.EXE
   ADARTL;2       Open Hdr Shar              Lnkbl
   BASRTL;1       Open Hdr Shar              Lnkbl
   BASRTL2;1
   VMSRTL;1       Open Hdr Shar              Lnkbl

DISK$VMSRL5:<SYS0.SYSCOMMON.SYSLIB>.TPU$SECTION
   EVE$SECTION;2  Open Hdr Shar              Lnkbl

DISK$TESTBDISK2:<INGRES.BIN>.EXE
   CREATEDB;30    Open             Prv
   DESTROYDB;120  Open             Prv
   INGCNTRL;19    Open             Prv

DISK$TESTBDISK2:<INGRES.LIBRARY>.EXE
   FRAMEFELIB;52  Open Hdr Shar              Lnkbl
   LIBQFELIB;62   Open Hdr Shar              Lnkbl
```

A listing of INSTALL command qualifiers follows:

/OPEN   Disk location information of the file is in memory. This
               eliminates searching for the file when the image is run.

/HEADER   File header information is in memory. Saves disk accesses
               when the image is run.

/PRIVILEGED   The image can use all privileges. Nonprivileged users can
               run the image which may perform privileged operations
               on behalf of the user. This in one way to give temporary
               privileges to nonprivileged users. All privileges are as-
               sumed unless some privileges are specified as in
               /PRIVILEGED = (CMKRNL, BYPASS)

/PROTECTED   Used for shared images. Specifies that the image contains code that can run in kernel or executive mode. The image can be used by nonprivileged users.

/NOPURGE	The installed image cannot be deinstalled by the IN-STALL PURGE command.
/SHARED	Used for sharable images. Images installed shared use global sections in memory.
/WRITABLE	Used for shared images. The image will be paged to the image on disk rather than the paging file if it has to be paged.

The INSTALL ADD command was shown above. The INSTALL commands are

ADD	Install the image file specified.
CREATE	Same function as ADD.
DELETE	Deinstall the image.
LIST	List all installed images with their attributes.
PURGE	Remove all installed images which were installed without the /NOPURGE qualifier.
REMOVE	Same function as DELETE.
REPLACE	Deletes an image and adds the latest version of the image.

Some commonly used system images like COPY.EXE and DIRECTORY.EXE are installed when the system boots. This installs are specified in the file SYS$MANAGER:VMSIMAGES.DAT which is accessed by SYS$SYSTEM:STARTUP.COM during the boot.

14.10   SYSTEM DUMP ANALYZER (SDA)

Normally, this utility is used by the experienced system manager. It can be used to examine system data structures while the system is running. It can also be used to analyze a crash dump file. VMS dumps memory to disk in the crash dump file, SYS$SYSTEM:SYSDUMP.DMP, under certain circumstances like when a fatal system bug occurs or when a crash dump is requested. The method for requesting a crash dump varies for the different types of VAXes. Some VAXes can be crash dumped from the console by

```
CTRL/P
>>>HALT
>>>@CRASH
```

or

```
CTRL/P
>>>@CRASH
```

SDA is used to examine data structures within VMS for the currently running system or for a crash dump file. To analyze the system use

```
$ ANALYZE/SYSTEM
```

To analyze a crash dump file use

```
$ANALYZE/CRASH_DUMP   SYS$SYSTEM:SYSDUMP.DMP
```

SDA automatically reads in symbol files: SYS$SYSTEM:SYS.STB and SYS$SYSTEM:SYSDEF.STB. These contain symbolic names for locations within the VMS executive. In fact, the commands

```
$ ANALYSE/SYSTEM
SDA> SHOW  SYMBOL /ALL
```

will display locations of major routines and data structures within VMS.

14.10.1 SDA commands

The EVALUATE command is used to evaluate an arithmetic expression. The DEFINE command is used to give a value to a symbol

```
SDA>DEFINE  TESTSYM = 5
SDA> EVALUATE  2 * (TESTSYM + 70)
Hex = 000000AA Decimal = 170
SDA>
```

All symbols having the evaluated value are also displayed. An instruction at a location can be displayed in mnemonic form by

```
SDA> EXAMINE/INSTRUCTION  3233A
0003233A:  LOCC  #09,#21,R8
SDA>
```

A few commands and their output are shown next. System debugging will require an extensive knowledge of VMS internal operations.

```
$ ANALYZE/SYSTEM
VAX/VMS System analyzer

SDA> EXAMINE 3A0
BUG$_RMSBUG: 00000000   "...."
SDA> SHO CRASH

System information
------------------
Version of system: VAX/VMS VERSION V5.1-1

System Version Major ID/Minor ID: 1/0


System type: VAX 8530

Primary CPU ID:  01
```

```
Bitmask of CPUs active/available:   00000002/00000002

CPU 01 database address:  80F0A000


SDA> SHO SYMBOL/ALL
(only some sybols shown in this output)

Symbols sorted by name
-----------------------
ACF$PROC_ADP     80003518 => 24A89F16
ACP$ACCESS       80002000 => A6439F17
ACP$ACCESSNET    80002008 => A6489F17
ACP$DEACCESS     80002010 => A6759F17


CLU$GW_QDSKVOTE  80008314 => 000A0001
CLU$GW_QUORUM    8000490C => 08C80000


SDA> EXAMINE /INSTRUCTION EXE$QIO+2
EXE$QIO+00002:  CHMK    #0022

SDA> SHO SUMMARY

Current process summary
-----------------------
 Extended Indx Process name    Username     State   Pri  PCB      PHD      Wkset
 -- PID --  ----  ----------------  -----------  -------  ---  --------  --------  ------
 00000101 0001 SWAPPER                        HIB    16 8019FD98 8019FC00      0
 00000104 0004 ERRFMT          SYSTEM       HIB     8 8048BA20 80F10400    113
 00000105 0005 OPCOM           SYSTEM       HIB     8 8048C2E0 80FF6000    160
 00000106 0006 JOB_CONTROL     SYSTEM       HIB     8 8048C530 81068E00    433
 00000107 0007 NETACP          DECNET       HIB    10 804A3980 810DBC00    451
 00000108 0008 EVL             DECNET       HIB     6 804A46E0 8114EA00     47
 00000109 0009 REMACP          SYSTEM       HIB     9 804B2690 811C1800     57
 0000010A 000A SYMBIONT_0001   SYSTEM       HIB     6 804BDCF0 81234600     88

 0000010B 000B RDMS_MONITOR    SYSTEM       LEF    15 804BE700 812A7400     53
 0000010C 000C RPC$SWL         SYSTEM       HIB     9 804BF290 8131A200    199
 0000010D 000D SMISERVER       SYSTEM       HIB     9 804C62F0 8138D000    492
 .
 .
 .
 00000162 0062 _RTA1:          TECH4        CUR    10 80549750 81C13A00   1515

SDA> SHOW PROCESS

Process index: 0062   Name: _RTA1:   Extended PID: 00000162
-----------------------------------------------------------------
Process status:  02040001   RES,PHDRES

PCB address            80549750   JIB address            80E3EAC0
PHD address            81C13A00   Swapfile disk address  00000000
Master internal PID    00010062   Subprocess count              0
Internal PID           00010062   Creator internal PID   00000000
Extended PID           00000162   Creator extended PID   00000000
State                       CUR   Termination mailbox        0000
Current priority              9   AST's enabled              KESU
Base priority                 5   AST's active               NONE
UIC            [00001,000011]     AST's remaining            9997
Mutex count                   0   Buffered I/O count/limit  20000/20000
Waiting EF cluster            1   Direct I/O count/limit    20000/20000
Starting wait time     1A001A15   BUFIO byte count/limit  999936/999936
Event flag wait mask   7FFFFFFF   # open files allowed left    299
Local EF cluster 0     E0000000   Timer entries allowed left  1000
Local EF cluster 1     C0000000   Active page table count        0
Global cluster 2 pointer 00000000 Process WS page count       1282
Global cluster 3 pointer 00000000 Global WS page count         233

SDA> SHOW LOCK
```

Lock database

```
Lock id:  00010001    PID:    00000000    Flags:    NOQUEUE SYNCSTS SYSTEM
Par. id:  00000000    Granted at    EX              CVTSYS
Sublocks:       3
LKB:       80EC49E0
Resource:        5F535953 24535953    SYS$SYS_   Status:   NOQUOTA
  Length   16    00000000 00004449    ID......
  Exec. mode     00000000 00000000    ........
  System         00000000 00000000    ........
Local copy
```

14.11 FURTHER READING

Systems Programming, Vol. 7B, VMS Programming Manuals.

SYSGEN, Vol. 1B, VMS Systems Management Manuals.

Install, Vol. 1B, VMS Systems Management Manuals.

Goatley, Hunter, "SDA: The Ultimate Management Tool" (3 parts), *VAX Professional*, August, October, December 1989.

Kenah, L. J., Goldberg, R. E., Bate S. F., *VAX/VMS Internals and Data Structures (Version 4.4)*, Digital Press, Maynard, Mass., 1988.

Goldberg, R. E., Kenah, L. J., *VMS Internals and Data Structures—Version 5 Update XPRESS* (Vols. 1, 2, and 3), Digital Press, Maynard, Mass., 1989.

15

Performance Monitoring and System Tuning

A properly installed VMS system is tuned for normal workloads. VMS has a number of system parameters (SYSGEN parameters) which can be tweaked to enhance system performance for specific requirements. The system can be monitored to see overall system performance, to determine bottlenecks, to solve specific performance problems, or for future capacity planning. Figure 15.1 shows parameters which are normally relevant to system performance.

Key utilities on the VAX for monitoring system performance are

- The MONITOR utility
- Software Performance Monitor (SPM)
- Vax Performance Advisor (VPA)

MONITOR displays snapshots (real-time displays) of system utilization. Typical displays include CPU, Direct (disk) I/O, memory usage, DECnet usage, and cluster statistics. The utility does not provide graphic reports, but it can generate an output binary file of performance data gathered at specified time intervals. Programs can be written to read this file and generate customized system utilization reports. MONITOR is supplied with the operating system.

SPM can be used to display real-time snapshots of system utilization or to log performance parameters to a file and create reports from this logged raw data. It can also be used to generate bills for system usage based on unit prices to be charged for usage of various resources. SPM has more features than MONITOR but it has to be ordered separately.

VPA collects and logs system parameters which can be used to gen-

Class	Information recorded
PROCESSES	For each process: UIC, state, priority, process name, count of process and global pages used, status (swapped?), count of direct I/Os, buffered I/Os and page faults.
STATES	Count of processes in each of the scheduler states. The state of each process could be current, computable, or waiting. Wait states are subclassified as collided page wait, miscellaneous resource wait, common event flag wait, page fault wait, local event flag wait (inswapped), local event flag wait (outswapped), hibernate (inswapped), hibernate (outswapped), suspended (inswapped), suspended (outswapped), and free page wait.
MODES	CPU time spent in kernel, executive, supervisory and user states. Time spent on interrupt stack and on synchronizing multiple CPUs.
PAGES	Systemwide page fault reads and writes. Page fault read and write I/Os. Faults on free page list, modified page list, demand-zero pages, system global pages, and system space. Pages read when they were in the process of being written to disk. Count of free and modified pages.
IO	Count of direct and buffered I/O, logical name translations, page faults, page reads and page I/Os, page writes, and page I/Os, free and modified pages, and inswaps.
FCP	Applies to the file system. Count of QIOs, QIOs causing disk space allocation, new files created, reads, writes, volume lock waits, CPU time used, and page faults generated by the file system, window turns, file name lookups, files opened, and erase operations.
POOL	Nonpaged dynamic pool statistics. Total space used and free. Blocks of memory unused. Largest and smallest block size. Count of blocks less than 33 bytes in size. Count of small, intermediate, and large request packets available and in use.
LOCK	Information similar to that of DLOCK class is displayed except that these locks are for the current system.
DECnet	Count of incoming and outgoing packets, congestion loss, receive buffer failure, and large request packets available.
FILE_SYSTEM_CACHE	Applies to memory cache. Count of hits and attempts on directory, directory data, file header, file id, extent, quota, and bitmap caches.
DISK	Count of I/O operations and I/O request queue entries for each disk.
DLOCK	Count of distributed locks created, deleted, and converted, and count of incoming and outgoing functions and blocking ASTs. Rate of deadlock messages.

Figure 15.1   MONITOR recording classes

Class	Information recorded
SCS	On a cluster, statistics are gathered on datagrams and sequenced messages from current node to each of the other members of the cluster.
SYSTEM	CPU busy time, total processes, total page faults, disk page fault read I/Os, pages in free and modified page list. Count of direct and buffered I/Os.
CLUSTER	Clusterwide CPU, memory, disk, and lock usage.
RMS	Statistics on each file specified on the command line with the /FILE qualifier. Some of the items displayed are count of KEY GETs, PUT bytes, counts of writes and delete operations, record locks for the file, and bucket splits for indexed files.
MSCP_SERVER	MSCP statistics.

Figure 15.1 *(Continued)*

erate reports on system behavior. It will give suggestions on what to do to gain better performance from the system. The latter feature is based on artificial intelligence techniques. VPA is an expert system with a rule database. The collected data is checked against the rules, and if the rules are being violated, VPA displays suggestions stored with the rules. VPA does not provide continuous displays of system usage.

In addition to the three utilities, some commands can help gain a better understanding of system usage:

```
$ SHOW SYSTEM                          !Summary of all processes
$ ACCOUNTING                           !Process resource usage
$ SHOW PROCESS processname             !Process information
$ SHOW PROCESS/CONTINUOUS/ID=nnnnnnnnn !Dynamic display of
                                        process state
$ SHOW USER                            !Users on the system (or
                                        cluster)
$ SHOW DEVICES                         !All devices on the system
$ MCR NCP SHOW KNOWN LINES COUNTERS    !Network information
$ MCR SYSGEN SHOW /ALL                 !System parameters
$ MCR SYSGEN SHOW /SPECIAL             !Special system parameters
```

The three performance monitoring and tuning utilities will be discussed here.

15.1 THE MONITOR UTILITY

MONITOR is simpler to use than SPM for on-line display of system activity. The utility is briefly described in Chapter 1. Here is an example usage.

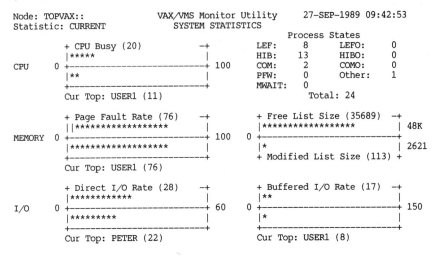

```
$ MONITOR SYSTEM

Node: TOPVAX::            VAX/VMS Monitor Utility    27-SEP-1989 09:42:53
Statistic: CURRENT           SYSTEM STATISTICS
                                              Process States
          + CPU Busy (20)      -+        LEF:    8    LEFO:    0
          |*****                 |        HIB:   13    HIBO:    0
CPU     0 +---------------------+ 100     COM:    2    COMO:    0
          |**                    |        PFW:    0    Other:   1
          +---------------------+         MWAIT:  0
          Cur Top: USER1 (11)                     Total: 24

          + Page Fault Rate (76)  -+      + Free List Size (35689)  -+
          ||****************      |       |****************          | 48K
MEMORY  0 +---------------------+ 100   0 +------------------------+
          |******************     |       |*                        | 2621
          +---------------------+         + Modified List Size (113) +
          Cur Top: USER1 (76)

          + Direct I/O Rate (28)  -+      + Buffered I/O Rate (17)  -+
          |***********           |        |**                       |
I/O     0 +---------------------+ 60    0 +------------------------+ 150
          |********              |        |*                        |
          +---------------------+         +------------------------+
          Cur Top: PETER (22)             Cur Top: USER1 (8)
```

The display shows:

- The CPU is 20 percent busy.

- The top CPU user is USER1 who uses 11 percent of the CPU time.

- 76 page faults per second are being generated. In this example all the page faults are by USER1.

- Direct I/O rate is 28 per second. Direct I/O is normally to disk and tape devices.

- Buffered I/O rate is 17 per second. Buffered I/O is mainly to terminals and mailboxes.

- Of the 24 processes in the system, 13 are hibernating, effectively waiting for some external process or VMS to wake them up.

On the VT series terminals, the screen display is updated at specified intervals (6 seconds by default) so that current system status is displayed. The data displayed can instead be recorded in a disk file (by default, MONITOR.DAT). These data can later be used via programs to generate custom reports. The data can also be used as input to MONITOR for generating screen displays. An example command to log data is

```
$MONITOR/RECORD/NODISPLAY SYSTEM
```

The contents of the recording file are binary and are described in the MONITOR section of the system management manual.

15.1.1 MONITOR CLASSES

MONITOR can be used to generate displays which are grouped by classes. The example command above displayed information on the SYSTEM class. The next command generates displays on all classes; each class information is displayed on the terminal for a few seconds before the next display:

```
$ MONITOR ALL_CLASSES
```

Figure 15.1 describes the information in the various classes. It gives you an idea on what is relevant when analyzing system behavior.

15.2 SOFTWARE PERFORMANCE MONITOR (SPM)

This product has to be purchased separately from DEC. SPM can be used to display a real-time snapshot of current system activity or it can be used to produce reports and graphs on system activity over a period of time, say CPU utilization from 9.00 a.m. to 5.00 p.m. yesterday.

The basic SPM commands for continuous monitoring of system are

```
$ PERFORMANCE DISPLAY = INVESTIGATE
$ PERFORMANCE DISPLAY = RESOURCE
```

A CRT terminal is required. Both forms display CPU, memory, and I/O information. The first command is particularly useful if the terminal supports ReGIS graphics (like a VT330 or a VT340).

To generate system usage reports, SPM has two components: the data collector and the report facility. The collector records system parameter values at specified intervals in a disk log file. The file is read later by SPM when it is used to generate reports. The basic commands are:

```
$ PERFORMANCE COLLECT = TUNE            !Start data collection
$ PERFORMANCE COLLECT = TUNE/STOP       !Stop data collection
$ PERFORMANCE REPORT = LOG_FILE         !Generate reports on the
                                         collected data
```

Here is an example:

```
$ PERFORMANCE COLLECT = TUNE/CLASS = ALL
```

SPM classes of data are different from that of MONITOR. Some classes are CPU, MEMORY, GLOBAL_SECTIONS and LOCK. In this example, information is collected on all classes. The command causes a process, SPM_TUNE, to run. The process collects and records parameters in a file, SPM$COLLECT_TUNE.DAT, in the current directory. The collection process can be stopped by the command:

```
$ PERFORMANCE COLLECT=TUNE/STOP
```

A report for 9.00 a.m. to 5.00 p.m. was generated from the data collected by the command:

```
$ PERFORMANCE REPORT=LOG_FILE SPM$COLLECT_TUNE.DAT -
/SINCE:28-SEP-1989:9:00 /BEFORE:28-SEP-1989:17:00
```

The report is 132 columns wide and, by default, is stored in the file LOGFILE.RPT. A detailed report can be generated by adding the qualifier /CLASS=ALL to the command line. Figure 15.2 is a report using the command

```
$ REPORT=LOG_FILE [SHAH]SPM$COLLECT_TUNE.DAT -
/SINCE=11-OCT-1989 09:00:00.00/BEFORE=11-OCT-1989 17:00:00.00
```

SPM can also be used to generate charge-back information for billing in a time-sharing environment. The charge file (SPM_-CHARGE.TXT) contains information on the charge per unit of a resource usage. An example line is

```
CPUSEC_PRICE = 0.01500
```

SPM uses output from the two VMS commands:

```
$ACCOUNTING /OUTPUT=ACC_CHARGE.DAT
$ANALYZE/DISK_STRUCTURE/USAGE=DISK_DUA2_CHARGE.DAT  DUA2:
```

To generate the bills, a command like this is issued

```
$ PERFORMANCE REPORT=CHARGE -
ACC_CHARGE.DAT SPM_CHARGE.TXT DISK_DUA2_CHARGE.DAT
```

15.2.1 Weekly and monthly performance reports

A set of collector log files may be created over a period of time. Say one file is produced every day; also, separate files may be created on each node of a cluster. These files could be merged and used to produce reports of the system activity over a period of days or even months. The merged file is called the history file. It can be created by a command like

```
$ PERFORMANCE ARCHIVE=HISTORY/CREATE   HISTORY.DAT
SPM$COLLECT_TUNE.DAT;*
```

To append new files to an existing history file, /CREATE should be replace by a /ADD.

The history file can now be used to produce a report covering, say, all the days from March 1, 1990 to March 31, 1990:

```
$ PERFORMANCE REPORT=HISTORY /SINCE:1-mar-1989/BEFORE:1-apr-1989
```

```
+-----------------------------------------------------------------------------------+
!                                                                                   !
!  ------------------------ VAX VMS System Configuration ------------------------   !
!                                                                                   !
!  Node : TOPVAX                                                                    !
!  Experiment name :                                                                !
!  Log File : SYS$SYSDEVICE:[SHAH]SPM$COLLECT_TUNE.DAT;1                             !
!  Data collection started :   10-OCT-1989 17:00:23.19                              !
!  Data collection ended :     17-NOV-2001 00:00:00.00                              !
!  Sample interval :               300 seconds /    5.000 minutes                   !
!  Report generated :          11-OCT-1989 17:11:52.36                              !
!  Processor type is : 8530                                                         !
!  Running VMS version V5.1-1                                                        !
!  TR 32   BI Disk Adapter (KDB50)                                                  !
!  TR 34   BI - NMI Adapter (NBIB)                                                  !
!  TR 37   BI - Combo Board (DMB32)                                                 !
!  TR 38   BI - LESI Adapter (KLESI-B)                                              !
!  TR 39   BI - NI Adapter (DEBNA)                                                  !
!  TR 48   BI Disk Adapter (KDB50)                                                  !
!  TR 50   BI - NMI Adapter (NBIB)                                                  !
!  TR 53   BI - NI Adapter (DEBNA)                                                  !
!  TR 54   BI Disk Adapter (KDB50)                                                  !
!  System Allocation Class :        0                                               !
!  Total memory :   65536 pages =   32.00 MB                                        !
!  Floating Point Accelerator Status:                                               !
!     None of the floating data types are emulated                                  !
!  Non-paged memory = 11673 pages (17.8% of total memory)                           !
!  Paged memory = 53863 pages (82.2% of total memory)                               !
!  System working set =     2623 pages ( 4.9% of paged memory)                      !
!  User memory (paged-system working set) =  51240 pages (95.1% of paged memory : 78.2% of total memory) !
+-----------------------------------------------------------------------------------+
```

Figure 15.2   An SPM report.

```
****************************                                                                       **************************
****************************                                                                       **************************
             FINAL Statistics
Data Analyzed: from  11-OCT-1989 09:00:56.76  to  11-OCT-1989 17:01:10.81
```

AVE Process-Memory Counts

Proc Count	Balset Count	Free Pages	Modify Pages
25	23	38829	187

Memory Utilization

Total MEMutl	Paged MEMutl	User MEMutl	Modify MEMutl
40.8%	23.0%	24.2%	0.4%

AVE Mem/CPU Queues

Mem	CPU
0	0

Swapper Counts

InSWP	OutSWP	Header InSWP	Header OutSWP	Swaper CPU %
0	0	0	0	0.0%

CPU Statistics

CPU ID	Total Idle	Busy Wait	Inter Stack	Kernel	Exec	Super	User	Compat	System	Task
1	96.3%	0.0%	0.8%	1.3%	0.3%	0.1%	1.3%	0.0%	2.3%	1.4%

Lost CPU / Page

Page Wait	Swap or Swp Wait
0.8%	0.8%
0.1%	0.8%

CPU and I/O Overlap

CPU+IO Idle	CPU Only	I/O Only	Multi I/O	CPU+IO Busy
93.9%	3.3%	2.3%	0.1%	0.4%

Paging Rates (per second)

Page Faults	System Faults	Pages Read	Read I/Os	Pages Writen	Write I/Os	Free List	Modify List	Bad List	Dzero Faults	Gvalid Faults	Trans Faults	WritIN Prog
10.5	0.0	6.9	0.3	1.3	0.0	2.8	1.1	0.0	3.7	2.6	0.0	0.0

Hard / Soft Faults

Hard Faults	Soft Faults
3.0%	97.0%

I/O Rates (per second)

Direct I/Os	Buffrd I/Os	Lognam Trans	Mailbx Reads	Mailbx Writes
1.4	3.9	2.3	0.1	0.0

File I/O Rates (per second)

Window Hits	Window Turns	Split I/Os	Erase I/Os	File Opens
1.0	0.0	0.1	0.0	0.1

AVE Open Files

AVE Open Files
224

Figure 15.2 *(Continued)*

```
+--------------------- File Cache Attempt Rate (per second) ---------------------+
!                                                                                !
!  Dir    Dir           File   File                 Bit                          !
!  FCB    Data   Quota    Id    Hdr    Extent       Map                          !
! ------ ------ ------ ------ ------ ------ ------ ------                         !
!  0.2    0.3    0.0    0.0    0.3    0.1    0.0                                  !
!                                                                                !
+--------------------------------------------------------------------------------+

+--------------------- File cache Effectivness ---------------------+
!                                                                   !
!  Dir    Dir          File   File                  Bit             !
!  FCB    Data   Quota   Id    Hdr    Extent        Map             !
! ------ ------ ------ ------ ------ ------ ------ ------            !
! 95.4%  95.9%  0.0%  99.1%  80.2%  98.0%        8.8%               !
!                                                                   !
+-------------------------------------------------------------------+
```

	Work Avail %	Paging %	Swping %	Contlr %	Rate (/s)	Read %	Remote I/O%	Serv Time (ms)	Resp Time (ms)	Queue Length	Space Used %
DJA1	0.6	35.2	0.0	25.0	0.2	65.7	0.0	32	32	0.0	99.2
DJA2	0.0	0.0	0.0	0.0	0.0	0.0	0.0	0	0	0.0	99.2
DJC8	0.0	0.0	0.0	0.0	0.0	0.0	0.0	0	0	0.0	99.2

Disk Statistics

Report Date: 11-OCT-1989 17:11   TOPVAX   VAX SPM V3.3-03   Page 3

	Work Avail %	Paging %	Swping %	Contlr %	Rate (/s)	Read %	Remote I/O%	Serv Time (ms)	Resp Time (ms)	Queue Length	Space Used %
DUA4	1.4	34.1	17.4	73.1	0.7	63.3	0.0	21	25	0.0	97.2
DUA5	0.0	0.0	0.0	1.9	0.0	44.5	0.0	21	22	0.0	98.0
DUB6	0.2	25.1	0.0	34.5	0.1	31.6	0.0	35	35	0.0	98.1
DUB7	0.6	1.2	0.0	65.5	0.2	26.6	0.0	32	43	0.0	85.5

Disk Statistics

	Work Avail %	Paging %	Swaping %	Queue Length
PUA	2.0	33.8	12.7	0.0
PUB	1.0	9.5	0.0	0.0
PUC	0.1	0.0	0.0	0.0

Server Statistics

Figure 15.2 (*Continued*)

249

Report Date: 11-OCT-1989 17:11   TOPVAX   VAX SPM V3.3-03   Page 4

CPU Utilization (Percent) vs. Time of Day
Each column = 300 seconds / 5.00 minutes

From: 11-OCT-1989 09:00:56.76   To : 11-OCT-1989 17:01:10.81

```
100% +
     -
     -
 90% +
     -
     -
 80% +
     -
     -
 70% +
     -
     -
 60% +
     -
     -
 50% +
     -
     -
 40% +
     -
     -
 30% +
     -
     -
 20% +
     -                                             U
     -                                             U
     -                                             U    U
     -              U                              UU UU
     -              UU             U               KUUEU                                            U   U
 10% +              UU           K KK              KK K UK                            U   U          U   E
     -     U        UU          KK K U UK         UKKKKK          U          U   U   U   U         U U K
     -     K        KK          IIKIIKIK KKKIIKKK UKKIIKKK       UKU      KUUUU KU   K   U        U U K    U
     -     IU       IUIII  UU   IIKIIKIK KKIIIKKK KIKK K  KKK K  KIKK  UU KUKUU KK   UU KKUIKKUII  IUI  KK K    S
        +----+----+----+----+----+----+----+----+----+----+----+----+----+----+----+----+----+----+----+----+----
09:00 09:25 09:50 10:15 10:40 11:06 11:31 11:56 12:21 12:46 13:11 13:36 14:01 14:26 14:51 15:16 15:41 16:06 16:31 16:56
```

"I" = Interrupt   "B" = Busy Wait   "K" = Kernel   "E" = Exec   "S" = Super
"U" = User   "C" = Compat   "." = Data Unavailable

Figure 15.2 (Continued)

Report Date: 11-OCT-1989 17:..   TOPVAX   VAX SPM V3.3-03   Page

Run Statistics

Total Intervals Found For Analysis: 96
Prime Hours: 08, 09, 10, 11, 12, 13, 14, 15, 16
Input Source: Log File V3.3

Command Line:

REPORT=LOG_FILE [SHAH]SPM$COLLECT_TUNE.DAT/SINCE=11-OCT-1989 09:00:00.00/BEFORE=11-OCT-1989 17:00:00.00

ELAPSED: 0 00:00:03.52   CPU: 0:00:01.97   BUFIO: 7   DIRIO: 46   FAULTS: 476

Figure 15.2 (*Continued*)

The report will be for the month with one column for each day of the month. The command has other useful qualifiers:

/WEEKLY	Produces a report for each week.
/MONTHLY	Produces a report for each month.
/P_HOURS	Produces a report on prime hours of each day. The default prime hours are 8 a.m. to 5 p.m. Prime hours can be specified as: /P_HOURS = (9:00-17:00).
/P_DAYS	Produces a report on prime days of the week: Monday through Friday. Prime day can be specified as: /P_DAYS = (MONDAY,TUESDAY,WEDNESDAY,THURSDAY,FRIDAY,SATURDAY,NOSUNDAY).
/HOLIDAYS = (DATE, ...)	Does not include the specified days in the report.
/NODE = nodename	The history file can consist of collector files from various nodes. This qualifier select a particular node for reporting.

15.3   VAX PERFORMANCE ADVISOR (VPA)

This product has to be purchased separately from DEC. VPA is the most versatile of the three utilities mentioned in this chapter. There are two phases to using VPA for generating reports and graphs. The first phase is data collection. The command to start data collection is

```
$ @SYS$STARTUP:VPA$STARTUP.COM
```

This command file creates a process, VPA_DC, which records various system parameters and resource usage metrics.

A report can be generated by a command like

```
$ ADVISE/REPORT=(PERFORMANCE_EVALUATION, ANALYZE)
```

The time interval covered is the start of day or start of data collection until the present time. The report gives a summary of CPU, memory, and I/O utilization, and, perhaps most importantly, the report also includes suggestions on what can be done to improve performance. A typical report appears at the end of this chapter. The output has been edited to reduce the number of pages.

Some interesting features of VPA are

- The ANALYSIS option when generating reports invokes a rule database which is used by VPA to make suggestions on how to improve performance. For example, there may be excessive page faulting because some users require more memory than their working set extent allows. VPA will give the names of users whose WSEXTENT parameter in the authorization file should be increased.

- The rule database can be customized to report potential combination of events depending on the site requirements.

- The report displays hot files. These are files accessed the most. These files can be made contiguous or placed on separate disks to improve peformance.

- On clusters, VPA produces clusterwide reports.

- VPA can be used to generate reports on a group of users called a workload. So, say, four users are working on a particular application, VPA could be set up to produce reports on system usage by the application.

- VPA can be used for capacity planning and modeling. For example, suppose a system has four applications divided into four workloads for VPA. Suppose the number of users of an application is likely to go up by 75 percent. VPA can be used to generate a report on the likely system performance when there are more users for a particular application. VPA can be used to model system performance to see the likely effect if ,say, a new disk and more memory is added to the system.

15.3.1 Data Collector

The collector is started by the command shown above. The collector stores the data in the directory VPA$DATABASE: with a file name like VPA$NODEA_1990JAN14.CPD where NODEA is the node name of the VAX. A new file is created for each new day. A file, VPA$SCHEDULE.DAT, also exists in VPA$DATABASE. This file determines when during the week data should be recorded and on what nodes (if the VAX is part of a cluster). The schedule file contents can be listed by

```
$ ADVISE/COLLECT/INQUIRE=SCHEDULE

SCHEDULE  FILE _____
             |    Node Names    |  |  Weekly Schedule for ALL nodes
Beginning    |------------------|  |-------------------------------------
  19-JAN-1990 | NODEA           |  |  Sunday      0-24
Ending        | TOPVAX          |  |  Monday      0-24
   1-JAN-2010 |                 |  |  Tuesday     0-24
Hot Files     |                 |  |  Wednesday   0-24
     0.33     |                 |  |  Thursday    0-24
Delete after  |                 |  |  Friday      0-24
     60 Days  |                 |  |  Saturday    0-24
```

The schedule file shows that data is collected for all 24 hours a day, seven days a week. Data is collected on two nodes of the cluster: NODEA and TOPVAX. The schedule can be modified by commands like

```
$ADVISE/COLLECT/SCHEDULE=(MONDAY=(9-17), NOSUNDAY)
$ADVISE/COLLECT/SCHEDULE/NODE_NAME=SCOOP
```

There is no need to stop the collection process explicitly since reports can be generated up to the current moment in time without having to stop the collector process (which is VPA_DC). The command to stop the collector is

```
$ ADVISE/COLLECT/STOP
```

15.3.2   Generating VPA reports

A typical command to generate a report is

```
$ ADVISE/REPORT=(PERFORMANCE_EVALUATION, ANALYSIS) -
/BEGINNING=29-SEP-1989:09:00 /ENDING=29-SEP-1989:17:00
```

The ANALYSIS option causes VPA to analyze the performance data and suggests what could be done to improve performance. Section 15.3.3 describes this feature in more detail.

An example performance report was shown previously. Some examples of qualifiers are

/BEGINNING=29-SEP-1989:09:00   Reports start date and time.

/ENDING=29-SEP-1989:17:00   Reports end date and time.

/IMAGE=applman   Generates image residency time histogram for the specified image.

/OUTPUT=vpa.report   Creates an output file rather than display the report on the terminal.

The performance reports include statistics on CI, NI and adapters, disks and tapes, hot files, locks, CPU modes, memory pool, processes, and SCS usage on clusters. The report output is quite self-documented.

15.3.3   Advice from VPA and the knowledge database

VPA is a rule-based expert system. It has a set of built-in rules which can be augmented by user-defined rules. Each rule has a five-character rule name. A rule file is also called a knowledge database. The file VPA$EXAMPLES:VPA$KB.VPR shows most elements of a rule file. Here is an example rule:

```
Rule R0030 Domain Summary
     Average_IRPs_InUse - SYSGEN_IRPCOUNT .ge. SYSGEN_IRPCOUNT *
                    td_pool_expansion_ratio;
     Evidence =
            SYSGEN_IRPCOUNT
            SYSGEN_IRPCOUNTV
            Average_IRPs_InUse
            Maximum_IRPs_InUse;
```

Conclusion
     The average number of IRPs in use during the report
     period exceeded the number of preallocated IRPs by at
     least 40%. This means that there was unnecessary VMS
     overhead to build additional IRPs from available
     physical memory. If more IRPs were preallocated at
     boot time, less overhead would have been incurred.
     However, be careful (in scarce memory situations) not
     to use more memory than is necessary.

     Use the AUTOGEN feedback mechanism to automatically
     increase the SYSGEN parameter IRPCOUNT. After
     successive uses of AUTOGEN, the AUTOGEN feedback
     mechanism provides the system with ample IRPs.

```
     Endrule
```

When generating a report with the ANALYSIS option, as in the sample command

```
$ ADVISE/REPORT=(ANALYSIS, PERFORMANCE_EVALUATION)
```

VPA analyzes the collected data against the built-in knowledge database (and the user-specified database if one is specified). Rules meeting specified conditions get fired and the analysis is written out. Here is a typical page from the analysis report. The output is based on the rule shown above.

```
VPA V2.0 Analysis           TOPVAX (VAX 6320)              PAGE 4
      Report          Friday 29SEP89 00:00 to 12:50

CONCLUSION 3.

                                                         {R0030}

        The average number of IRPs in use during the report
        period exceeded the number of preallocated IRPs by at
        least 40%. This means that there was unnecessary VMS
        overhead to build additional IRPs from available
        physical memory. If more IRPs were preallocated at
        boot time, less overhead would have been incurred.
        However, be careful (in scarce memory situations) not
        to use more memory than is necessary.

        Use the AUTOGEN feedback mechanism to automatically
        increase the SYSGEN parameter IRPCOUNT. After
        successive uses of AUTOGEN, the AUTOGEN feedback
        mechanism provides the system with ample IRPs.

    CONDITIONS

        1. AVERAGE_IRPS_INUSE - SYSGEN_IRPCOUNT .GE.
           SYSGEN_IRPCOUNT * 0.40
```

EVIDENCE

```
Current IRPCOUNT.......1607
Current IRPCOUNTV......4821
Avg IRPs in use........2841
Max IRPs in use........2973
```

To create your own knowledge database, use the file VPA$EXAMPLES:VPA$KB.VPR as a template creating, say, NEWRULES.VPR in your directory. The rule file must be built by VPA

```
$ ADVISE/BUILD   NEWRULES.VPR
```

The output will be a "compiled" knowledge base NEWRULES.KB. This file can be specified for analysis by

```
$ ADVISE/REPORT=ANALYSIS/RULES=NEWRULES.KB
```

VPA will first scan the factory rules and then these rules during the analysis phase.

15.3.5 Workloads: system usage reports based on user groups

The VPA reports discussed up to now are based on the three types of images on the system: interactive, batch and network. When a number of independent applications are running on the system, reports based on resource utilization by individual applications may be more insightful. To do this, it is necessary to create workloads of users or program images. For example, a system may be running two major applications, word processing and an on-line banking application. The ADVISE/EDIT command can be used to create two user workloads:

```
$ ADVISE/EDIT
VPA-EDIT> ADD /WORKLOAD  WORD_PROCESSING
                              /USERNAMES=(ZITTO,PAUL,BROWN)
VPA-EDIT> ADD /WORKLOAD  BANKING /USERNAMES=(BLY,SHAH)
```

The commands modify a parameter file, VPA$DATABASE:VPA$PARAMS.DAT. Workloads have to be grouped into families for reporting purposes. The two workloads created can be placed in a family called MY_VAX_USERS:

```
VPA-EDIT> ADD/FAMILY   MY_VAX_USERS
   /WORKLOAD=(WORD_PROCESSING,BANKING)
```

Now, a report can be created which contains subreports on the two workloads:

```
$ ADVISE/REPORT=PERFORMANCE_EVALUATION
  /CLASSIFY_BY=USERGROUPS=MY_VAX_USERS
```

There are two types of workload families: user group and transaction. The user group would normally contain workloads with groups of users in each workload while the transaction workloads contain related set of images like say all the compiler images. Reporting is similar for the two types of families. The major difference is that the transaction family report also contains an implicit workload, Z-Frequency, which consists of all images which were not terminated during the reporting period. Here are some predefined families and workloads.

```
VPA-EDIT>SHOW/FAMILY *

    Workload  Family                Workload Member(s)
-------------------------   ------------------------------------------
MODEL_USERGROUPS            SYSTEM_USER, OPERATOR, DECNET
MODEL_TRANSACTIONS          SYSMAN, UTILITIES, EDITORS, COMPILES, NETWORK
EACH_USER                   EACH_USER


VPA-EDIT>SHOW/WORKLOAD *

        Workload                  Selection Criteria
-------------------------   ------------------------------------------
SYSTEM_USER                 Match is based on EITHER username or imagename.
          Usernames:        SYSTEM
OPERATOR                    Match is based on EITHER username or imagename.
          Usernames:        OPERATOR
DECNET                      Match is based on EITHER username or imagename.
          Usernames:        DECNET
SYSMAN                      Match is based on EITHER username or imagename.
          Imagenames:       APLIC, ARRAY, BACKUP, BUTTON, CALC$MAIN, CALNOTICE, CDU,
                            CLEAR, CLR, CMS, CONFIGURE, CSP, DBMMON, DIRFMT, DQS$SMB,
                            DTM$FILTER, DVI2LN3, EPC$REGIS, ERRFMT, EVL, HISTORY,
                            HOSTCHECK, INSTALL, JOBCTL, MONITOR, NOTICE, OPCOM, PAVN,
                            PLOT, PROCNAM, PROTS, QUEMAN, SCHED, SETRIGHTS, STARTUP,
                            SYSGEN, VAXSIM, VPA$ADVISOR, VPA$BLDKB, VPA$DC_V5,
                            VPA$GRAPH, VPA$VME, VPA$EDIT, WHAT, WHYBOOT
COMPILES                    Match is based on EITHER username or imagename.
          Imagenames:       BASIC, BLISS32, LINK, MACRO32, VAXC
UTILITIES                   Match is based on EITHER username or imagename.
          Imagenames:       COPY, CREATE, CREATEFDL, DELETE, DIFF, DIRECTORY, DTM,
                            ENOTES, LNGSPLCOR, LOGINOUT, LPS$SMB, MAIL, NOTES$MAIN,
                            NOTES$SERVER, PHONE, QUOTE_V0, RECOLOR, RENAME, REPLY,
                            RUNOFF, SEARCH, SET, SETP0, SHOW, SHWCLSTR, SORTMERGE,
                            SSU, SUBMIT, TYPE, VMSHELP, VTXPAD
EDITORS                     Match is based on EITHER username or imagename.
          Imagenames:       EDT, EMACS, EMACSSHR, LSEDIT, SED, TECO32, TEX, TPU
NETWORK                     Match is based on EITHER username or imagename.
          Imagenames:       ELF, FAL, FILESERV, LATCP, LATSYM, NCP, NETACP,
                            NETSERVER, NM$DAEMON, NM$QUEMAN, NML, REMACP, RTPAD
EACH_USER                   Unique Workload for each Username
```

15.3.6 Capacity planning and modeling

Capacity planning is the process of planning for future growth in system usage. Modeling allows you to study system performance on a hypothetical system. Typically, the current system is used as a basis and then VPA is asked to generate performance reports assuming that the workload has increased by, say, 50 percent, or assuming that a new disk drive has been added.

The two steps for modeling are

1. Create a model file which contains a description of the current hardware, workload, and performance parameters

   ```
   $ ADVISE/MODEL/BUILD   ENVIRON.MDL /BEG=9:00/END=17:00
   ```

   The command has qualifiers similar to that used with the /REPORT qualifier. The model file will have performance information based on the time interval specified.

2. Use the model file to generate a prediction report. This report will show system performance assuming workloads 25 percent, 50 percent, 75 percent, and 100 percent of current workload

   ```
   $ ADVISE/MODEL/REPORT=PREDICTION ENVIRON.MDL
   ```

   Here is a prediction report.

```
VPA V2.0 Modeling              Model: ENVIRON                    PAGE 1
          Prediction Report


                                   load increase (%) -->
                                   -----------------------
                          0%      25%     50%     75%     100%    1928%
                      (baseline)                                  (critical)
          --------------------------------------------------------------------

Most Utilized Components

System      Name
Component   or Id.
-------     ------------
   CPU        TOPVAX     4.4%    5.5%    6.7%    7.8%    8.9%    90.0%
   DISK       VMSRL5     1.7%    2.2%    2.6%    3.0%    3.5%    35.1%
   DISK       USER1DISK  0.7%    0.9%    1.1%    1.3%    1.5%    15.1%
   DISK       BANK2PRIM  0.5%    0.6%    0.8%    0.9%    1.0%    10.4%

   CPU Utilizations

   Type      Name or Id.
------------  ----------
   6400       TOPVAX     4.4%    5.5%    6.7%    7.8%    8.9%    90.0%

Workload Throughputs
  (transactions/sec)
------------------------
        Z-FREQUENCY:    0.008   0.010   0.012   0.015   0.017   0.168
           SYSMAN:     0.001   0.001   0.002   0.002   0.002   0.020
        UTILITIES:     0.019   0.024   0.029   0.033   0.038   0.385
          EDITORS:     0.003   0.004   0.004   0.005   0.006   0.059
         COMPILES:     0.001   0.001   0.001   0.001   0.002   0.016
          NETWORK:     0.000   0.000   0.000   0.000   0.000   0.004
            Other:     0.003   0.003   0.004   0.005   0.006   0.057
```

```
Workload Response Times
     (seconds)
------------------------
     Z-FREQUENCY:    1.44    1.53    1.61    1.69    1.77    7.17
         SYSMAN:    28.49   29.36   30.22   31.05   31.87   87.82
      UTILITIES:     1.54    1.62    1.69    1.76    1.83    6.42
        EDITORS:     3.73    3.97    4.21    4.43    4.66   19.55
       COMPILES:    21.02   21.99   22.94   23.86   24.76   85.57
        NETWORK:     2.59    2.75    2.92    3.07    3.23   13.44
          Other:     9.23    9.61    9.99   10.36   10.72   35.09
```

NOTE: "Critical" load is the load at which the utilization
of one or more components in the system exceeds 90%

The report shows that at 1928 percent of current utilization, one component, the CPU in this case, will exceed 90 percent utilization. Clearly, the system is not heavily utilized and no hardware upgrade is required in the near future. A more detailed report can be printed by using the qualifier /REPORT=ALL.

The model file can be modified to create hypothetical hardware environments (say, adding two new disks) or workload characteristics. The file can then be used to generate modeling reports. Another method to generate "what-if" reports is to use the /PROMPT qualifier

```
$ ADVISE/MODEL/PROMPT ENVIRON.MDL
```

The potential workload can be entered from the terminal as a percentage change from the current workload. The report will reflect the specified workload.

15.4 APPENDIX. SAMPLE PAGES FROM A VPA REPORT

Selected pages from a VPA report are shown on pages 260 to 269.

15.5 FURTHER READING

VAX Performance Advisor User's Guide.
Performance, Vol. 4, System Management Manuals.
VAX SPM Manuals (Vols. 1 and 2).

VPA V2.0 Analysis   TOPVAX (VAX 6320)   PAGE 1
        Report   Thursday 12OCT89 00:00 to 23:59

CONCLUSION 1.

{M0010}

There are excessive page faults from the following
processes.   This might happen if the application's
design induces heavy page faulting such as an AI type
or CAD application. Possible remedies include:

1. Increase User's Working Set Quota (WSQUOTA)

2. Reschedule the application to run during non-peak
    times

3. Redesign the application for improved memory
    efficiency.

Please note below the image(s) that is (are) causing
the problem and the number of occurrences.

        ImageNames   No. of times
        ----------   ------------
        DEBUGSHR   10

Total number of samples supporting this conclusion: 10

CONDITIONS

        1. SOFT_FAULT_RATE .GE. 100.00 * SOFT_FAULT_SCALING
           .OR. HARD_FAULT_RATE .GE. 10.00 *
           HARD_FAULT_SCALING
        2. WORKING_SET_FAULT_RATE .GE. 500.00
        3. PROCESS_CPUTIME .GE. 400.00
        4. PROCESS_UPTIME .GE. 30.00
        5. OCCURRENCES .GE. 1

EVIDENCE

| | | Image | System wide | |
Image Name	User Name	Flts/Cpusec	Flts/sec	Time of occurrence
DEBUGSHR	USERAP1	520	219	12-OCT 11:52:00
	USERAP1	706	151	12-OCT 20:58:00
	USERAP3	1198	255	12-OCT 12:00:00
	USERAP6	562	192	12-OCT 17:58:00
	USERAP6	1057	216	12-OCT 19:02:00
	SHAH1	589	161	12-OCT 20:44:00

VPA V2.0 Analysis   TOPVAX (VAX 6320)   PAGE 2
     Report   Thursday 12OCT89 00:00 to 23:59

CONCLUSION 2.

                                                                        {M0030}

        There are many page faults associated with many image
        activations in the system as a whole. This might
        happen if applications or command procedures   are
        causing   too   many image activations or users are
        activating too many images.

        Most likely, the total system workload is causing the
        problem, in which case, there is no practical action to
        take in order to rectify the situation.   However, if
        particular users and/or images are suspected, attempt
        to identify them using VPA as a tool for further
        investigation.   Issue   the ADVISE/REPORT= DUMP_PROCESS
        command for the reporting interval in which the heavy
        image activation rate occurred, and then analyze the
        executing images during that time slice, paying close
        attention to the following: USERNAME, IMAGENAME, and
        TM (the image termination flag).

        Total number of samples supporting this conclusion: 13

     CONDITIONS

        1. SOFT_FAULT_RATE .GE. 100.00 * SOFT_FAULT_SCALING
           .OR. HARD_FAULT_RATE .GE. 10.00 *
           HARD_FAULT_SCALING
        2. IMAGE_ACTIVATION_RATE .GE. 0.50 *
           IMG_ACT_RATE_SCALING
        3. IMG_ACTIVATIONS_PER_PID .LT. 0.50 *
           IMG_ACT_RATE_SCALING
        4. OCCURRENCES .GE. 10

     EVIDENCE

PageFaults/sec   Image
  Total   Hard   Act./sec   Time of occurrence
 ------- -------   --------   --------------------
     115   11.3   0.82   12-OCT 16:46:00
     122   13.9   0.79   12-OCT 19:48:00
     115   12.4   0.77   12-OCT 20:28:00
     114   12.3   0.71   12-OCT 22:24:00
     108   12.2   0.76   12-OCT 22:26:00
     131   14.7   0.82   12-OCT 22:34:00
     137   13.9   0.77   12-OCT 22:42:00

VPA V2.0 Analysis   TOPVAX (VAX 6320)   PAGE 3
       Report   Thursday 12OCT89 00:00 to 23:59

CONCLUSION 3.

{R0070}

    The Resource Hash Table is becoming congested by the
quantity of LOCK MANAGER resource names.   If more
entries were preallocated to the Resource Hash Table at
boot time, less overhead would have been incurred when
searching for the resource names.

    Use the AUTOGEN feedback mechanism to automatically
increase   the   SYSGEN parameter RESHASHTBL.   After
successive uses of AUTOGEN, the AUTOGEN   feedback
mechanism provides the system with ample RESHASHTBL
entries.

CONDITIONS

    1. SYSGEN_RESHASHTBL .LT. 4097.00
    2. AVERAGE_RESOURCES_INUSE − SYSGEN_RESHASHTBL .GE.
       SYSGEN_RESHASHTBL * 0.05

EVIDENCE

    Current RESHASHTBL..................2048
    Avg number of known resources.......4647
    Max number of known resources.......5934

VPA V2.0 Analysis   TOPVAX (VAX 6320)   PAGE 4
       Report   Thursday 12OCT89 00:00 to 23:59

CONCLUSION 4.

{R0080}

    Unnecessary overhead occurred to build additional Lock
Id Table entries. If more entries were preallocated to
the Lock Id Table at boot time, there would have been
no additional overhead incurred.

    Use the AUTOGEN feedback mechanism to automatically
increase   the   SYSGEN parameter LOCKIDTBL.   After
successive uses of AUTOGEN, the AUTOGEN   feedback
mechanism provides the system with ample LOCKIDTBL
entries.

CONDITIONS

    1. AVERAGE_LOCKS_INUSE .GT. SYSGEN_LOCKIDTBL * 2.00

EVIDENCE

    Current LOCKIDTBL...................1891
    Avg # of locks in existence........4844
    Max # of locks in existence........6250

```
VPA V2.0 Analysis              TOPVAX (VAX 6320)                    PAGE 5
         Report            Thursday 12OCT89 00:00 to 23:59


              ANALYSIS SUMMARY for node TOPVAX

         Number of Records Processed.......................720
         Number of Records satisfying rule conditions......192
         Number of Records not satisfying rule conditions..528
         Number of Conclusions.............................4


VPA V2.0 Histogram             TOPVAX (VAX 6320)                    PAGE 6
                           Thursday 12OCT89 00:00 to 23:59

                                             *---------------------*
                                             |                     |
                                             |    Legend:          |
                                             |                     |
                                             | D   DECnet jobs     |
                                             | I   interactive     |
                                             | B   batch           |
                                             | O   overhead        |
                                             |     (swapper+netacp)|
                                CPU utilization              | X   interrupts      |
%used                          ---------------              | *   other           |
 100 !                                       *---------------------*
  95 !
  90 !
  85 !
  80 !                                              IB B
  75 !                                       '    IIIII
  70 !                               I          IIIIIII  I  I
  65 !                               I   I   IIIIIIIIIIII III
  60 !                         I     I   I   IIIIIIIIIIIIIIII
  55 !               B        IB     I  II   IIIIIIIIIIIIIIII
  50 !              BBB       II      I  II   IIIIIIIIIIIIIIII
  45 !              BBBB      II     II III   IIIIIIIIIIIIIIII
  40 !              BBBBBI    BII    II III   IIIIIIIIIIIIIIII
  35 !              BBBBBIIB  IIII   IIIIII   IIIIIIIIIIIIIIII
  30 ! BBB          IBBBIIIBB IIII  IIIIIII   IIIIIIIIIIIIIIII
  25 ! BBB         IIIBIIIIBB I IIIIIIIIIIIII IIIIIIIIIIIIIIII
  20 ! BBBB        IIIIIIIIBBIIIIIIIIIIIIIIIIIIIIIIIIIIIIIIIII
  15 ! BBBB      I IIIIIIIIIIIIIIIIIIIIIIIIIIIIIIIIIIIIIIIIIII
  10 ! IIIB      IIIIIXXXXXXXXXXOOXXXXXXXXXXXXXXIXXXXIXIIIIIIIII
   5 ! XXXXXXXXXXXXXXXXXXXXXXXXXXXXXXXXXXXXXXXXXXXXXXXXXXXXXXXXXXX
     ! ---01-02-03-04-05-06-07-08-09-10-11-12-13-14-15-16-17-18-19-20-21-22-23-
```

Each Column represents approximately 20 minutes starting from
12–OCT 00:00:00 to 12–OCT 23:59:00. An "N" indicates NO DATA.

VPA V2.0 Histogram   TOPVAX (VAX 6320)   PAGE 7
                            Thursday 12OCT89 00:00 to 23:59

```
                                              *--------------------*
                                              |      Legend:        |
                                              |                     |
                                              |  m Modified List    |
                                              |  . Free List        |
                                              |  u User Ws          |
                                              |  s Tot Wss For All  |
                                              |    'System' Users   |
                       PHYSICAL MEMORY USAGE  |  v VMS Allocated    |
  % of memory          ---------------------  *--------------------*
    100 ! ................................................................
     95 ! ................................................................
     90 ! ................................................................
     85 ! ......................................................uu...u....
     80 ! ...................................................uuuuuuuu..uuu.
     75 ! ..................,............................uuuuuu..uuuuuuuuuuuuuuuuu.
     70 ! ...........................................uuuuuuuuuuuuuuuuuuuuuuuuuuuuuu.
     65 ! ...................................uuuuuuuuuuuuuuuuuuuuuuuuuuuuuuuuuuu.
     60 ! .........................uuuuuuuuuuuuuuuuuuuuuuuuuuuuuuuuuuuuuuuuuuuu.
     55 ! ...................uuuuuuuuuuuuuuuuuuuuuuuuuuuuuuuuuuuuuuuuuuuuuuuuuuu
     50 ! uuuu...............uuuuuuuuuuuuuuuuuuuuuuuuuuuuuuuuuuuuuuuuuuuuuuuuuuuu
     45 ! uuuuuuuuuuuuuuuuuuuuuuuuuuuuuuuuuuuuuuuuuuuuuuuuuuuuuuuuuuuuuuuuuuuuuuu
     40 ! uuuuuuuuuuuuuuuuuuuuuuuuuuuuuuuuuuuuuuuuuuuuuuuuuuuuuuuuuuuuuuuuuuuuuuu
     35 ! uuuuuuuuuuuuuuuuuuuuuuuuuuuuuuuuuuuuuuuuuuuuuuuuuuuuuuuuuuuuuuuuuuuuuuu
     30 ! uuuuuuuuuuuuuuuuuuuuuuuuuuuuuuuuuuuuuuuuuuuuuuuuuuuuuuuuuuuuuuuuuuuuuuu
     25 ! sssssssssssssssssssssssssssssssssssssssssssssssssssssssssssssssssssss
     20 ! vvvvvvvvvvvvvvvvvvvvvvvvvvvvvvvvvvvvvvvvvvvvvvvvvvvvvvvvvvvvvvvvvvvvvvv
     15 ! vvvvvvvvvvvvvvvvvvvvvvvvvvvvvvvvvvvvvvvvvvvvvvvvvvvvvvvvvvvvvvvvvvvvvvv
     10 ! vvvvvvvvvvvvvvvvvvvvvvvvvvvvvvvvvvvvvvvvvvvvvvvvvvvvvvvvvvvvvvvvvvvvvvv
      5 ! vvvvvvvvvvvvvvvvvvvvvvvvvvvvvvvvvvvvvvvvvvvvvvvvvvvvvvvvvvvvvvvvvvvvvvv
        ! ---01-02-03-04-05-06-07-08-09-10-11-12-13-14-15-16-17-18-19-20-21-22-23-
```

Each Column represents approximately 20 minutes starting from
12-OCT 00:00:00 to 12-OCT 23:59:00. An "N" indicates NO DATA.

```
VPA V2.0 Histogram                  TOPVAX (VAX 6320)                      PAGE 8
                              Thursday 12OCT89 00:00 to 23:59

                                                    *------------------*
                                                    |   Legend:        |
                                                    |                  |
                                                    | * user io        |
                          DISK I/O PER SECOND        | P pag+swping     |
IOs per sec               --------------------      *------------------*
 150 !
 145 !
 140 !
 135 !
 130 !
 125 !
 120 !
 115 !
 110 !
 105 !
 100 !
  95 !
  90 !
  85 !
  80 !
  75 !
  70 !
  65 !
  60 !
  55 !
  50 !                              *   *
  45 !                            ******
  40 !                            ******                   *
  35 ! **                         *******          *   **                   *
  30 ! ***                        ********          *   ******    *    *
  25 ! ***                        *********     *    *   **  ******    **  **
  20 ! ****             ***********  *  **  *    **   ***  ****************
  15 ! ****             *********** ******    *********P****PPPPPP*PPP
  10 ! ****        *   ********P******P*****PP**P**PPPPPPPPPPPPPPPP
   5 ! ****            PPPPPPPPPPPPPPPPPPPPPPPPPPPPPPPPPPPPPPPPPPPPPPPPPPP
     ! ---01-02-03-04-05-06-07-08-09-10-11-12-13-14-15-16-17-18-19-20-21-22-23-
```

Each Column represents approximately 20 minutes starting from
12–OCT 00:00:00 to 12–OCT 23:59:00. An "N" indicates NO DATA.

VPA V2.0 Histogram   TOPVAX (VAX 6320)   PAGE 9
                            Thursday 12OCT89 00:00 to 23:59

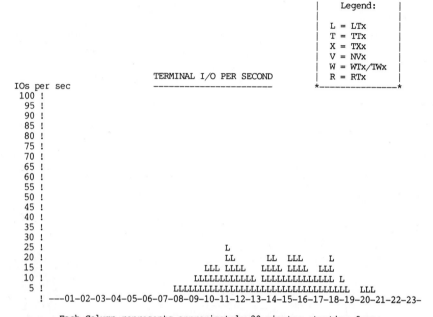

```
                                                         *----------------*
                                                         |    Legend:     |
                                                         |                |
                                                         |  L = LTx       |
                                                         |  T = TTx       |
                                                         |  X = TXx       |
                                                         |  V = NVx       |
                                                         |  W = WTx/TWx   |
                                TERMINAL I/O PER SECOND   |  R = RTx       |
IOs per sec                     ----------------------   *----------------*
 100 !
  95 !
  90 !
  85 !
  80 !
  75 !
  70 !
  65 !
  60 !
  55 !
  50 !
  45 !
  40 !
  35 !
  30 !
  25 !                              L
  20 !                              LL        LL  LLL      L
  15 !                         LLL LLLL     LLLL LLLL   LLL
  10 !                    LLLLLLLLLLLLL LLLLLLLLLLLLLL L
   5 !                 LLLLLLLLLLLLLLLLLLLLLLLLLLLLLLLLLLLL   LLL
     ! ---01-02-03-04-05-06-07-08-09-10-11-12-13-14-15-16-17-18-19-20-21-22-23-
```

        Each Column represents approximately 20 minutes starting from
        12-OCT 00:00:00 to 12-OCT 23:59:00. An "N" indicates NO DATA.

```
+----------------------------------------------------------------------+
| The table below lists observed workload characteristics of all the   |
| interactive images that were run during the given interval. Note     |
| that Diskio, Bufio and Cputim are percentage contributions of the    |
| respective images to the total workload. Working set size and        |
| working set faults are the average for the respective images. In     |
| the case of 0 image activations, the Uptime/image and Cputim/image   |
| actually report the cumulative Uptime and Cputim for the image.      |
+----------------------------------------------------------------------+
```

Node Name: TOPVAX   INTERACTIVE JOBS

Image Name	# of activ- ations	Page Faults per Image -Soft--Hard		Avg. Ws size	% of Direct I/O	% of Buffered I/O	% of Cputim	Uptime/ image (sec)	Cputim/ image (sec)
(not all images shown in this output)									
(dcl)	0	12531	4506	427	0.63	1.25	1.02	385367	1758.98
ANALYZRMS	2	60	6	619	0.00	0.01	0.00	19	0.27
AUDIT_SERVER	0	0	0	216	0.00	0.00	0.03	86400	56.61
BACKUP	38	221	29	2801	14.58	3.45	1.10	277	49.88
CMS	2	252	45	877	0.03	0.08	0.01	3041	4.81
CONFIGURE	0	0	0	180	0.00	0.00	0.00	86400	5.63
CONVERT	11	1246	20	3153	1.63	0.15	0.26	91	40.65
COPY	184	82	3	515	6.31	0.52	0.11	27	1.04
CREATE	12	33	3	432	0.01	0.02	0.00	23	0.18
CREATEFDL	61	52	9	563	0.21	0.09	0.03	6	0.72
CREATE_TEST1	11	96	13	618	0.00	0.01	0.01	2	1.01
SAMPLE_APPLI	4	263	36	1226	0.18	0.01	0.01	32	5.66
WI_POSN	4	409	33	1929	2.94	0.02	0.15	322	62.72
WI_RATE	22	464	32	1347	0.06	0.59	0.06	128	4.61
WI_START	3	1033	61	1698	0.28	0.01	0.03	70	17.51
VAXSIM	0	75	0	754	0.05	0.02	0.00	86400	4.41
VMOUNT	12	33	14	535	0.01	0.03	0.00	15	0.24
VMSHELP	10	136	8	646	0.01	0.06	0.00	102	0.62
VPA$DC_V5	0	0	0	1918	0.33	0.58	0.55	86400	942.51
Totals	16493				79.52	93.26	23.67		

```
VPA V2.0 Performance              TOPVAX (VAX 6320)                  PAGE 13
        Evaluation        Thursday 12OCT89 00:00 to 23:59
```

+--+
| The table below lists observed workload characteristics of all the |
| batch jobs that were run during the given interval. |
+--+

Node Name: TOPVAX   BATCH JOBS

Image Name	# of activ- ations	Page Faults per Image -Soft--Hard		Avg. Ws size	% of Direct I/O	% of Buffered I/O	% of Cputim	Uptime/ image (sec)	Cputim/ image (sec)
(dcl)	0	318	0	314	0.00	0.01	0.00	57	2.75
BACKUP	3	130	27	949	0.01	0.01	0.00	2	0.78
CONVERT	3	373	20	777	0.02	0.01	0.00	5	2.21
COPY	6	107	4	613	0.73	0.10	0.01	60	4.22
CREATE	8	75	4	324	0.00	0.01	0.00	2	0.27
CREATEFDL	11	66	9	547	0.02	0.02	0.00	2	0.78
CREATE_TEST1	3	57	12	632	0.00	0.00	0.00	3	0.95
DELETE	56	132	3	408	0.08	0.12	0.02	2	0.47
WI_POSN	1	468	24	861	0.00	0.00	0.00	6	3.87
WI_START	3	422	79	1764	0.29	0.01	0.03	57	16.27
WI_TURN_OFF	3	163	16	647	0.00	0.00	0.00	2	1.21
WI_TURN_ON	3	187	16	678	0.00	0.00	0.00	3	1.63
LINK	195	1203	5	1278	7.69	1.57	1.04	100	9.26
LOAD_CURR_2	3	269	29	1293	0.14	0.00	0.01	23	3.97
Totals	936				20.22	6.06	3.41		

```
VPA V2.0 Performance              TOPVAX (VAX 6320)                  PAGE 19
        Evaluation        Thursday 12OCT89 00:00 to 23:59
```

+--+
| The table below lists observed workload characteristics of all the |
| network jobs that were run during the given interval. |
+--+

Node Name: TOPVAX   NETWORK JOBS

Image Name	# of activ- ations	Page Faults per Image -Soft--Hard		Avg. Ws size	% of Direct I/O	% of Buffered I/O	% of Cputim	Uptime/ image (sec)	Cputim/ image (sec)
(dcl)	0	75	0	303	0.00	0.00	0.00	1	0.29
EVL	0	12522	199	68	0.00	0.01	0.00	86400	5.77
FAL	16	35	3	587	0.02	0.09	0.00	10	0.37
WIDE_CHECK21	7	170	12	518	0.02	0.02	0.00	4	1.05
LOGINOUT	14	141	5	425	0.02	0.02	0.00	2	0.32
NETSERVER	23	30	2	548	0.03	0.02	0.00	107	0.21
SET	33	78	5	498	0.02	0.03	0.01	2	0.42
Totals	93				0.10	0.19	0.02		

```
VPA V2.0 Performance              TOPVAX (VAX 6320)                PAGE 20
       Evaluation        Thursday 12OCT89 00:00 to 23:59
```

```
+-------------------------------------------------------------------+
| The following table summarizes the workload  characteristics  of  |
| all interactive,  batch  and  network jobs.  It  lists  the number  of  |
| intervals  in  which  the  respective  processes  were busy, along with  |
| the average values of some important metrics. Note that  values  would  |
| be zeros if total number of image activations is zero.            |
+-------------------------------------------------------------------+
```

Node Name: TOPVAX

# of Intvls	# of active proc's	Avg. WSiz/ image	Avg. Soft flts/ image	Avg. Hard flts/ image	Avg. Direct IO/ image	Avg. Buff'd IO/ image	Avg. Cputim/ image	Images per Second	Workload Name
720	12.8	1180	247.5	18.1	42.1	57.0	2.48	0.19	Inter
392	1.6	1049	1024.7	16.5	188.6	65.2	6.30	0.01	Batch
387	1.0	83	210.5	6.5	9.8	20.2	0.46	0.00	Netwrk

```
+-------------------------------------------------------------------+
| The following table summarizes the workload characteristics for all  |
| the processes in the system plus the number of swaps per second and  |
| CPU utilization.   Note that values would be zeros if total number of  |
| image activations is zero.                                        |
+-------------------------------------------------------------------+
```

Node Name: TOPVAX

# of intrvls	Avg. # of proc's	Avg. WSiz/ image	Avg. Soft flts/ image	Avg. Hard flts/ image	Avg. Direct IO/ image	Avg. Buff'd IO/ image	Avg. % CPU Util	Avg. # of Swaps	Images per Second
720	68.4	1016	259	17.0	44.7	51.6	34.6	0.00	0.23

```
+-------------------------------------------------------------------+
| The following table gives the average pool resources used and     |
| allocated on this node.  N/A means not applicable.                |
+-------------------------------------------------------------------+
```

	LRP	IRP	SRP	NP-POOL	LOCKS	RESOURCES
Avg number in use	42	4561	5573	1360618	4845	4647
Max number in use	49	4823	7085	1537296	6250	5934
Number of intvls w/expansns	0	0	13	2	1	N/A
Allocation (xRPCOUNT)	128	1607	6122	1426944	1891	2048
Virtual Alloc (xRPCOUNTV)	512	4821	24488	2982912	N/A	N/A

```
VPA V2.0 Performance              TOPVAX (VAX 6320)                PAGE 21
       Evaluation        Thursday 12OCT89 00:00 to 23:59
```

```
+-------------------------------------------------------------------+
| The following table gives the average percent of time in each of the  |
| various CPU modes for each active processor in the local node.    |
| "Samples" is the record count contributing to the summary line.   |
+-------------------------------------------------------------------+
```

CPU No.	Kernel	Exec	Supervisor	User	Interrupt	Compat	Null	MP Synch	Samples
1	15.1	1.2	0.1	4.7	10.4	0.0	66.8	1.7	720
2	22.4	2.3	0.2	8.8	0.2	0.0	64.0	2.0	720

User Command: ADVISE/REPORT=PERFORM/BEGIN=12-OCT-1989 00:00:00.00

16

The VAX Architecture

The VAX architecture is implemented on all the VAXes from the smallest desktop models to the largest multiprocessing clusters. While the architecture is the same on all the machines, the physical implementation techniques vary among the various series of VAXes. So, the VAX 8700 series central processing unit (CPU) uses ECL and TTL logic circuitry with a 64-Kbyte cache memory while the MicroVAX II CPU is on a single board using variations of NMOS circuitry without cache memory. The low-end VAXes use single-bit parity main memory while the larger machines use error correcting (ECC) memory. Listed below are some of the features of the VAX architecture

1. 32-bit virtual addressing. Total address space is 4,294,967,296 bytes. Demand paged memory management hardware.
2. Sixteen 32-bit general purpose registers.
3. Memory-mapped I/O.
4. Four levels of privileges for CPU operations.
5. 16 priority levels for hardware interrupts.
6. 15 priority levels for software interrupts.
7. Over 400 instructions.
    a. Instructions for switching program context in a multiprogramming environment.
    b. Queue manipulation instructions for linked list manipulation.
    c. Bit manipulation instructions.
    d. Packed decimal arithmetic instructions.
    e. 4-, 8-, and 16-byte floating point number instructions.
    f. Indexed and based (register deferred) data addressing.
    g. Vector processing instructions.

16.1 OVERVIEW

The VAX has *32-bit memory addressing*, allowing the CPU to access more than 4 Gbytes (2^{32} bytes) of main memory. This address range is virtual since none of the VAXes supports that much physical memory. The memory management hardware maps the virtual memory onto physical memory (or disk) using the demand paging technique (explained later). The large address space for programs is the basis for the name VAX, which is derived from *Virtual Address eXtension*.

The VAX is designed for multiprogramming applications. Fast-context switching instructions allow the CPU to service a number of programs with minimum overhead. To ensure that programs do not access unauthorized memory or adversely affect system resources the CPU can operate in one of four modes of privileges: *kernel* (most privileged state), *executive*, *supervisor*, and *user* (least-privileged state). Special interlock instructions allow multiple processes to systematically share system resources.

The VAX is a CISC (complex instruction set computer) as opposed to a RISC (reduced instruction set computer). It has about 400 instructions. The instruction set is highly symmetric, which means that most of the instructions can be used with most of the data types and data addressing modes. Position independent code (PIC) can be written using program counter relative addressing, allowing programs to be loaded at any location in the address space. The CPU has several instructions for bit manipulation. The largest data type is 128-bit floating point numbers.

The CPU has sixteen 32-bit general purpose registers. A 32-bit *processor status longword* (PSL) contains the execution state of the CPU. The lower 16 bits of the PSL are known as the *processor status word* (PSW).

Input/output (I/O) on the system is *memory-mapped*. There are no special instructions for I/O. Devices are controlled by means of *control and status registers* (CSRs) which are within the device but mapped to locations in the memory (called I/O space). I/O space is set up by the operating system so that it cannot be directly accessed by user programs. Devices return status information in the status registers and optionally generate a hardware interrupt. Hardware interrupts have 16 levels of priority. Devices, like disk drives, generating interrupts at high priority are serviced before low-priority devices like terminals.

Vector processing instructions allow efficient processing of DO and FOR loops. These instructions are not discussed in this book.

16.2   MEMORY MANAGEMENT

16.2.1   Virtual to physical memory translation

Processes on the system can be considered to be running user programs. Processes have a large (contiguous) address space starting at location 0. Different processes' address space cannot correspond to the same physical memory locations. Each process actually has a virtual address space. When a process accesses a memory location, the location is in the process' virtual address space, which is translated by the memory management hardware into a physical address. The translation is based on a table in memory called the page translation table. The table is created and maintained by the operating system. Each element of the table is called a *page table entry* (PTE).

Memory is allocated in chunks of 512 bytes called pages. A process using 1800 bytes of virtual memory will be allocated 4 virtual pages. These virtual pages will be mapped into 4 physical pages by the *memory management hardware* (MMH). Hypothetically, two processes, each using two virtual pages, can be mapped as seen in Fig. 16.1.

In this case, if an instruction in process p1 writes into location 12, the physical memory location is 1036, while if the write is by process p2, then the physical memory location is 10764.

This technique of mapping virtual memory to physical allows multiple processes to have a linear address space starting at 0.

16.2.2   A large address space

Let us say that three processes use 20 Mbytes of virtual memory each and the physical memory available for processes is 8 Mbytes. Obviously, virtual to physical memory translation cannot map the 60 Mbytes of total virtual memory into the 8 Mbytes of physical memory. In this case the MMH has some of the virtual pages mapped into physical memory while the operating system stores the remaining virtual pages on disk. The component of the O/S which handles pages on disk is called the *pager*. See Fig. 16.2.

When a process addresses a location in a page in its virtual memory and the page does not have a corresponding physical page, the MMH generates a page fault which interrupts execution of the process and the pager loads the page from disk, updates the page translation tables, and resumes execution of the interrupted process. On VAX/VMS the main paging file on the disk is SYS$SYSTEM:PAGEFILE.SYS. The scheme of fetching pages from disk when required is called *demand paging*. If the disk space for paging is limited, then the operating system has various options:

Virtual memory

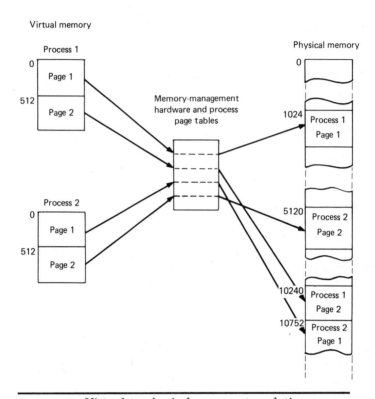

Figure 16.1   Virtual to physical memory translation example.

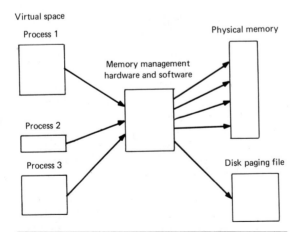

Figure 16.2   Process pages on disk or physical memory.

1. Limit the address space of processes. (The working set parameters in the authorization file on VAX/VMS effectively specify maximum process size.)

2. Limit the number of processes on the system. (SYSGEN parameter MAXPROCESSCNT specifies the maximum number of processes allowed.)

3. Crash or "hang" the system.

16.2.3 Sharing memory

The page table entries used by MMH can be set up so that part of the virtual address space of a number of processes map to the same physical memory pages. This feature is exploited by sharable installed images and global sections in VAX/VMS. Each page table entry contain 4 bits which specify whether a process has read, write, read/write, or no access to the physical page depending on which of the four modes of privileges the process is operating in. See Fig. 16.3.

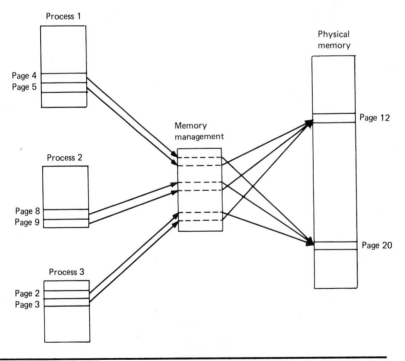

Figure 16.3 Sharable image example. A sharable image resides in pages 12 and 20 of physical memory. Two pages from each of the three processes' virtual memory is mapped into the sharable image, effectively allowing the processes to access the code (or data) in the sharable image.

Sharing memory has two major advantages:

1. A number of processes sharing a set of library routines consume less memory than if each processes includes the routines in their virtual memory.

2. Memory sharing is used for interprogram communications. Passing data between processes using shared memory (global sections) is very efficient.

16.2.4 A closer look at the memory management function

The 4,294,967,296 (2 to the power of 32) byte address range on the VAX is divided into two equal halves known as the process space (or the per-process space) and the system space. Half of the system space is used by the operating system and the other half is currently unused by VAX/VMS. The process space is again divided into two equal halves known as the *P0 program region* (for user program and data) and the *P1 control region* (for stack and process contextual information). The P0 and system space grow downward, the P1 space grows upward. The virtual address space for a system running four processes is shown in Fig. 16.4. The largest user program and data cannot exceed 2 to the power of 29 (about 1 billion) bytes.

The translation from virtual to physical addresses is performed using three translation tables:

- The system page table (SPT) translates addresses in system space.

- The P0 process page table (P0PT) translates addresses in P0 process space. There is one P0PT for each process.

- The P1 process page table (P1PT) translates addresses in P1 process space. There is one P1PT for each process.

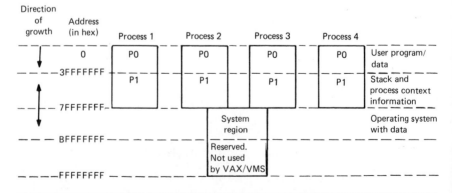

Figure 16.4 Virtual memory addressing limits.

SBR	System page table base register
SLR	System page table length register
P0BR	P0 region page table base register
P0LR	P0 region page table length register
P1BR	P1 region page table base register
P1LR	P1 region page table length register

Figure 16.5 CPU internal registers which define page tables.

The tables consist of 32-bit page table entries (PTEs). The operating system creates these entries for use by the MMH. Each PTE contains information on one virtual page to physical page translation. All the translation tables are stored in system space. Each table has a base address and a specific length. The length determines the size of the virtual memory space. For example, if a P0 table has a length of 200 bytes, then it has 50 PTEs (since each PTE is 4 bytes) and it maps 25,600 bytes of virtual space to physical memory (Each PTE maps one page). The starting address and length of each table are stored in base and length registers in the processor shown in Fig. 16.5.

These registers are accessible to the MMH. The SPT is stored in contiguous pages of physical memory. The size of the table is fixed when the operating system is loaded. P0PT and P1PT for each process are stored in system virtual memory. The operating system maintains one set of P0PT and P1PT for each process.

16.2.5 The translation process

Each virtual address can be depicted as shown in Fig. 16.6. Corresponding to each *virtual page number* (VPN) there is a PTE in one of the three types of tables. Each PTE can be depicted as shown in Fig. 16.7.

The MMH determines the table to be used by inspecting bits 30 and 31 of the virtual address. The VPN is used as an index in the page table to determine the address of the PTE. Bits 0 through 20 of the

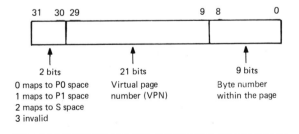

Figure 16.6 A virtual address.

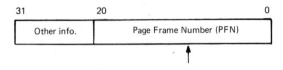

Figure 16.7 A page table entry (PTE).

PTE contain the physical page number (also called the page frame number or PFN). The details are shown in Fig. 16.8 where a virtual address in system space is being translated.

The translation for P0 and P1 spaces takes place as shown in the figure except that the PTE is in system virtual space so to derive the physical address of the PTE there is one more translation in the system space. Figure 16.9 shows a simplified example.

16.2.6 The PTE

A *page table entry* can be depicted as shown in Fig. 16.10. When a virtual page for a process is to be translated into a physical page, the hardware first determines the PTE address. The PFN is extracted from the PTE only if two conditions are met:

1. The *protection field* of the PTE has a bit pattern which specifies the type of access (read or write) which is valid for the currently executing process. The table illustrates this. For example, if the pro-

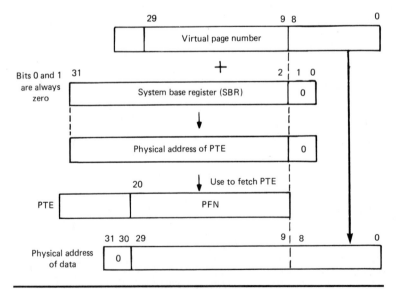

Figure 16.8 Virtual to physical address translation.

tection field contains 1101 and the current process is executing in kernel privilege mode then the process can read from or write into the page. If the process were in user mode then a write access to the page will be invalid (the process would be terminated with an error message). See Fig. 16.11.

2. The *valid bit* in the PTE is set. For example, this bit is zeroed by the pager when a previously mapped page is now paged out onto disk. In this case, a translation invalid fault is generated by the hardware and the pager then retrieves the corresponding page from disk, modifies the PTE to point to the correct PFN, sets the valid bit, and the translation continues.

The *modified bit* is set by the hardware when any of the 512 bytes in the physical page has been written into. When physical memory is running short and the pager has to write some pages out to disk, pages

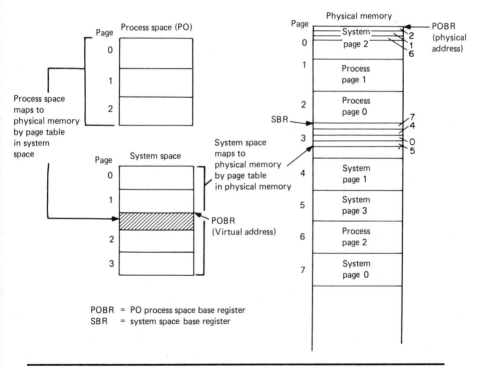

Figure 16.9 Example of process virtual address translation. The process page table entries are in system virtual page 2. Since the system space is virtual, the process page table is, in this case, in physical page 0. Here, process virtual pages 0, 1, and 2 are mapped to physical memory pages 2, 1, and 6. System virtual pages 0, 1, 2, and 3 are mapped to physical memory pages 7, 4, 0, and 5.

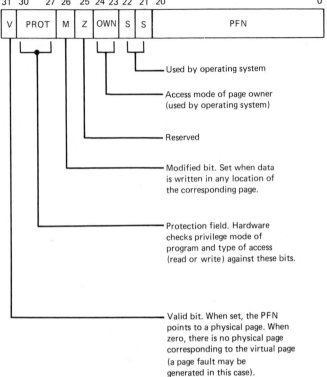

Figure 16.10 Details of a PTE.

Protection field binary	Privilege mode of program (specified in PSL)			
	Kernel	Super	Exec	User
0000	NO	NO	NO	NO
0001		RESERVED		
0010	RW	NO	NO	NO
0011	R	NO	NO	NO
0100	RW	RW	RW	RW
0101	RW	RW	NO	NO
0110	RW	R	NO	NO
0111	R	R	NO	NO
1000	RW	RW	RW	NO
1001	RW	RW	R	NO
1010	RW	R	R	NO
1011	R	R	R	NO
1100	RW	RW	RW	NO
1101	RW	RW	R	R
1110	RW	R	R	R
1111	R	R	R	R

NOTE: R = read ,W = write ,NO = no access.

Figure 16.11 Access based on protection field and privilege mode.

with the modified bit set recently are unlikely candidates since they are more likely to be used soon.

The pager maintains a list of free physical memory pages. When a new process is run on the system, the pager allocates pages from this list for the process's virtual memory. When a process terminates, all physical pages allocated to it are returned to the free page list. If there are no more free pages and a new process is created then the pager selects a few of the allocated pages, stores their contents on the disk paging file, updates the list of pages it has for pages on disk, resets the valid bit of the PTEs in the page tables of the processes which had "owned" the pages, and allocates these physical pages to the new process. In this way large amounts of virtual memory can be allocated to each process on the system.

16.3   THE I/O SUBSYSTEM

I/O is usually handled by circuit boards in the back plane of the processor cabinet. These boards are called *controllers*. The controllers are connected to the CPU and memory by a bus. Figure 16.12 shows some controllers. Four major types of buses are supported on VAXes: *Qbus*, *Unibus*, and *VAXBI* and *XMI*. Qbus is the slowest of the three and is used on the microVAXes while the XMI is the fastest and is used on the larger machines like the 6000 series VAXes.

I/O is memory mapped so some physical memory is actually within controllers. Commands to controllers and status or data information received from them are placed in system virtual memory and pass through the memory management hardware. Most controller can also generate hardware interrupts to gain attention of the CPU.

Controller name	Bus supported	Function
KDA50	Qbus	Controls up to 4 RA series drives.
KDB50	VAXBI	Controls up to 4 RA series drives.
KDM70	XMI	Controls up to 8 RA series drives and TA series tape drives.
UDA50	Unibus	Controls up to 4 RA series drives.
DELQA	Qbus	VAX to Ethernet interface.
DELUA	Unibus	VAX to Ethernet interface.
DEBNI	VAXBI	VAX to Ethernet interface.
CIBCA	VAXBI	VAXcluster interface.
DMB32	VAXBI	8 asynchronous lines (can be used for terminals). plus 1 synchronous line (can be used for a SDLC connection).

Figure 16.12   Example of controllers.

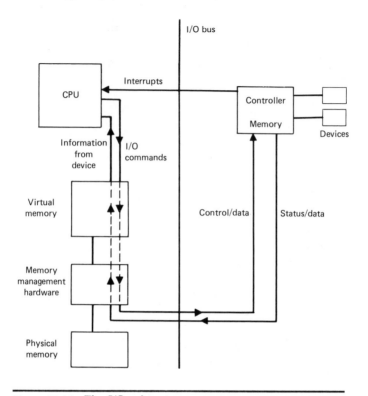

Figure 16.13   The I/O subsystem.

On the VAX/VMS operating system I/O is handled by system software called device drivers. User programs access I/O devices by means of standard high-level language statements (like OPEN and WRITE in COBOL) or by using operating system calls generically known as queued I/Os or QIOs. See Fig. 16.13.

16.4   EXCEPTIONS AND INTERRUPTS

Programs consist of instructions which specify the flow of execution. Typically, the processor will execute instructions sequentially unless a branch is specified in which case the instructions are executed starting at another location in the same program. This flow of execution is interrupted under certain conditions. For example, if the program attempts to execute an instruction which involves division by zero, control passes to the operating system which then aborts execution of the program with an error message. This type of program interruption is called an *exception*. Program execution also stops temporarily when a device interrupts the CPU to signal completion of an output operation.

Exception	Description
Abort	Leaves registers and memory in unpredictable state. Process must be terminated.
Fault	Interruption occuring during instruction execution. Process can continue after the fault condition has been corrected. For example, an access to a page with the protection field in the PTE set so that the current process has no access will cause a access control violation fault. The operating system can change the protection field to allow access to the process and let the process continue execution.
Trap	Interruption occurs after instruction execution. Process execution can continue after the trap. An example is integer division by zero trap.

Figure 16.14   The three types of exceptions.

In this case the operating system performs housekeeping operations for the device and allows the interrupted program to continue. This type of program execution is called an *interrupt*.

Exceptions are interruptions caused in the context of the executing process, while interrupts are interruptions caused because of events external to the executing process. There are three kinds of exceptions: aborts, faults and traps. Figure 16.14 explains them.

16.5   REGISTERS

The VAX processor has sixteen 32-bit registers available to nonprivileged and privileged programs. The registers are labeled R0 through R15. While these are called general-purpose registers, Fig. 16.15 shows that actually a number of them are dedicated for specific use. By convention, R0 is used by subprograms to return values or status information to calling programs.

The *processor status longword* (PSL) contains a collection of fields defining the current execution state of the processor. The low-order 16 bits are called the *processor status word* (PSW). These bits are set or reset as a side effect when many of the instructions are executed. The high-order 16 bits are available to programs running in the kernel privilege mode (usually it is the operating system). See Fig. 16.16.

16.5.1   Privileged registers

The VAX processor also has a number of registers which can be accessed only by processes in the kernel privilege mode. The registers hold information for use mainly by the systems software. These registers are shown in the Fig. 16.17. The registers are also known as internal processor registers.

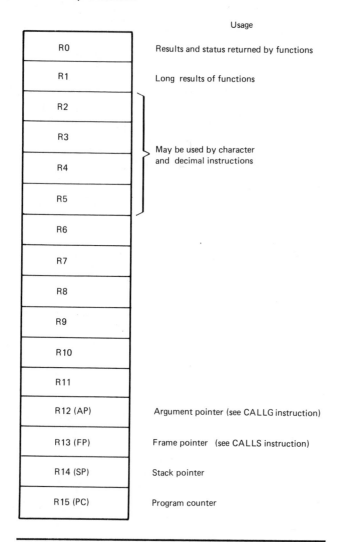

Figure 16.15   General purpose registers in the CPU.

The registers can be accessed by two instructions:

1. MTPR. (move to processor register)
2. MFPR. (move from processor register)

For example,

```
MTPR   R1,P0LR      ;move contents of general
                    ;register R1 to processor
                    ;register P0 process-space
                    ;length register.
```

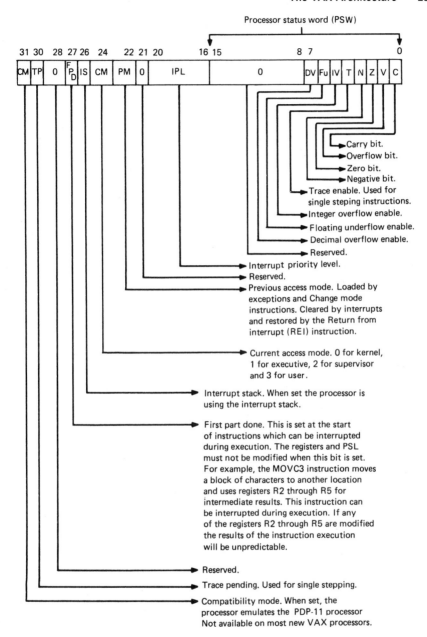

Figure 16.16   Processor status longwood.

Name	Symbol	Type
Kernel stack pointer	KSP	Per process
Executive stack pointer	ESP	Per process
Supervisor stack pointer	SSP	Per process
User stack pointer	USP	Per process
Interrupt stack pointer	ISP	System
P0 base register	P0BR	Per process
P0 length register	P0LR	Per process
P1 base register	P1BR	Per process
P1 length register	P1LR	Per process
System base register	SBR	System
System length register	SLR	System
Process control block base	PCBB	System
System control block base	SCBB	System
Interrupt priority level	IPL	System
AST level	ASTLVL	Per process
Software interrupt request	SIRR	System
Software interrupt summary	SISR	System
Time of year	TODR	System
Memory management enable	MAPEN	System
Translation buffer invalid:		
all	TBIA	System
single	TBIS	System
System identification	SID	System
Translation buffer check	TBCHK	System

Figure 16.17   Privileged registers (internal processor registers).

When the CPU is to be allocated to a new process, the registers marked PROCESS in the table have to be loaded. The system software can load these registers using only one instruction: load process context (LDPCTX). The operating system maintains a *process control block* (PCB) for each process. Part of this PCB is called *hardware PCB*, which contains the registers shown in Fig. 16.18.

When the CPU is to be allocated to a new process, the operating system ,among other tasks, loads the address of the hardware PCB of the process into the PCB base register (PCBB) and executes the LDPCTX instruction. The CPU is then set to execute the new process. The save process context instruction (SVPCTX) saves the context of the Hardware PCB from the processor to memory. The two instructions facilitate fast switching of the CPU among running processes.

16.6   PROGRAMMING THE MACHINE

16.6.1   The assembly language

While the machine language can be used for low-level programming, for most purposes the assembly language is more convenient. The VAX assembly language is called Macro-32 or simply, Macro. A Macro

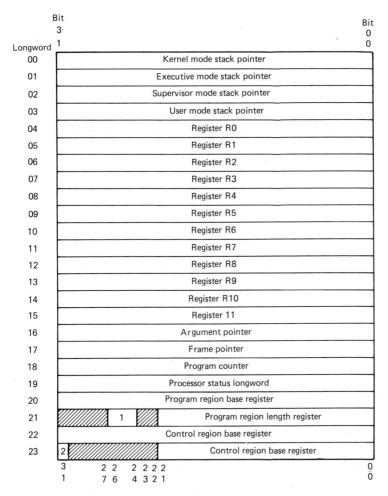

NOTES:
1. Asynchronous trap pending field
2. Enable performance monitor field

Figure 16.18   The hardware process control block (PCB).

program consists of assembler directives and VAX instructions. Assembler directives are used by the assembler during the assembly phases. No code is generated by the directives. The VAX instructions are mnemonic forms of the machine language instructions.

16.6.1.1   Assembler syntax

Here is a simple assembly language program.

```
      .TITLE  Sample Program
      .ENTRY  MAINPR, ^M<>   ;Start of main program
      MOVL    #24,R2         ;Register2 = 24
INPPTR: INCL  R3.            ;Register3 =
                             ;  Register3 + 1
      ADDL    R2,R3          ;Register3 =
                             ;  Register2 + Register3
      .END
```

An assembler statement has up to four fields:

Label: Operator   Operand(s)   ;Comment

- *Label* defines the current location in a program.

- *Operator* specifies a machine instruction operation code or an assembler directive.

- *Operand(s)* zero, one, or more argument(s) for the machine instruction or assembler directive.

- *Comment* Program documentation. Ignored by the assembler.

Further details on the assembler are in the chapter on Macro programming. In this chapter the emphasis is on the architectural aspects of the machine instructions.

Data type	Mne-monic	Representation or precision	Size, bytes	Range of values Low	High
Integers					
Byte	B	Signed	1	-128	127
		Unsigned		0	255
Word	W	Signed	2	$-32,768$	32,767
		Unsigned		0	65,635
Longword	L	Signed	4	$-2,147,483,648$	2,147,483,647
		Unsigned		0	4,294,967,295
Quadword	Q		8		
Octaword	O		16		
Floating point numbers					
F_Floating	F	7 digits	4	0.29×10^{-38}	1.7×10^{38}
D_floating	D	16 digits	8	0.29×10^{-38}	1.7×10^{38}
G_Floating	G	15 digits	8	0.56×10^{-308}	0.9×10^{308}
H_Floating	H	33 digits	16	0.84×10^{-4932}	0.59×10^{4932}
Variable length bit-field	V		0–32 bits		
Packed decimal string	P		0–16		
Queue					
Character strings			0–65,535		

Figure 16.19 Data types.

16.6.2 Data types

Consider the statement

```
MOVL #24,R2   ;Register2 = 24
```

The instruction is manipulating longwords. A longword is a 32-bit integer. The VAX instructions support various other data types. Figure 16.19 describes each one.

Figure 16.20 describes the format of floating point numbers.

16.6.3 Instruction formats

Consider the Clear (CLR) instruction. It zeroes the contents of the location specified by the operand. The operand can be specified in various ways. Here are some examples:

```
CLRL    #1000       ;Clear the longword at memory
                    ;location 1000.
CLRL    @1000       ;Clear the longword at the memory
                    ;location whose address is in ;memory location
                        1000.
CLRL    R2          ;Clear register R2.
CLRL    (R2)        ;Clear the longword at the memory
                    ;location whose address is in
                    ;register R2.
```

The various ways in which operands can be specified are called operand addressing modes. Figure 16.21 summarizes these modes.

Here are some examples of usage of the addressing modes. The instructions should be read in the sequence given since the operations performed by preceding instructions may be relevant to the current instruction.

```
MOVL    3000,R2     ;Operand 1: Program Counter Relative Addressing
                    ;Operand 2: Register Addressing
                    ;R2=3000.
CLRL    @1000       ;Program Counter Relative Deferred Addressing
                    ;Clear memory location 1000.
CLRB    (R2)        ;Register Deferred Addressing
                    ;Clear byte at location 3000.
CLRW    (R2)+       ;Autoincrement Deferred Addressing
                    ;Clear word at location 3000. Increment
                    ;register 2 by two (since the operand is
                    ;a longword).
MOVL    4000,(R2)   ;Operand 1: Program Counter Relative Addressing
                    ;Operand 2: Register Deferred Addressing
                    ;Move the longword value 4000 to memory
                    ;location 3000.
CLRQ    @(R2)+      ;Autoincrement deferred addressing
                    ;Clear quadword (8 bytes) at location 4000
                    ;and then R2=4008.
CLRW    24(R2)      ;Displacement Addressing.
                    ;Clear word at location 4032 (4008+24).
MOVL    3000,R5     ;
```

```
CLRB   14(R2)[R5]  ;Indexed Addressing. The base is using
                   ;Displacement Addressing.
                   ;R2 contains 4032, R5 contains 3000.
                   ;Clear byte at location 7046 (4032+3000+14).
```

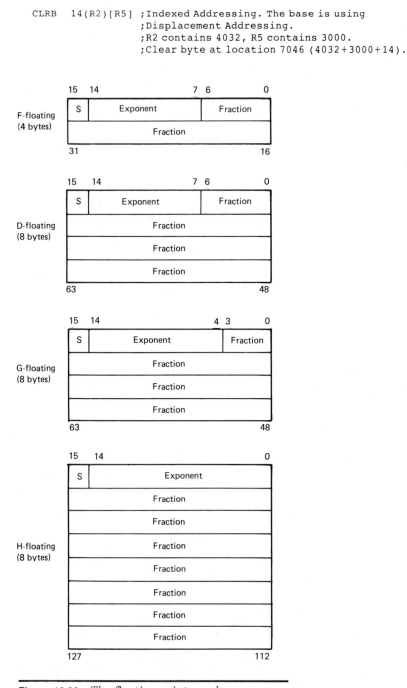

Figure 16.20   The floating point numbers.

Addressing mode	Format	Description
Literal	#literal	The literal value is part of the instruction. Example: MOVL #20,R3
(Program counter) relative	address	The address can be prefixed with B^, W^ or L^ for a byte, word or longword address value. Example: CLRL W^2000. The longword at location 2000 is zeroed.
(Program counter) relative deferred	@address	The address points to a location which in turn contains the address of the operand. This is also known as indirect addressing.
Register	Rn	The operand is the contents of the register.
Register deferred	(Rn)	The operand address is in the register. Example: CLRL (R3). If R3 contains 2121, the contents of location 2121 are zeroed.
Autodecrement	–(Rn)	The register content is decremented by the size of the operand (specified by the instruction mnemonic). The operand address is then the register contents. Example: CLRW -(R3). If R3 contains 2121, the instruction decrements it by 2 (since the operand is a word) to make it 2019. The memory location 2019 is then zeroed.
Autoincrement	(Rn)+	The operand address is in the register. The contents of the register are incremented by the size of the operand after the operation.
Autoincrement deferred	@(Rn)+	The operand address is in the memory location whose address is in the register. The contents of the register are incremented by the size of the operand after the operation. This addressing mode is useful when a single operation is to be performed on each element of an array. Note that autodecrement deferred does not exist. (Why?).
Displacement	disp(Rn)	The content of the register is added to the displacement to derive the effective address. This addressing mode is useful when elements of record structures have to be accessed. Example: CLRL 14(R3). If R3 contains 2121, the longword at 2135 is zeroed.

Figure 16.21   Operand addressing modes.

Addressing mode	Format	Description
Displacement deferred	@disp(Rn)	The content of the location derived by adding the register contents and the displacement is the address of the operand. The displacement can be specified as byte, word or longword. Example: CLRL @W^14(R3). As in the previous example, the location 2135 is derived. This location's content is used as an address for the longword operand to be zeroed.
Index	base	Used for array indexing. The base (of the array) is formed by one of the other valid addressing modes. Register Rn is then multiplied by size of each element and added to the base to form the effective address. Example: CLRL W^2100[R5]. If R5 contains 6 then the effective word address is 2124. The longword at location 2124 is zeroed.

Figure 16.21 *(Continued)*

16.6.4   The instruction set

The instructions are classified in the following groups:

1. Arithmetic and logical instructions

2. Character string instructions

3. Control instructions

4. Procedure call instructions

5. Queue instructions

6. Variable length bit field instructions

7. Miscellaneous instructions

A real instruction is formed using the generic instruction, operand data type and the number of operands. For example,

```
MULL2   M1,M2     ;M2 = M1 * M2
```

is formed from the generic instruction MUL (for multiply), the operand data type L (for longword) and the number of operands which is 2 in this instruction.

The instructions are listed here in their generic form along with a brief description.

16.6.4.1   Arithmetic and logical instructions

ADAWI   Add aligned word interlocked. Adds two words and prevents other processors in a multiprocessor system from executing a similar operation. The destination must be aligned on a word boundary.

ADD	Add.
ADWC	Add with carry.
ASH	Arithmetic Shift.
BIC	Bit clear. A mask specifies the bits to be zeroed.
BIS	Bit set. A mask specifies the bits to be set.
BIT	Bit test.
CLR	Clear. Zero the operand.
CMP	Compare.
CVT	Convert. Converts data from one form to another like packed decimal to string.
DEC	Decrement. Decrement operand by one.
DIV	Divide. Returns the quotient.
EDIV	Extended divide. Returns the quotient and remainder.
EMOD	Extended multiply and integerize. Multiplies two floating point numbers and stores the integer and fractional parts of the result in separate operands.
EMUL	Extended multiply. Multiplies two longwords and forms a quadword result.
INC	Increment. Increment by one.
MCOM	Move complemented. Moves the one's complement of the source operand to the destination.
MNEG	Move negated.
MOV	Move.
MOVZ	Move zero-extended. The source, with zeroes padded at the left, is moved to the destination which is greater in size than the source.
MUL	Multiply.
PUSHL	Push longword (on the stack).
ROTL	Rotate longword. Rotate a given number of times.
SBWC	Subtract with carry.
SUB	Subtract.
TST	Test. Modifies condition codes.
XOR	Exclusive OR.

16.6.4.2 Character string instructions

CMP	Compare two character strings.
LOCC	Locate character. Locate a given character in a string.

MATCHC	Match character. Search for a substring in a main string.
MOVC	Move character. Block data movement.
MOVTC	Move translated character. Moves characters from a source string to a given destination after translating each character using a translation table. Useful, say, to convert ASCII characters to EBCDIC.
MOVTUC	Move translated until character. Similar to MOVTC except that the translation and movement stops when the specified escape character is encountered as the translated character.
SCANC	Scan characters. Every byte in the specified string is used to look up a character in the specified 256-byte table. The character from the table is logically ANDed with a specified mask. The operation continues until the result of the AND operation is nonzero or the input string is exhausted. The instruction can be used, say, to search for the position of the first nonalphanumeric character in a string.
SKPC	Skip character. Used to search for the first character in a string not matching a given character.
SPANC	Span characters. Similar to SCANC except that the operation continues until the result of the AND operation is zero.

16.6.4.3 Control instructions

The VAX maintains a difference between a branch and a jump. A branch instruction contains the displacement of the branch location from the current location. The displacement is a byte or word value. The jump (and call) instructions contain the longword address of the jump location. Branches are usually more efficient than jumps.

ACB	Add compare and branch. Operand 2 is added to operand 3 and the result placed in operand 3. The branch is effected if the absolute value of operand 3 is less than or equal to the absolute value of operand 2. This instruction efficiently implements the DO and FOR loops of high level languages.
AOB	Add one and branch.
B	Branch (on condition). The branch is effected depending on the value of condition codes.
BB	Branch on bit. The branch is effected if a particular bit is set in the base operand.
BB	Branch on bit (and modify without interlock). The branch is effected if a particular bit is set or clear. Regardless of whether the branch is taken or not, the bit is set or cleared as specified.
BB	Branch on bit interlocked. This is similar to the above instruction except that the operation is an atomic one. This in-

struction is useful when multiple processes are implementing common semaphores.

BLB Branch on low bit. Bit 0 is tested and the branch is effected if the bit is set or cleared as specified in the instruction.

BR Unconditional branch. The displacement is stored in a byte or word so a branch to a location further away must be implemented using the JMP instruction.

BSB Branch to subroutine. The PC is pushed on the stack and the branch taken.

CASE Case. Implements the CASE and SWITCH statements of high-level languages

JMP Jump. Similar to BR except that the jump can be to any location in the address space.

JSB Jump to subroutine. Similar to BSB except that the jump can be to any location in the address space.

RSB Return from subroutine. Used to return from subroutines called by the BSB and JSB instructions.

SOB Subtract one and branch.

16.6.4.4 Procedure call instructions

These instructions implement subroutine calls and returns. They adhere to the VAX Procedure Calling and Condition Handling standard described in the chapter on advanced programming features.

CALLG Call procedure with general argument list. The address of the list of arguments passed is given in the instruction. The instruction, when executed, stores the AP (Register 12) on the stack and stores the argument list base address in AP. The subroutine accesses the arguments via the AP. The instruction also saves specified registers on the stack.

CALLS Call procedure with stack argument list. The arguments are passed on the stack. The stack pointer, SP, is stored in the frame pointer, FP, for use by the RET instruction to restore the stack pointer after the subroutine is executed. The instruction also saves specified registers on the stack. The instruction is particularly useful for recursive programming.

RET Return from procedure. The instruction restores the state of the FP, SP, AP and saved registers to their pre-CALL state.

16.6.4.5 Queue instructions

A queue on the VAX is a circular, doubly linked list. Each queue entry has a forward pointing address, a backward pointing address, and zero or more bytes of data. While linked lists can be implemented using other instructions, the VAX has hardware instructions for efficient list manipulation. The basic queue operations are inserts and deletes of entries. All queue operations are interlocked to avoid concurrent access by multiple processes or processors.

INS   Insert entry into queue, interlocked. The entry can be inserted at the head, tail or in between the queue.

REM   Remove entry from queue, interlocked. The entry to be removed can be at the head, tail or in between the queue.

16.6.4.6 Variable-length-bit field instructions

These instructions are useful for efficient bit manipulation. The size of a bit field can be from 0 to 32 bits (yes, up to 33 bits). The branch on bit (set or reset) instructions described above are also used for bit manipulation.

CMP   Compare field. Compare a bit field with a longword. Used to set condition codes.

EXT   Extract field. Move the given bit field to a longword location.

FF   Find first. Find the position of the first bit set (or reset, if specified in the instruction) in the given bit field. The search starts at the least significant bit and proceeds "left."

INSV   Move as many bits as required to fill up the bit field from a longword.

16.6.4.7 Miscellaneous instructions

BPT   Break point fault. Along with the T-bit in the PSL, the instruction is used for program tracing.

BUG   Bugcheck. Used to generate a fault. These instructions are inserted at points where the code should never be reached.

CHM   Change mode. Change mode to kernel, executive, supervisor, or user.

CRC   Calculate cyclic redundancy check. The CRC of a specified string of data is calculated using a specified polynomial.

EDITPC   Edit packed to character string. The source string is edited using a specified pattern. The instruction is useful for output formatting of data (like in the PICTURE clause of COBOL).

HALT   Halt. Halts the processor.

INDEX   Compute index. Used to compute the address of an element in an array.

LDPCTX   Load process context. Loads processor registers from memory. Used for rapid switching of processor from one process to another.

MTPR   Move to processor register. Used to load processor registers (like the memory management registers) excluding the general purpose registers.

NOP   No operation.

POLY   Polynomial evaluation. Accepts a table of polynomial coefficients and an argument (X value) to evaluate the polynomial. All mumbers are floating point.

POPR   Pop registers (on the stack). The registers are specified in the operand.

PROBE   Probe accessibility. Checks read or write accessibility of a memory region.

PUSHR   Push registers (from the stack). The registers are specified in the operand.

REI   Return from exception or interrupt.

SVPCTX   Save process context. Saves processor registers to a specified memory address. Used for rapid switching of processor from one process to another.

XFC   Extended function call. Used to implement customer-defined instructions.

16.7 VECTOR PROCESSING

Special instructions for efficient vector arithmetic are offered with the release of VAX 9000 series mainframes. These instructions are implemented in hardware and extend the basic instruction set explained above. The VAX 6000 series computers will have to be upgraded with CPU cards if vector processing is to be performed on them. Vector processing in hardware is not supported on the smaller VAX 4000 and microVAX series computers. A detailed discussion on vector processing is beyond the scope of this book.

16.8 FURTHER READING

Leonard, Timothy (ed), *VAX Architecture Reference Manual*, Digital Press, Bedford, Mass., 1986.
Levy, H. M., and Eckhouse, R. H., *Computer Programming and Architecture: The VAX*, 2d ed., Digital Press, Bedford, Mass., 1989.
VAX Architecture Handbook
Digital Technical Journal, Issue 7: "CVAX-based Products," Digital Press, Bedford, Mass., 1988.

17

The Assembly Language: MACRO-32

The material in this chapter is closely related to the material in the chapter on the VAX architecture. It will be a good idea to read that chapter before this. The assembly language on VAX/VMS is called MACRO-32 or simply, MACRO. Its structure is similar to many other assembly languages like that of IBM 3090 series mainframe computers. By convention, MACRO program files have a file type of ".MAR". Here is a hypothetical MACRO program:

```
        .TITLE  Sample Program
        .ENTRY  MAINPR, ^M<R2,R3>    ;Start of main program.
        MOVL    #24,R2               ;Register2 = 24
INPPTR: INCL    R3                   ;Register3 = Register3 + 1
        ADDL    R2,R3                ;Register3 = Register2 + Register3
        .END    MAINPR
```

An assember statement has up to four fields:
   Label: Operator   Operand(s)   ;Comment

- *Label* defines the current location in a program.

- *Operator* specifies a machine instruction operation code or an assembler directive.

- *Operand(s)* zero, one or more argument(s) for the machine instruction or assembler directive.

- *Comment* Program documentation. Ignored by the assembler.

While the order of the fields is important in a statement, the fields can begin in any column. Conventionally, the field positions are

Label at 1st tab position (1st column)

Operator at 2nd tab position (8th column)

Operands at 3rd tab position (17th column)

Comments at 5th tab position (33rd column)

Each of the machine instructions of the VAX has a corresponding assembly language instruction. The instruction mnemonics are described in the chapter on the VAX architecture.

17.1 INSTRUCTIONS AND ASSEMBLER DIRECTIVES

All assembly language statements are classified as machine instructions or directives to the assembler. Assembler directives begin with a dot. Examples of directives are

```
.TITLE  Sample Program
.ENTRY  MAINPR, ^M<R2,R3>    ;Start of main program
.END    MAINPR
```

The .ENTRY directive specifies a register mask, ^M<R2,R3>. CPU registers 2 and 3 will be stacked when the macro program is entered. The registers are poped at the end of the program. This way, the original contents of these registers are maintained even if the program uses them during execution.

17.2 OPERANDS AND OPERATORS

The instruction:

```
MOVL    #24,R2        ;Register2 = 24
```

has two operands: #24 and R2. Operand addressing modes are described in the chapter on the VAX architecture.

When values have to be specified in operands they can be specified as expressions or constants in various forms. Here are some examples of operands:

24   ;The constant 24. The base is decimal by default but it
                  ;can be changed to hex by a preceding assembler directive.

^B1001   ;Binary for decimal 9.

^X0A1   ;Hexadecimal for decimal 161.

^F2E14   ;Floating point number 2 * (10 ** 14).

^A/abc/   ;ASCII string abc.

2 + (3+4)*6   ;Expression which the assembler evaluates to 44.

2+CNT	;CNT must be defined before by, say,
	; CNT .byte 13
^B01 & ^B11	;Logical bit-wise AND.
^B01 ! ^B11	;Logical bit-wise OR.
^B01 \^B11	;Logical bit-wise exclusive-OR.

Some instructions require a subset of the 16 CPU registers to be specified. These instructions have 16-bit register masks, one bit for each register. If a bit is set, the corresponding register is assumed to be specified. To specify a register mask, the ^M form is used:

```
PUSHR  ^M<R2,R3,R12)    ;Registers 2,3 and 12 are pushed
                        ;on the stack.
```

17.3 CURRENT LOCATION COUNTER

The current location counter for a program is defined by the dot. For example,

```
SYMA  = .+10
```

The symbol, SYMA, points to the present location (where code is next going to be generated) plus 10.

17.4 MACROS

Macros are similar to subroutines; the main difference is that code for the macro is inserted in-line in the program while for a subroutine, there is a CALL statement. Macros are very common within VMS systems software and are used in most useful assember programs, which is the key reason for calling the assembler MACRO. Here is an example macro definition:

```
.MACRO  ADDMUL  ARG1,ARG2
ADDL3   ARG1,ARG2,R3         ; R3 = ARG1+ARG2
MULL3   ARG1,ARG2,R4         ; R4 = ARG1*ARG2
.ENDM   ADDMUL
```

The macro, ADDMUL, takes two arguments, adds them and puts the result in register 3, and multiplies them and puts the result in register 4. ARG1 and ARG2 are called formal or dummy parameters. To use the macro, statements like the following can be used within the program after the macro is defined:

```
        ADDMUL 12 , 34
A1 = 5
A2 = 6 + A1
        ADDMUL A1 , A2
```

Macros can be used to form new "instructions" which have syntax similar to normal machine instructions. A single macro instruction is expanded into normal instructions by the assembler depending on how the macro is defined.

17.4.1   Local macro labels

A macro can be expanded at more than one place in the program. So, if normal labels are used within the macro definition, the program will have the same label expanded at more than one place. This will cause a "multiply defined label" error during assembly. To avoid this, labels within macros must be local labels. These are "dummy" labels which are expanded to actual labels during macro expansion. The actual labels are unique for each expansion. The assembler generates unique actual labels when expanding the macro. Here is a simplified example. The assembler will generate code during macro expansion such that the greater of the two values of ARG1 and ARG2 will be stored in R4:

```
; a macro to store the greater of two values in R4.
;
        .MACRO COMPARE ARG1,ARG2, ?label1, ?LABEL2
        CMPL ARG1,ARG2          ;Compare arguments
        BLEQ    ?LABEL1
        MOVL    ARG1,R4         ;If ARG1 > ARG2 then R4 = ARG1
        B       ?LABEL2
?LABEL1:
        MOVL    ARG2,R4         ;If ARG1 <= ARG2 then R4 = ARG2
?LABEL2:
        .ENDM
```

Local labels are declared in the macro definition command line. They must start with the question mark character. Each time the macro is used as, say,

```
COMPARE      A1 , A2
```

the assembler will assign new values to the labels ?LABEL1 and ?LABEL2. The actual label names should not be of concern to the programmer.

17.5   ASSEMBLER DIRECTIVES

Assembler directives are commands to the assembler; usually no machine code is generated directly. These commands begin with a dot. Here are examples of the commonly used directives:

```
.CROSS       ;Generate cross reference listing in the
             ;listing file.
```

The .BLKx directives are used to reserve storage:

```
.BLKB 12        ;Reserve 12 bytes of memory.
.BLKW 12        ;Reserve 24 bytes (12 words) of memory.
.BLKL 12        ;Reserve 48 bytes (12 longwords) of memory.
```

The next set of directives reserve memory and put specified values in the memory locations:

```
.BYTE   3, 2+A, 2*12      ;Reserve 3 bytes. Place 3, 2+A and 24 in them.
.WORD   3, 2+A, 2*12      ;Reserve 3 words (6 bytes). Place 3, 2+A and
                          ;24 in them.
.LONG   3, 2+A, 2*12      ;Reserve 3 longwords (12 bytes). Place 3, 2+A
                          ;and 24 in them.
.FLOAT  21.23, 0.2E12     ;Reserve space for 2 floating point numbers
                          ;(8 bytes). Put the values 21.23 and 0.2E12
                          ;in them.
.ASCII  /ABC/             ;Stores the characters A,B and C in the next
                          ;three bytes.
.ASCIZ  /ABC/             ;Stores the characters A,B and C in the next
                          ;three bytes. The fourth byte contains 0.
.ASCID  /ABC/             ;Creates a string descriptor in the next two
                          ;longwords. Stores the characters A,B and C in
                          ;three bytes following.
.PACKED 2453, -832        ;For packed decimal arithmetic. Storage is
                          ;2 digits per byte. There can be up to 31
                          ;digits with a sign. In this example, each of
                          ;the two decimal numbers occupy 4 bytes.
```

Conditional assembly can be performed by the .IF directive:

```
.IF     EQUAL A-B    ;IF A-B = 0
MOVL    #23 , R3
.ENDC                ;End of IF (condition).
```

The .SHOW (or .LIST) directive is used to have the assembler write optional information to the listing file (which has a file type of ".LIS" by convention):

```
.SHOW EXPANSIONS     ;Lists expanded macros wherever macros are
                     ;used (invoked).
```

The .TITLE directive is used to give a name to the program, this title is used as the object module name and is displayed at the top of every listing page. An optional comment string can be present:

```
.TITLE  ADPROG   "Adds two arrays"
```

17.6 A SAMPLE MACRO PROGRAM

Here is a program which reads a file name from the terminal and displays all the records in the file:

```
                .TITLE DISPLAY_FILE    Display file specified
; The program accepts file name from the terminal and then displays the file.
; The program makes extensive use of RMS macros and like most macro programs,
; has a number of system calls like LIB$GET_INPUT. The system library
; SYS$SHARE:STARLET.MLB is automatically used by the linker to include
; RMS macros like $FAB. The commands to run the program are:
;
; $ MACRO  DISPLAY_FILE.MAR /LIST
; $ LINK   DISPLAY_FILE.OBJ
; $ RUN    DISPLAY_FILE.EXE
;
; Many macros are used ("invoked") within this program but none are defined.
;
; In many system calls a string descriptor is used to specify string data.
; The descriptor consists of two longwords, the first contains the string
; length (and type and class which are defaulted to 0) and the second the
; string address.

;program data area

FILE_FAB:                               ;File attributes block data structure macro
        $FAB    FNA=FILE_NAME,-
                FNS=255                 ;File name string maximum size

FILE_RAB:                               ;Record attributes data structure macro
        $RAB    FAB=FILE_FAB,-          ;Address of FAB
                UBF=RECBUF,-            ;Address of record buffer
                USZ=MAX_REC_SIZ ;Maximum allowed size of any input record
MAX_REC_SIZ = 2000                      ;File record size and storage area
RECBUF: .BLKB   MAX_REC_SIZ

RECBUF_DESCR:                           ;Descriptor used for record display
REC_SIZ:
        .WORD   0                       ;Length of record, will be filled in run time
        .WORD   0                       ;String type and class are 0
        .LONG   RECBUF

PROMPT:                                 ;string descriptor
        .ASCID  /File to be displayed: /
FILE_NAME_SIZE:
        .BLKL   1
FILE_NAME:
        .BLKB   255                     ;255 bytes for filename
FILE_NAME_DESCR:                        ;Descriptor for filename
        .LONG   255                     ;Length=255, type=0, class=0
        .LONG   FILE_NAME               ;Address of file name string

;program code

        .ENTRY  DISFIL,^M<>             ;Start of program. Register mask specifies
                                        ;that no registers are to be saved on stack
;get file name
        PUSHAB  FILE_NAME_SIZE  ;File specification (name) size

        PUSHAB  PROMPT
        PUSHAB  FILE_NAME_DESCR ;File name descriptor
        CALLS   #3,G^LIB$GET_INPUT
                                        ;System Library routine to get file name
                                        ;from user
                                        ;CALLS accepts parameters on the stack
        BLBS    R0, OPENFILE    ;Error?
        BRB     ERROR

OPENFILE:
        $OPEN   FAB=FILE_FAB    ;Open file macro
        BLBC    R0,ERROR        ;Error?
        $CONNECT  RAB=FILE_RAB  ;Macro to sets various pointers
        BLBC    R0,ERROR        ;Error?
```

```
READFILE:
        $GET    RAB=FILE_RAB     ;Macro to get one record
        BLBS    R0, DISPLAY_RECORD
        CMPL    R0, #RMS$_EOF    ;End of file?
        BEQL    ENDFILE
        BRB     ERROR

DISPLAY_RECORD:
        MOVW    FILE_RAB+RAB$W_RSZ, REC_SIZ
                                 ;Move record size from FAB to string
                                 ;descriptor
        PUSHAB  RECBUF_DESCR     ;Address of record (data) string descriptor
        CALLS   #1,G^LIB$PUT_OUTPUT
                                 ;System library routine for output
        BRB     READFILE         ;Go to display next record from file
ENDFILE:
        $CLOSE  FAB=FILE_FAB     ;Close the file
        RET


ERROR:  RET                      ;Return with error status in R0. An
                                 ;error message will be displayed on the
                                 ;terminal by the operating system.
        .END    DISFIL
```

The listing file created by the assembler is shown on pages 306 to 309. The machine code should be read right to left.

17.7 FURTHER READING

VAX Macro, Vol. 9, VMS Programming Manuals.
Leonard, Timothy (ed.), *VAX Architecture Reference Manual*, Digital Press, Bedford, Mass., 1986.
Levy, H. M., and Eckhouse, R. H., *Computer Programming and Architecture: The VAX*, 2d ed., Digital Press, Bedford, Mass., 1989.
VAX Architecture Handbook.

```
0000                            1                    .TITLE DISPLAY_FILE   Display file specified
0000                            2
0000                            3  ; The Program accepts file name from the terminal and then displays the file.
0000                            4  ; The Program makes extensive use of RMS macros and like most macro programs,
0000                            5  ; has a number of system calls like LIB$GET INPUT. The system library
0000                            6  ; SYS$SHARE:STARLET.MLB is automatically used by the linker to include
0000                            7  ; RMS macros like $FAB. The commands to run the program are:
0000                            8  ;
0000                            9  ;
0000                           10  ; $ MACRO   DISPLAY_FILE.MAR /LIST
0000                           11  ; $ LINK   DISPLAY_FILE.OBJ
0000                           12  ; $ RUN   DISPLAY_FILE.EXE
0000                           13  ;
0000                           14  ; Many macros are used ("invoked") within this program but none are defined.
0000                           15  ;
0000                           16  ; In many system calls a string descriptor is used to specify string data.
0000                           17  ; The descriptor consists of two longwords, the first contains the string
0000                           18  ; length (and type and class which are defaulted to 0) and the second the
0000                           19  ; string address.
0000                           20
0000                           21  ;program data area
0000                           22
0000                           23  FILE_FAB:   $FAB   FNA=FILE_NAME,-    ;File attributes block data structure macro
0000                           24                     FNS=255            ;File name string maximum size
0000                           25
0050                           27  FILE_RAB:   $RAB   FAB=FILE_FAB,-     ;Record attributes data structure macro
0050                           28                     UBF=RECBUF,-       ;Adress of FAB
0050                           29                     USZ=MAX_REC_SIZ    ;Address of record buffer
0050                           30                                        ;Maximum allowed size of any input record
                                                                         ;File record size and storage area
000007D0                       31  MAX_REC_SIZ = 2000
00000864                       32  RECBUF:  .BLKB   MAX_REC_SIZ
0864                           33
0864                           34  RECBUF_DESCR:                         ;Descriptor used for record display
0864                           35  REC_SIZ:
0000       0866                36        .WORD   0                       ;Length of record, will be filled in run time
0000       0868                37        .WORD   0                       ;String type and class are 0
00000094'  086C                38        .LONG   RECBUF
                               39
           086C               40  PROMPT:  .ASCID  /File to be displayed: /   ;string descriptor
74 20 65 6C 69 46 0000087A'010E0000' 62 20 6F
79 61 6C 70 73 69 64 20 65 64 20 3A 65
           086A               41
           088A               42  FILE_NAME_SIZE:
0000088E   088A               43        .BLKL   1
           088E               44  FILE_NAME:
0000089D   088E               45        .BLKB   255                      ;255 bytes for filename
```

DISPLAY_FILE   Display file specified

```
0000088E  0991        48          .LONG   FILE_MASK        ;...
          0995        49  ;program code
          0995        50
          0995        51
0000      0995        52          .ENTRY  DISFIL,^M<>      ;Start of program. Register mask specifies
          0995        53                                    ;that no registers are to be saved on stack
FEEF CF 9F 0997       54  ;get file name
          0997        55          PUSHAB  FILE_NAME_SIZE   ;File specification (name) size

                 099B 9F FECD CF   56          PUSHAB  PROMPT
                 099F 9F EB AF     57          PUSHAB  FILE_NAME_DESCR   ;File name descriptor
00000000'GF 09A2 FB 03            58          CALLS   #3,G^LIB$GET_INPUT  ;System Library routine to get file name
          09A9                     59                                     ;from user
          09A9                     60                                     ;CALLS accepts parameters on the stack
          09A9                     61
          09A9 E8 02 50            62          BLBS    R0, OPENFILE       ;Error?
          09AC 11 55               63          BRB     ERROR
          09AE                     64
          09AE                     65  OPENFILE:
          09AE E9 47 50            66          $OPEN   FAB=FILE_FAB       ;Open file macro
          09B9 11                  67          BLBC    R0,ERROR           ;Error?
          09BC E9 39 50            68          $CONNECT RAB=FILE_RAB      ;Macro to sets various pointers
          09C7 11                  69          BLBC    R0,ERROR           ;Error?
          09CA                     70
          09CA                     71  READFILE:
00000000'8F 09CA E8 0B 50          72          $GET    RAB=FILE_RAB       ;Macro to get one record
          09D5 D1 50               73          BLBS    R0, DISPLAY_RECORD
          09D8 13 16               74          CMPL    R0, #RMS$_EOF      ;End of file?
          09DF 11 20               75          BEQL    ENDFILE
          09E1                     76          BRB     ERROR
          09E3                     77
          09E3                     78  DISPLAY_RECORD:
FE7A CF F68B CF 09E3 B0            79          MOVW    FILE_RAB+RAB$W_RSZ, REC_SIZ  ;Move record size from FAB to string
          09EA                     80                                     ;descriptor
          09EA                     81
FE76 CF 09EA 9F                    82          PUSHAB  RECBUF_DESCR       ;Address of record string descriptor
00000000'GF 09EE FB 01            83          CALLS   #1,G^LIB$PUT_OUTPUT ;System library routine for output
          09F5 D3                  84          BRB     READFILE           ;Go to display next record from file
          09F5                     85  ENDFILE:
          09F7 04                  86          $CLOSE  FAB=FILE_FAB       ;Close the file
          09F7                     87          RET
          0A02                     88
          0A03                     89
          0A03                     90
          0A03 04                  91  ERROR:  RET                        ;Return with error status in R0. An
          0A04                     92                                     ;error message will be displayed on the
          0A04                     93                                     ;terminal by the operating system.
          0A04                     94          .END    DISFIL
```

22-FEB-1990 13:02:07   VAX MACRO V5.0-8
21-FEB-1990 17:48:37   DISFIL.MAR;1

Display file specified

```
DISPLAY_FILE
Symbol table

$$.TAB          = 00000050 R       01
$$.TABEND       = 00000094 R       01
$$.TMP          = 00000000         01
$$.TMP1         = 00000001
$$.TMP2         = 000000CF
DISFIL            00000995 RG
DISPLAY_RECORD    000009E3 R       01
ENDFILE           000009F7 R       01
ERROR             00000A03 R       01
FAB$C_BID       = 00000003         01
FAB$C_BLN       = 00000050         01
FAB$C_SEQ       = 00000000         01
FAB$C_VAR       = 00000002         01
FAB$L_ALQ       = 00000010         01
FAB$L_FOP       = 00000004         01
FAB$V_CHAN_MODE = 00000002         01
FAB$V_FILE_MODE = 00000004         01
FAB$V_LNM_MODE  = 00000000
FAB$W_GBC       = 00000048         01
FILE_FAB          00000000 R       01
FILE_NAME         0000088E R       01
FILE_NAME_DESCR   0000098D R       01
FILE_NAME_SIZE    0000008A R       01
FILE_RAB          00000050 R       01
LIB$GET_INPUT     ******** X       01
LIB$PUT_OUTPUT    ******** X       01
MAX_REC_SIZ     = 000007D0         01
OPENFILE          000009AE R       01
PROMPT            0000086C R       01
RAB$B_RAC       = 0000001E         01
RAB$C_BID       = 00000001         01
RAB$C_BLN       = 00000044         01
RAB$C_SEQ       = 00000000         01
RAB$L_CTX       = 00000018         01
RAB$L_ROP       = 00000004         01
RAB$W_RSZ       = 00000022         01
READFILE          000009CA R       01
RECBUF            00000094 R       01
RECBUF_DESCR      00000864 R       01
REC_SIZ           00000864 R       01
RMS$_EOF          ******** X       01
SYS$CLOSE         ******** GX      01
SYS$CONNECT       ******** GX      01
SYS$GET           ******** GX      01
SYS$OPEN          ******** GX      01
```

PSECT name	Allocation		PSECT No.		Attributes
. ABS .	00000000	(0.)	00	(0.)	NOPIC USR CON ABS LCL NOSHR NOEXE NORD NOWRT NOVEC BYTE
. BLANK .	00000A04	(2564.)	01	(1.)	NOPIC USR CON REL LCL NOSHR EXE RD WRT NOVEC BYTE
ABS	00000000	(0.)	02	(2.)	NOPIC USR CON ABS LCL NOSHR EXE RD WRT NOVEC BYTE

DISPLAY_FILE   Display file specified   22-FEB-1990 13:02:07   VAX MACRO V5.0-8   Page   4

VAX-11 Macro Run Statistics   21-FEB-1990 17:48:37   DISFIL.MAR;1   (1)

```
+------------------------------+
! Performance indicators !
+------------------------------+
```

Phase	Page faults	CPU Time	Elapsed Time
Initialization	104	00:00:00.05	00:00:00.35
Command processing	817	00:00:00.19	00:00:00.38
Pass 1	154	00:00:01.54	00:00:02.15
Symbol table sort	0	00:00:00.12	00:00:00.13
Pass 2	10	00:00:00.21	00:00:00.55
Symbol table output	0	00:00:00.02	00:00:00.02
Psect synopsis output	0	00:00:00.00	00:00:00.00
Cross-reference output	0	00:00:00.00	00:00:00.00
Assembler run totals	1088	00:00:02.13	00:00:03.64

The working set limit was 10000 pages.
19177 bytes (38 pages) of virtual memory were used to buffer the intermediate code.
There were 20 pages of symbol table space allocated to hold 359 non-local and 0 local symbols.
94 source lines were read in Pass 1, producing 16 object records in Pass 2.
23 pages of virtual memory were used to define 17 macros.

```
+----------------------------------+
! Macro library statistics !
+----------------------------------+
```

Macro library name	Macros defined
SYS$COMMON:[SYSLIB]STARLET.MLB;1	14

592 GETS were required to define 14 macros.

There were no errors, warnings or information messages.

MACRO DISFIL.MAR/LIST

18

The VAX/VMS Hardware Environment

Many actual hardware components are mentioned in this chapter. Actual device names are used as examples. These components may become obsolete in the future. The architecture underlying the use of these components is usually valid for replacement components. Rather than explaining the underlying concepts in abstract, I have chosen to use illustrative examples from current available hardware. It will help in understanding more innovative hardware which will be available in the future.

A VAX CPU cabinet has a "card cage" which contains a backplane and a set of cards. The backplane is where the bus (like VAXBI) is located. More cabinets and card cages may be present to extend the bus. There are three main types of cards: *CPU*, *memory*, and *device controllers*. On clusters, each of the VAXes are similarly configured except that some devices are shared by them.

There are four major types of I/O buses on VAXes: *Qbus*, *Unibus*, *VAXBI* and *XMI*. The Qbus is a 16-bit bus used on most microVAXes. Unibus is a 16-bit bus used on older VAXes; it is being phased out. VAXBI and XMI are 32-bit and 64-bit buses used on larger VAXes like the 6000 and 9000 series. The industry standard bus, SCSI, is also used on the smaller VAXes.

The CPUs are made from various technologies like CMOS for the microVAX 3500 and ECL for the VAX 8700. Rather than specifying CPU speed in MIPS, DEC measures CPU speed in terms of VAX units of performance (VUPs). The standard is VAX 11/780 which is a 1 VUP machine. As examples, microVAX II is rated at 0.9 VUP, microVAX 3500 at 2.7 VUP, VAX 8810 at 6 VUP and VAX 6310 at 3.8 VUP.

DEC also measures speed in microVUPS (MVUPS). In this case, the standard is the microVAX II which is a 1 microVUP machine.

Memory is 8-bit plus a parity bit on smaller VAXes while *error correcting code* (ECC) based memory is used on larger VAXes; 16-Mbyte of memory is supported on most VAXes; the larger VAXes normally have 128 Mbytes.

Many device controllers are semiintelligent in the sense that they use *direct memory access* (DMA) techniques, use interrupts to signal completion of operations to the CPU and perform check-sum type of operations when accessing disk blocks. But the I/O is initiated and followed through by the CPU. Where offloading I/O processing from the CPU would substantially improve performance, DEC has developed intelligent microcomputers which work in conjunction with the main VAX CPU. Examples of these are the HSC70 disk and tape controller and the SNA gateway.

DEC offers a set of devices, like the RA60 removable disk drive, which can be installed on many VAX systems. The controllers would be different depending on the bus used on the VAX. For example, the RA60 drive can be connected to any of the VAXBI bus–based VAXes (like the VAX 6000-320) by the KDB50 controller. To connect the same drive to a Qbus-based VAX (like the microVAX 3600), a KDA50 controller is required. Both the KDA50 and KDB50 controllers can be connected to up to 4 RA series drives. The RA60 can be connected to an XMI bus–based VAX (like the VAX 9000-210) by the KDM70 controller. Other commonly used controllers are Ethernet controllers (DELUA for Qbus, DEUNA for Unibus and DEBNT for VAXBI), tape controllers (TSV05 for Qbus VAXes attached to TU-81 PLUS standard tape drives and TMSCP for VAXes attached to TK70 cartridge tape drives) and communications controllers (DMV-11 for 56Kilobytes/second synchronous lines and DMB32 for 8 asynchronous lines and 1 synchronous line on VAXBI).

DEC device and controller offerings change as time passes by. Usually, the newer offerings have better functionality and performance. A number of third-party vendors also offer DEC-compatible and specialized devices and controllers. Figure 18.1 shows a MicroVAX II configuration.

18.1 SOFTWARE DEVICE DRIVERS

Each device is connected to a controller which is accessed by the CPU using memory mapped I/O. Each controller has control and status registers (CSRs) which are actually memory locations which are accessed by the CPU. The operating system has a driver for each type of device. To see the list of drivers currently being used by the operating system use:

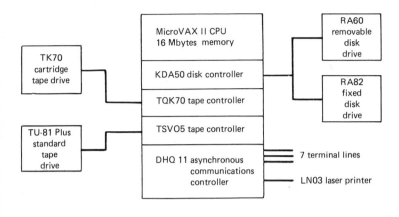

Figure 18.1   A small VAX configuration.

```
$ SYSGEN      :==$SYSGEN !Make SYSGEN a DCL command
$ SYSGEN>SHOW /DRIVER
__Driver_____Start_____End___
SPMTIMER   803DEE60 803DFAD0
LTDRIVER   803C57D0 803C8C00
RTTDRIVER  803C2370 803C2D90
NETDRIVER  803B2E30 803B6B30
ETDRIVER   803AB9F0 803B1330
TUDRIVER   803A8A60 803AB6A0
LIDRIVER   80678C30 80679200
DUDRIVER   806741F0 80677B99
PUDRIVER   806728D0 806741E9
TTDRIVER   8066D570 806728C0
OPERATOR   800018CE 8000196E
NLDRIVER   80001895 80001ED2
MBDRIVER   8000185C 80001E5E
```

The start and end columns refer to virtual memory locations. Many drivers are loaded by the operating system just after the system is booted and the base operating system is loaded. Which drivers are loaded depends on which controllers are connected in the backplane of the computer. The drivers are loaded from files in directory SYS$SYSTEM:. An example driver file is ETDRIVER.EXE, which is used for the Ethernet controller. Users can write I/O drivers for controllers not supplied by DEC. Drivers can be explicitly loaded by the SYSGEN LOAD command.

18.2   DEVICES

18.2.1   Disk drives

One of the most common disk drives on the larger VAXes are called the RA series drives. These drives have various disk storage sizes but the same controllers can operate any of these drives. The RA60's are removable drives with 205 Mbytes capacity; the RA81, RA82 and RA90 are fixed-drive. The RA90 has about 1.2 Gbytes of storage and is probably the least expensive per byte of storage.

Disk drives are magnetic devices and bad blocks develop on them for various reasons. The RA series drives along with their controllers are designed to revector bad blocks to some extra blocks on the disk. The systems software will not be aware of revectoring. So, software can access the disks starting at logical block 0 thru the disk limit wihout encountering any bad blocks. When a bad block on disk is to be accessed, the controller actually accesses the re-vectored block.

The software name of many drives start with "DU" for fixed drives and "DJ" for removable drives. Examples are DUA0:, DUC8: and DJB2:. To see the disk drives on the system use:

```
$ SHOW DEVICES D        !Display devices whose name start with D.
```

The RA series drives can be dual-ported so that they are connected to two VAXes. Only one VAX can access the drive at any particular time; the drive can be switched to the other VAX by a push-button switch on the drive panel. This scheme is useful to "move" files from one system to another when a system fails.

DEC also has an "electronic" disk drive, the ESE20. This is a drive emulated using memory chips. It is expensive but it can be justified for fast transaction processing applications. Optical and floppy disk drives are also offered by DEC.

Some of the smaller VAXes have a SCSI bus which supports a separate variety of disk drives.

18.2.2   Tape drives

Some of the standard 9-track $\frac{1}{2}$-inch spool tape drives are:

TU81-Plus   6250 bpi, streaming at 75 inch/sec, standard speed is 25 inch/sec

TA79   6250 bpi, 125 inch/sec read/write speed.

Cartridge tape drives:

TK50   95-Mbyte capacity, 75 inch/sec

TK70   290-Mbyte capacity, same form factor as TK50 drives.

A TK50 tape is called Compactape and a TK70 tape is called Compactape II. A TK70 drive can read a TK50 tape but cannot write to it.

The TA90 cartridge tape subsystem can be used on VAXclusters for backing up large amounts of data. It uses IBM 3480-compatible cartridges. Each cartridge has a capacity of 200 Mbytes and, depending on the configuration, up to 12 cartridges can be stacked to provide 2.4 Gbytes of unattended data storage capability.

Tape drive software device names usually start with MU or MS. An example name is MUA0:.

The command:

```
$ DISMOUNT  MUA0:/NOUNLOAD
```

will rewind the tape to the BOT mark and leave it online while

```
$ DISMOUNT  MUA0:/UNLOAD
```

will set the drive offline and unload the tape ready to be removed from the drive.

18.3 TERMINALS AND TERMINAL SERVERS

Currently, the most common terminal is VT320. This has 25 lines of 80 or 132 characters on the screen. The 25th line is normally used for status messages. Other terminals are

VT100 Obsolete, VT220 can emulate this terminal.

VT220 Obsolete, VT320 can emulate this terminal.

VT240 Graphics terminal. Obsolete. VT340 can be used instead.

VT330 Monochrome graphics terminal. Supports ReGIS, SIXEL and Tektronix 4010 graphics commands. 800 by 500 pixels.

VT340 Color graphics terminal. Supports ReGIS, SIXEL and Tektronix 4010 graphics commands. 800 by 500 pixels.

These terminals use asynchronous RS232 or RS423 communications protocol with the host. The terminals can be directly connected to controller cards in the CPU cabinet or they can be connected to terminal servers on Ethernet.

18.3.1 Terminal servers

Terminal servers are semiintelligent communications controllers which connect terminals, via terminal ports, to Ethernet. The terminals can then communicate with VAXes on the Ethernet. There are various types of terminal servers:

DECserver 200 !Up to 8 terminals can be connected to Ethernet.

DECserver 300 !Up to 16 terminals can be connected to Ethernet.

DECserver 500   !Up to 128 terminals can be connected to Ethernet.

DECserver 550   !Up to 128 terminals can be connected to Ethernet.

Terminals on servers are called local terminals. The server normally issues a prompt:

```
Local>
```

VAXes on the network offer LAT services (using the LATCP program). Typically, a VAX offers a service with the same name as its nodename. Multiple services can be offered by a VAX. VAXes may offer no LAT service in which case terminals on the DECservers cannot connect to these VAXes (directly).

The user can show the services on the Ethernet by using:

```
Local> SHOW SERVICES
```

The user can log into a node by, say,

```
Local> CONNECT TOPVAX
```

The BREAK key on the terminal (usually the F5 key) can be used to temporarily break the connection with the host computer and return back to the local server. Another CONNECT can be issued to log into the same or another node on the Ethernet. Multiple sessions can be establised in this way. CTRL/F (for FORWARD) can be pressed to go to the next session. The sessions other than the current session remain in a state of hibernation. All sessions can be terminated by

```
Local> LOGOUT      !Disconnect all sessions
```

The servers contain software which is loaded from any VAX on the Ethernet (which has the software). A load can be forced from a VAX by the LOAD or TRIGGER commands. A load can be requested by the terminal server broadcasting a "please load me" multicast message over the Ethernet. A number of parameters can be changed in the servers from the VAXes on the Ethernet. Some of these are

- Forcing a terminal to use a particular node only. (SET PORT 3 DEDICATED SCOOP).

- Setting a password on the server. Users on terminals connected to the server have to enter the password before any operations can be performed.

- Offer a service which is actually a number of VAXes on the Ethernet. When a user connects to the service, he or she will be connected to the VAX which is least busy. If some of the VAXes are down, a connection will be established with a running VAX.

- Establish a port as a printer service. This port, which may be connected to a printer, can then be used by VAXes on the network. The port is set for ACCESS REMOTE and is called a "reverse LAT" port (since the connection is initiated by a VAX when a job is to be printed).

If power fails and comes back up, the servers automatically ask for a boot and the VAX containing the server software loads it. If a number of VAXes have the server software, then the one which responds first will be able to load the software.

18.4   VAXclusters

A cluster is a collection of VAXes sharing resources like disk and tape drives. Files on disks can be shared by users on different nodes on the cluster. The advantage is that the cluster acts as a computer with an effective CPU speed of the total CPU speeds of all the VAXes on the cluster. Also, if some VAXes on the cluster do not function, terminals on DECservers can automatically be routed to other VAXes. CI-based VAXclusters and not Local Area VAXclusters are alluded to in this discussion. The VAXes on a cluster communicate with each other and with shared resources over a bus called Computer Interconnect (CI). The speed of CI is 70 Mbits/sec. Physically, the bus is a set of cables from the CI controller of each VAX joined together at a point called the star coupler (SC008). The shared disk and tape drives are on a microcomputer called HSC70 which is also connected to the star coupler. The logical bus structure is similar to Ethernet except that a node wishing to send a message to another node has to wait for the bus to be free, take control of it, perform the message transfers, and then release the bus somewhat like "token-passing." On Ethernet, the nodes send out messages and retransmit if there was a collision with messages from other nodes.

VAXes in a cluster can be (actually, should be) interconnected by Ethernet. Ethernet should be used for DECnet communications rather than CI for better efficiency of cluster operations. Further details on the cluster are given in the chapter on VAXclusters. Figure 18.2 shows a medium-sized VAX installation set-up.

18.5   FURTHER READING

The DECconnect Communications System Handbook.
Device Support Manual, Vol. 8, VMS Programming Manuals.
VAX/VMS Hardware Handbook.
Digital Technical Journal, Issue 8: "Storage Technology," Digital Press, Bedford. Mass., 1989.

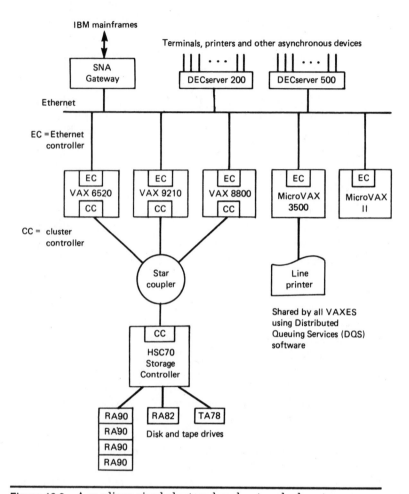

Figure 18.2   A medium-sized clustered and networked system.

Glossary

Abort An exception during process execution which leaves registers and memory in an unpredictable state. The process will be terminated by VMS. Also see *exceptions*.

Access control entry (ACE) What each entry in an ACL table is called.

Access control list (ACL) A protection table associated with an object. The table specifies the users and the type of access allowed. Objects are files, devices, logical name tables, queues and global sections.

Access control string A string specifying a username and password when accessing another node on the network. For example: $ DIR TOPVAX"SHAH TIPJAM"::

Addressing mode The method of specifying addresses of operands in an assembly language (MACRO) statement. Examples of addressing modes are immediate value where the operand is part of the instruction or register deferred where the operand is in the location pointed to by the specified register.

Anciliary control program (ACP) A process interfacing between user processes and an I/O device driver. The ACP process performs higher-level functions than those handled by drivers. An example is the NETACP process which handles network functions.

Area Logical subdivisions in a DECnet Phase IV network. They are created for efficient routing of packets. Nodes which can route packets within an area are level 1 routers and nodes which can route packets from one area to another are level 2 routers. Areas in an indexed file are subsections of the file. Each subsection contains logically related data. For example, keys can be in one area while actual records can be in another area.

Asynchronous system trap (AST) A software interrupt to a program by the operating system. The normal flow of execution is suspended, a previously specified routine (within the program) is executed, and then execution resumes at the point where it was suspended.

Autoconfigure On power up and system boot, the device drivers for all attached devices are loaded by VMS. If new devices are connected later, the SYSGEN AUTOCONFIGURE command can be used to load the new drivers.

Autogen The command file SYS$UPDATE:AUTOGEN.COM is used to resize all system parameters when some parameters are modified by specifying them in SYS$SPECIFIC:[SYSEXE]MODPARAMS.DAT.

Balance set Set of processes resident in memory as opposed to processes swapped out to disk.

Block spanning The concept of file records on disk continuing from one block to the next. Block size is 512 bytes.

Bucket An area of up to 63 blocks in memory used as a buffer by RMS for storing data from an open relative or index file. It is the quantum of I/O when performing disk data read and write operations.

Buffered I/O I/O (like that to terminals or mailboxes) which use system pool buffer for the data being transferred. Contrast with Direct I/O.

Captive account A user account which limits the set of operations the user can perform on the system. The user will not be able to execute DCL commands directly.

Circuit A logical DECnet connection, normally from one process to another on a different or the same node.

Cluster A VAXcluster is two or more VAXes which can share resources like disk and tape drives, act as one high availability system and allow common system management.
  A disk cluster is a set of contiguous disk blocks which are used as the mimimum size for disk allocation. The cluster size is defined when the disk pack is initialized. A common value is 3 blocks.

Command file A file containing a set of DCL commands which can be executing by specifying the file name preceded by an @ sign.

Command line interpreter (CLI) The interface between the user and the operating system is called a CLI. A CLI accepts and parses user commands before notifying the corresponding components of VMS. DCL is the usual CLI on VMS.

Computer interconnect (CI) The hardware bus interconnecting VAXes in a CI VAXcluster. Physically, the bus consists of coaxial cables with a bandwidth of 70 Mbits/sec.

Console terminal The terminal which communicates with the CPU even when VMS is not running. An operator console is any terminal which has been enabled to receive operator messages by the REPLY/ENABLE command.

Context switching The action of setting up CPU registers and performing other house-keeping functions by VMS when switching the CPU from one process to another.

CPU access mode One of the four modes in which the CPU can operate: kernel, executive, system, or user. Kernel is the most privileged and user is the least.

DDCMP Acronym for Digital Data Communications Protocol. This protocol is used when VAXes are networked using communications lines. It is a point-to-point protocol.

DECnet Networking component of VAX/VMS.

DECwindows   DEC's implementation of windowing system using X-windows developed at MIT.

Delta time   Time specified as a difference of two absolute times. For example, 5 days and 10 hours is specified as "5-10:00:00"

Demand zero paging   A page initialized to zero when allocated during a page fault. The page is not written to the disk paging file during a write operation if the page has not been modified. This way, disk space is conserved and page faults are serviced faster.

Detached process   A process that has no owner process. Normally, these are the top processes of process trees. The process created when a user logs in is a detached process. Detached processes can be created by the RUN/DETACH command or the $CREPRC system service.

Direct I/O   I/O (like that to disks) where data is transferred directly from the process memory to the device. Contrast with Buffered I/O.

Distributed lock manager   Used to synchronize operations between nodes in a cluster. It is used by other cluster software like the distributed file service and distributed job controller. It is a superset of the lock manager on individual VAXes. Users can synchronize clustered applications by using $ENQ and $DEQ system calls.

EEPROM   Electrically erasable programmable read-only memory.
Customized BOOT commands and some other parameters can be stored in EEPROM connected to the CPU. The EEPROM does not loose data on power failure so the commands can be used to quickly bring up the system when power resumes.

Ethernet   One of the communications standards used by DECnet, Ethernet has a maximum theoretical bandwidth of 10 Mbits/sec and is mainly used for local area networks. Ethernet physical layer specifications is defined in the IEEE 802.3 Standard.

EVE   Extensible VAX editor. EVE is a screen oriented text editor programmed using the text processing utility (TPU). The editor can be enhanced for customized functions.

Event flag   A bit used to indicate completion of an event either by the system or by a process. They are typically used for synchronization.

Exceptions   Interruptions caused in the context of the executing process while interrupts are interruptions caused because of events external to the executing process. There are three kinds of exceptions: aborts, faults, and traps.

Executor   The node on which NCP commands will be executed. NCP is a component of DECnet.

Exit handler   A routine which is executed just before an image exits. The handler normally performs cleanup tasks. It executes even when the image terminates abnormally, say, by a CTRL/Y entered at the terminal.

Fault   Interruption occurring during instruction execution. Process can continue after the fault condition has been corrected. For example, an access to a virtual memory location which is not mapped to actual physical memory will generate a page fault. The operating system will decide further course of action. Also see exceptions.

File access block (FAB) A data structure used by RMS to store file related information.

Folder Within the MAIL utility, a directory of mail messages.

Foreign tape A tape mounted with the /FOREIGN qualifier (or the equivalent when mounted using the $MOUNT system service). ANSI standard label processing is bypassed by the system.

Global section A set of memory pages whose contents can be accessed by one or more processes.

Hierarchical storage controller (HSC) A hardware device on a VAXcluster which efficiently utilizes attached disks and tape drives on behalf of the cluster. HSCs can be used with nonclustered VAXes also but a CI bus interconnection is required.

Identifier See *rights identifier.*

Interrupt See *exception.*

Interrrupt priority level (IPL) A value from 1 to 31. Software interrupts have a priority from 1 through 15 and hardware interrupts have a priority from 16 through 31. A low-priority interrupt processing routine can be preempted by a higher-priority interrupt but not vice versa.

LANBRIDGE A hardware component which connects two separate Ethernet segments.

Lexical functions A set of functions which can be called from DCL at a terminal or from DCL command files. For example, im = f$getjpi("SHAH","IMAGNAME") returns the name of the image currently being executed by process SHAH into the symbol im.

License The authorization to use a (software) product. The product license has to be registered in VMS before the product can run.

Line A physical link from a node to a DECnet network.

Link A session between two nodes over DECnet. A number of links can use one circuit.

Local Area VAXcluster (LAVc) A cluster using Ethernet rather than the CI (bus) for cluster communications. Also known as NI cluster.

Lock Locks are a VMS-supported synchronization mechanism. Locks on a cluster are clusterwide even if created and used only on one node.

Logical names A name which, when used, gets translated to a string of characters by VMS. VMS searches logical name tables for the translation. Logical names can be created by the DEFINE command.

Login directory The default directory when a user logs in. The logical name SYS$LOGIN created by VMS for each process points to this directory.

Mailbox A software device which can be used for (stream oriented) communications by two or more processes. Mailboxes are node-specific even on a cluster.

Mass storage control protocol (MSCP) A protocol used for handling disk and tape I/O for some devices.

Null device A software device, NL:, which accepts and discards data sent to it and returns an end-of-file when accessed for input.

On Disk Structure - 2 (ODS-2) The disk structure for FILES-11 disks on the VAX. ODS-1 is an older version of disk structure which is also used on some PDP-11 computers.

OPCOM A process which accepts and processes messages sent to the operator by users or other processes. Users can send a message to the operator by the DCL REPLY command; programs can do the same with the $SNDOPR system service routine.

Options file A file used by the LINKER which specifies files and other parameters to be used during a link operation.

P0 space Virtual memory region where program code and data resides for a process.

P1 space Virtual memory region where stack, DCL, and process contextual information resides for a process.

Password encryption The process of storing user passwords in the authorization file using a one-way encryption algorithm. This way, even privileged users cannot determine the password of another user, although they can change it.

Priority A value from 0 through 31 assigned to each process on the system for CPU scheduling.

Privileges A set of values, one or more of which can be owned by each process on the system. Each privilege permits the owning processes to perform a set of operations which would not be possible if the privilege were not owned by the process. For example, if a process has the READALL privilege, it can read any file on any disk.

Procedure calling standard A standard method used by all VMS software products for calling subprograms in the run time library and system services, and within modules written in any of the VMS languages. The standard defines parameter types, parameter passing mechanisms and conventions for returning status values. The standard also allows programs written in one language to "call" routines written other languages.

Process An independent, executable entity running under VMS. The two major software components on the system are the operating system and processes.

Process identification (PID) A unique 8 hexadecimal digit number assigned to each process on the system. On a cluster, this number is unique to each process on the cluster.

Processor status longword (PSL) A 32-bit register in the CPU.

Proxy account A proxy account on a VAX allows a user on another VAX to access the first VAX without having to specify passwords.

Qbus A 16-bit data bus used on many microVAXes.

Queued input/output (QIO)   Generic term for all user-level I/O under VMS.

Quorum   An integer which determines whether the Votes of VAXes in a cluster are sufficient for the cluster to be allowed to operate.

Quorum disk   A disk which contributes votes in a cluster. The quorum disk cannot be shadowed.

Record access block (RAB)   A data structure where RMS stores record related information like maximum record size for a file.

Record management services (RMS).   The file management system on the VAX.

ReGIS   Remote graphics instruction set. A set of commands used to display graphical output on a terminal or printer.

Rights identifier   A rights identifier is a name stored in the rights database, SYS$SYSTEM:RIGHTSLIST.DAT. A rights identifier is used for protecting objects against unauthorized access. Users can hold one or more of these identifiers. Objects can be protected so that they can be accessed only by holders of a specific identifier.

Run time library (RTL)   A set of VMS utility routines which can be called from programs.

Save set   A (container) file which contains a set of RMS files. Save sets are created by BACKUP utility commands.

Screen management routines (SMG)   A set of utility routines for performing terminal independent screen oriented output and keyboard input.

Security alarm   A message sent to the operator console and the operator log file when there is a security event (like a security breach).

SIXEL graphics   A form of bit-image graphics for terminal and printer output.

Spawn   The command used to create a subprocess of the current process.

Spinlock   In a multiprocessor VAX like the VAX 6000-420, a spinlock is a lock shared by multiple CPUs. When one CPU has access to the lock, another CPU wishing to acquire the lock will loop until the lock is released—hence the term spinlock. A spinlock can simply be a bit in memory.

Star coupler   A junction box in a VAXcluster where the CI cables from all the nodes on the cluster are interconnected.

String descriptor   A data structure used for passing string parameters from one program to another. The descriptor consists of a string address, string size and string type.

Symbiont   A process which interfaces between a user process and record-oriented devices like printers and card readers.

Symbol   A DCL variable.

System communications services (SCS)   SCS is the software on each node of a VAXcluster which implements communications on a cluster. It makes use of the VAXport drivers.

System services   A set of VMS utility routines which can be called from programs.

Terminal server   A hardware device which allows a number of terminals to access VAXes over Ethernet using an efficient protocol called LAT.

TPU   Text processing utility. A programming tool for manipulating text oriented data.

Trap   A type of exception where interruption occurs after instruction execution at the machine level. Process execution can continue after the trap. An example is integer division by zero trap. Also see exceptions.

Unibus   A 16-bit I/O bus used on older VAXes.

User authorization file (UAF)   An indexed file containing security and quota related information on all users who can access the system. The file is SYS$SYSTEM:SYSUAF.DAT. The file is normally accessed by the AUTHORIZE utility.

User environment test package (UETP)   A set of programs which are bundled with VMS for testing VMS software and hardware components.

User identification code (UIC)   An UIC consists of two numbers; a group and a member number. Each user on the system is assigned an UIC. UICs are used in the VMS protection scheme.

VAX units of processing (VUP)   A common basis for measuring VAX CPU performance. One VUP is the processing power of a VAX 11/780.

VAXBI   A 32-bit I/O bus found on some of the VAXes like the VAX 6000 series.

VAXELN   A real-time operating system based on VAX/VMS.

VAXsim   A software tool for diagnosing system malfunctions.

Volume shadowing   The VMS feature which allows data to be written to two or more identical disks in a single I/O operation for redundancy.

Votes   A value contributed by each VAX in a cluster which is used to determine if the cluster is valid. See *Quorum*.

Working set   The number of physical memory pages being used by a process.

XMI   A 64-bit I/O bus which is being used on some of the VAXes like the 6000 and 9000 series.

Index

ABOUT THE AUTHOR

Jay Shah is a specialist in VAX computer technology. He has been working in VAX environments since 1983. Mr. Shah is presently a senior software engineer at Chase Manhattan Bank in New York City. He also conducts in-house training on the use of DEC products.